JAY RAYNER

Jay Rayner is an award-winning writer, journalist and broadcaster with a fine collection of floral shirts. He has written on everything from crime and politics, through cinema and theatre to the visual arts, but is best known as restaurant critic for the *Observer*. For a while he was a sex columnist for *Cosmopolitan*; he also once got himself completely waxed in the name of journalism. He only mentions this because it hurt. Jay is a former Young Journalist of the Year, Critic of the Year and Restaurant Critic of the Year, though not all in the same year. He chairs BBC Radio 4's *The Kitchen Cabinet*, and is a regular on British television, where he is familiar as a judge on *Masterchef* and, since 2009, as the resident food expert on *The One Show*. He likes pig.

JAY RAYNER

A GREEDY MAN IN A HUNGRY WORLD

WHY *ALMOST* EVERYTHING YOU THOUGHT
YOU KNEW ABOUT FOOD IS WRONG

**WILLIAM
COLLINS**

First published in 2013 by William Collins
An imprint of HarperCollins*Publishers*
77–85 Fulham Palace Road
Hammersmith, London W6 8JB

www.harpercollins.co.uk

10 9 8 7 6 5 4 3 2 1

Text © Jay Rayner 2013

Jay Rayner asserts his moral right to
be identified as the author of this work

A catalogue record for this book is
available from the British Library

ISBN 978-0-00-723759-3

Printed and bound in Great Britain by
Clays Ltd, St Ives plc

MIX
Paper from
responsible sources
FSC C007454
www.fsc.org

FSC™ is a non-profit international organisation established to promote
the responsible management of the world's forests. Products carrying the
FSC label are independently certified to assure consumers that they come
from forests that are managed to meet the social, economic and
ecological needs of present and future generations,
and other controlled sources.

Find out more about HarperCollins and the environment at
www.harpercollins.co.uk/green

For Sarah and Jerry, who have always fed me well.

CONTENTS

AUTHOR'S NOTE

I am a greedy bastard. For the sake of appearances, I could lie about this. I could tell you that my appetites are entirely unremarkable; that my relationship with food does not dominate my every waking moment. But we both know this would be a lie as big and fat as each of my really quite awe-inspiring thighs. I have earned those thighs. Every shadowed dimple of cellulite has been put there courtesy of a restaurant bill. If you are eating while reading this book, if perhaps you thought that a book about food culture in the twenty-first century would be the perfect companion to a meal taken alone, and the image of my over-engineered, middle-aged, lard-heavy thighs is now putting you off your food, then obviously I apologize. That said, I can't really empathize with you. Nothing puts *me* off my dinner.

This is less a confession than a vital piece of background information. Otherwise you might assume, as I lead you on a journey through the knotty complexities of how and what we eat now, that it was all merely some academic exercise on my part. It is nothing of the sort. It is motivated by lust and appetite. Even as I'm typing I'm thinking about what I'll be having for dinner later on. At some restaurant with the word 'pig' in the title. I like pig. I admire the way its skin crisps so perfectly, the way the fat melts, the way it takes a cure so enthusiastically, producing the very best of charcuterie; salamis spiked with fennel or green peppercorns; chorizos so heavy with paprika they stain your fingertips orange as you get the oily slices from cutting board to mouth. There's intense, earthy black pudding, and its Spanish cousin *morcilla*; bacons, singed rust and bronze in the pan, and pork scratchings that threaten to take out a filling, and …

Sorry. I think I got a little distracted there. Where was I? Oh yes. Greed, namely mine, and its impact upon my work. The point is that a lot of books written about food policy, responding to the undeniably serious issues involved, can take on a pinched and troubled aspect, as if the subject under discussion were the correct interpretation of something profound but strangely unintelligible uttered by the Dalai Lama, rather than an examination of what may well end up as lunch. Whenever I am thinking, asking questions or writing about food, the one question I am always asking myself is: how will this eventually impact upon my lunch?

Some may regard this as a moral failing, will think that too much appetite can get in the way of a cool and collected appraisal of the facts. I see it differently. Just as there's no point reading a book about sex written by a nun, or a book about morals written by a banker, there's also no point reading a book about food written by a picky eater. Sometimes gluttony isn't a vice, it's a virtue, and this is one of those occasions. Though I accept I may just be attempting to excuse my own failings. If I am, I'm doing a bloody good job of it, don't you think?

Either way the fact remains: my name is Jay Rayner and I am a greedy bastard.

Live with it.

1.

THE £31 CHICKEN

It would suit the narrative if I could claim that, from the moment I laid eyes upon the chicken, I knew I had to have it; that I was overcome by a greed and hunger verging on the carnal. Granted it was one damn beautiful chicken: good sturdy legs for the brown meat fetishists, a robust skin with the ivory promise of plentiful fat deposits underneath; breasts big enough to make Pamela Anderson wince with jealousy. But the truth is it wasn't the chicken I saw first, but the entire meat carnival of the butcher's shop. I had heard tell of Lidgate's in Holland Park before, of course. It's one of those high-end butchers that food obsessives dribble into their computer keyboards over, when describing their shopping adventures. It's the kind of place you visit with more money than sense.

Lidgate's has been trading for 150 years, has remained in the same family throughout that time and has won countless awards for what, in cheaper parts of town, would be called their ready meals but here are called 'baked goods'. The window is full of their ready-to-cook shepherd's pies, the surface of the mash as carefully raked as the gravel outside a stately home. There are boeuf bourguignon pies and pesto-smeared saddles of lamb, and their own enormous sausage rolls, wrapped in the flakiest of butter-rich pastry. The shop is tiled inside and out in Edwardian shades of jade green. The butchers wear straw boaters as if it's an entirely reasonable thing to do. (It isn't.)

I stepped inside and waited in the narrow space in front of the counters with the Holland Park yummy mummies, smelling of Jo Malone products – jasmine and mint, wild fig – while others were served. I was not entirely sure what I was going to do. I like butcher's shops, worked in one of them at weekends as a kid. I like the promise of all that meat; like to think about what it could become. I like to think about what pleasure it could give me. I particularly like high-end butcher's shops, as if the pleasure I can achieve can in some way be correlated on a graph against the cost of the produce on offer. I like all this, while also knowing it is wrong and deluded, that the quality of the meal will actually depend on my ability to cook those ingredients sympathetically. I listened to a butcher weigh off a piece of beef and quote the price. My eyes widened. I have spent big money on my dinner before, paid unconscionable sums for bits of dead animal, but this was in a new category.

Then my gaze fell upon a small chicken, slapped with the label 'organic free range', from Otter Farm. Yours for £12 a kilo. Later I would check the going rate for whole fresh chicken in the supermarkets that week – from £2.04 a kilo to as much as £6 a kilo for a free-range organic bird – but even without checking I knew that this wasn't just expensive; that this chicken laughed in the face of expensive. It had migrated to a new and unique category located somewhere between nose-bleeding and paralysing.

In its favour these were small birds of little more than a kilo, and so, individually, a whole chicken was likely to come in at less than £20. I had paid £18 for a bird once before, a free-range organic number from Borough Market in south London, a place so expensive I never went there carrying plastic, only cash so as to put a limit on what I could spend. This would, in turn, enable me to carry on buying shoes for my children. Buying the £18 chicken had made me feel dirty and wrong, albeit in a good way; but the point is that these Lidgate's birds were within my tolerances for excess.

That's when I saw it, on a glass shelf, creamy-coloured arse to the shop, as though its skin tones had been picked out of a Farrow & Ball catalogue. This free-range, non-organic chicken was big. Very big. I asked the butcher to put it on the scales. It weighed just over 3.2kg. At £9.90 a kilo. 'That will be £31.78,' he said, his straw boater rested at a jaunty angle. I let out a hiss of breath, like the air leaking from a punctured bicycle tyre. Did I want it? the nice chap asked me.

Did I want it? Yes. Yes, I did want it. Who wouldn't? A chicken costing more than £31? What would that be like? Surely it had to be the ultimate chicken, the king (or, more precisely, the queen) of birds? Surely if I paid – I did the sums quickly – over 75 per cent more for a chicken than I had ever paid before I would accrue an equivalent amount more pleasure from the experience than I ever had before? At the very least wasn't it my responsibility to find out? Wasn't that what I did these days? As I left the shop, I noticed a sign in the window signed by David Lidgate, the current family member to be custodian of the business, to the effect that all their chickens were bred and supplied by small farms. 'We pay our farmers a fair price.' It felt like he was getting his apology in first.

Before leaving I asked the butcher where this particular chicken had come from. 'It's an Elmwood chicken, I think,' he said. Back home I Googled the words 'Elmwood' and 'chicken'. It turned out to be an odd thing to have said. Elmwood isn't really a place, or at least it isn't a place any more. It's an idea. While there is an Elmwood Farm somewhere in East Anglia, today the word is a registered marketing label, used by the Co-op – and only the Co-op – to describe a higher-quality, more expensive bird than the bog-standard, fast-grown cheap chickens they sell. The higher welfare standards started at the original Elmwood Farm have now been pressed into service at farms across Britain. The label is now applied to all birds grown under those standards.

This is a familiar ploy by the big food retailers. Marks & Spencer has its Oakham chicken, which some might assume comes from the environs of the town in Rutland of the same name. It doesn't. It's just a brand name for chickens grown at farms all over the country, none of which is called Oakham. Tesco has a range of chickens called Willow Farm, which are reared on a few dozen farms across the south-west of England and Northern Ireland, none of which is called Willow Farm. The labels may portray bucolic scenes of olde farming life. They may be sold with images of carefully drawn ears of corn, but they are still birds raised on an industrial scale.

Whatever my £31 chicken was, it had nothing to do with Elmwood. I phoned Lidgate's and asked again if they could say where it was from. 'It's from Willow Field in Norfolk,' I was told by another butcher. Right. That's more like it. Willow Field actually sounds like a real place. It had the word 'field' in the name. That made it sound just like a farm. Back I went to Google, but found nothing online about a chicken farm in

Norfolk called Willow Field, save for a planning application to the local council for the placement of a mobile home. Conceivably the mobile home was for luxury chickens to live in, but I thought it unlikely.

I was becoming obsessed with this chicken. I had begun to fantasize about its life. Maybe its coop was completely pimped: ermine trim, leather seats, a sound system with serious bass, and a drinks cabinet heavy with vintage Crystal. At this price surely it had to be the most pampered chicken ever? Maybe they fed it on the ground-up bones of delicate songbirds? Perhaps it was watered with Evian? How else could the price be justified?

To bring things back into focus I called Lidgate's yet again. This time I spoke to David Lidgate's son, Danny. He could not explain the misinformation I had been given but he could categorically confirm that it had come from a farm in Suffolk which didn't want any publicity because they couldn't produce any more birds and didn't want any more trade. But he could tell me that they were slow-grown, hand-plucked, and hung for seven days before being dispatched. I wanted to ask him about the ermine-trimmed coop, but couldn't quite summon the will.

One afternoon I went onto Twitter and asked people there to tell me the most they'd ever spent on a whole chicken. There were a few who had never gone beyond a tenner. Quite a number of people had spent sums in the mid-teens. A small number had gone over the £20 mark. Curiously, people had very specific memories. 'Eighteen pounds for a rooster in Montpellier. Nineteen ninety-one. It was worth every penny,' said one person. 'On one memorable occasion enough to feel obliged to give it a name,' said another, without revealing what the sum might be. 'Eighteen pounds,' said a third. 'Big

bugger. Think they might have killed it for scaring the cows.'
One tweeter talked proudly of the two chickens they had
picked up for a fiver in a supermarket deal; another said they
had never spent more than £8 and wouldn't dream of doing
so. As these things do, the singular question about the price
of a chicken had quickly become a debate about welfare
standards, food poverty, excess and the morality thereof. And
every now and then someone chipped in with a tweet
announcing the enormous sum they had once spent on a
chicken as if it were a mark of commitment.

I nodded sagely. As I had suspected, this was a game I was
going to win. I gave them the big reveal, told them about
Lidgate's and the £31 chicken. There was an electronic gasp of
horror. Thirty-one pounds? Too much. Absurd. Ludicrous.
Bizarre.

Just wrong.

'I once saw a woman run out of Lidgate's in tears over the
price of a chicken,' one person said. I answered that I could
well imagine such a thing.

My warped, obsessive, competitive streak now took me on
a tour of London's classiest butchers, desperate to prove that
I had spent the most it was possible to spend on a chicken. For
some reason it mattered that the bird which now sat in my
freezer awaiting its moment, the bird which had become such
a talking point on Twitter, should be able to hold onto its title.
I saw birds that were local and free-range and hand-reared
and hand-plucked and hung with their guts in. I went to
Harrods, where the food hall throngs with tourists who have
no intention of buying anything other than tins of branded
tea, and looked at shrink-wrapped birds from unpronounce-
able places in France. I did kilo-to-pound-weight calculations
in my head, asked bored butchers to weigh chickens for me

and pronounce on the price, and moved on, each time satisfied I was still ahead.

And then I went to the meat counter at Selfridges' food hall, which is run by a highly respected butcher called Jack O'Shea. There I met the £51 chicken. It was a Poulet de Bresse, a particular breed which was granted *Appellation d'origine contrôlée*, or AOC, status in 1957, protecting it as a name for a particular type of bird, prized for its gamey flavour and rich fat. A nice chap behind the counter called Les, who wasn't wearing a straw boater, told me they were special 'because of their diet. They're treated like royalty, they are.' The bird I was looking at, with its head, neck, and feet on, and guts in – when you bought a bird from Bresse you got to pay for a lot of things you might not actually want – cost over £22 a kilo, and it was well in excess of two kilos.

Damn.

Damn, damn, damn.

There was I thinking I had bought the Bentley of chickens, with metallic paint and sports settings on the gearbox, when it was nothing of the sort. It was just a mid-range BMW. It was an Audi with under-seat heating, the kind of thing a desperate sanitary-ware salesman trying to prove his worth might buy as a way of declaring he had arrived, when in truth all it did was signal loud and clear to anybody who could bother to be interested that he had barely got started.

I wondered, even then, whether I had finally reached the zenith of the luxury chicken business and quickly discovered I had not. One evening, in the kitchens of London's Savoy Hotel, I came across Heston Blumenthal, the chef of the famed Fat Duck in Bray, which has three Michelin stars. He was there overseeing the preparation of the starter for a big charity dinner I was attending. I had snuck away from the velvet plush and precious gilding of the ballroom to the bright lights and hard surfaces of the kitchen, where I always felt more comfortable, and stood there in my dinner jacket, picking his brains about chickens. A few years before he had made a TV series called *In Search of Perfection* which involved finding and then roasting the perfect chicken. I wondered how much he had spent on the birds. He thought about £45 each. He talked about the quality of Label Anglais chickens, a British-reared bird which was supposed to challenge the big names of the chicken world.

'But there are even more expensive ones.' Like what? He mentioned the birds from Bresse. Well yes, I knew all about those. 'It's the cockerels, though. They only sell them for about two weeks of the year around Christmas,' he said, hand-sown into muslin bags. 'They have this fabulous skin. 'It's like silk.'

And how much would one of these Bresse cockerels set me back?

'About £120.'

There was, it seems, always a more expensive chicken out there somewhere.

I went to university in the eighties with a bloke called Eugene, who was thinner than me, smarter than me, and got much more sex than me. His name isn't really Eugene; it is, naturally enough, something far cooler than that, but it pleases me to take my revenge by giving him a really crass pseudonym, because he was horribly annoying. Though obviously not to the parade of pretty girls who were willing to go to bed with him.

Eugene had read an awful lot of Jacques Derrida and Roland Barthes and, *pace* the kings of postmodern philosophy, liked to refer to things as 'signifiers' and 'symbols'. Nothing was merely itself. In his universe everything was representative of its place within a long-drawn-out discourse; the physical world in which we lived was merely a set of these signifiers and symbols that had to be reconfigured and understood through their conversion to language. Or something. A pint of beer was never just a pint of beer. It was a signifier for the pursuit of a certain type of human experience, a way of managing communication, usually with one of the women who, a few drinks to the bad, had failed to recognize Eugene as the sociopath he was. (I'm really not bitter.) A bike was actually a signifier for modes of property ownership and an understanding of forward motion. A five-pound note was ... something he cadged off you just before last orders in the back end of term when his money was running out, so he could buy this girl he'd just met another drink. Can you see just how bloody irritating Eugene was?

Which was why it was all the more infuriating that thinking about the £31 chicken had in turn made me think about Eugene and his tiresome language of symbols and signifiers. For it was clear to me that this ridiculously expensive bird was so much more than just three kilos of prime protein, delicious fat and potentially luscious crisp skin. It could stand – Lord help me – as a symbol for so many of the arguments and battles that we are, and need to be, fighting over food in the early years of the twenty-first century.

Certainly it couldn't be dismissed as an object that was merely about wealth. I have long said that there is nothing wrong with paying large amounts of money for food experiences. Some people like to shell out for opera tickets or seats at cup finals to watch their team compete. They are buying memories, and an expensive restaurant experience is no different.

But an expensive restaurant experience is only that. You can't go to, say, the Fat Duck for something as banal as chicken nuggets. You can't even go there for deconstructed, ironic chicken nuggets (yet). You can only go there for a luxury experience. And sure, my £31 chicken could be given the full de luxe treatment: it could be pelted with truffles, stuffed with lobes of foie gras and basted with the richest of butters. (I can recommend a great place for something like that if you fancy it.) On the other hand it really could just be turned into chicken nuggets. However expensive the raw ingredient, it can still be converted into something very ordinary, which is precisely why the debate on Twitter had kicked off. Hell, it's just a bloody chicken, and you make broth out of those for loved ones when they're snotty and feverish. You barbecue their wings and drumsticks for kids' parties, and put the breasts into pies with leeks and the kind of mustard-heavy cheese sauce that completely obscures the nature of the bird that provided the meat in the first place.

It was clear to me that wrapped up in this single bird were arguments over how we rear our livestock and the amount we are willing to pay for it: about provenance, sophisticated food marketing, the supply chain, and the value of small, local shops over large supermarkets; about the imperative to eat meat and the competing imperative to cut down on it; about the roles of money, status and class in what we eat; and the difference between what we want and what we need. In short, this one big-titted hen had become what Eugene would have called a huge signifier for the warped morality of our food chain.

That's the point. I am in no doubt that the way we in the developed world think and talk about food has become warped; that most of the time we are completely missing the point. On television, online and in the glossy press we are bombarded with pornified images of food which attempt to cast the most expensive of ingredients as less a luxury than an ideal to which we should all aspire. In this world view any form of mass production or mass retailing is an evil; any attempt to engage with issues around food which doesn't fetishize the words 'local', 'seasonal' and 'organic' is plain wrong. In short, too many of us have mistaken a whole bunch of lifestyle choices for the affluent with a wider debate on how we feed ourselves, when they are nothing of the sort.

We need to get real. The term 'food security' is occasionally bandied around, but it has failed to take its place right at the heart of our conversation about what and how we eat, even though it has to be there. Because, be in no doubt: a combination of world population growth – expected to hit nine billion by 2050 – climate change, appallingly misguided policies on biofuels and an ingrained Luddite response in parts of the West to biotechnology risks coming together into a perfect storm; one which will make the sight of young chefs on the telly talking about their passion for cooking and their commitment to local and seasonal ingredients sound like the screeching of fiddles while Rome burns. According to the United Nations, by 2030 we will need to be producing 50 per cent more food, and a system built around that holy trinity of local, seasonal and organic simply won't cut it.

Indeed, while self-appointed food campaigners are banging on about that, an entirely different conversation has been going on elsewhere, within university faculties and government departments as well as at an inter-governmental level. In that world they use not three words, but two: sustainable intensification. It is about the need to produce more food, in as sustainable a manner as possible, which means thinking about far more than just how close to you your food was produced. It's about carbon inputs all the way down the production system. It's about water usage, land maintenance and the careful application of science. According to Oxfam, between 1970 and 1990 global agricultural yield grew 2 per cent a year. Between 1990 and 2007 the yield growth dropped to 1 per cent. We are close to a standstill on producing more food, and that is not a good place to be. In January 2011 the British government's Chief Scientific Adviser, Sir John Beddington, published a major report entitled 'The Future of Food and Farming'. It drew on the work of dozens of experts; over 100 peer-reviewed papers were commissioned in its writing. In that report there were 39 references to 'sustainable intensification', and the single word 'sustainability' cropped up 242 times. Where food is concerned there is a new lexicon, and it has nothing to with farmers' markets or growing your own vegetables or fruit.

I hate polarized arguments. They serve no one, because nothing is ever black and white. Even while I pick fights with the diehard foodinistas, and I do on a regular basis, it's obvious to me that there is a lot of good stuff in what they are saying. When they describe the modern food chain and the way we eat its product as being deformed they are absolutely right. A lot is wrong. The problem lies in the solution they propose, which is too often based on a fantasy, mythologized version of agriculture, one that isn't much different from those lovingly drawn ears of corn slapped on the packaging for Oakham or Willow Farm chickens to suggest their bucolic origins when in fact they've been reared in gigantic industrial sheds.

As a newspaper and television journalist I spend an awful lot of my time travelling around Britain (and abroad) finding out how our food is produced. It's fascinating. I have watched tons of carrots being lifted in the darkest, small hours of the night because, if harvested during the day, they would start to decay under the sunlight. I have dodged fountains of stuff from the wrong end of a cow to help milk the herd on a traditional dairy farm and visited a cow shed that can house up to 1,000 milkers at a time. I have fished for langoustine off the very northernmost tip of Scotland, helped make bespoke salt from the waters off the Kent coast, chosen beef animals for slaughter and followed them to the abattoir so I could witness them take the final bolt. I have driven a £360,000 harvester that vines peas, tried to keep my balance on the slopes of the island of Jersey that give us their sweet, nutty Royal potatoes, and stood in the rafters of an ex-Cold War aircraft hangar atop fifty foot of drying onions. I have even visited a pork scratchings factory and discovered that there is a limit to the amount of pork scratchings an eager man can eat in a day (six packs, as you ask).

From these experiences, and many others like them, I have become convinced that we are disconnected from what real food production means, and therefore afraid of it. We need to understand how it works, be unembarrassed about it, because only then can we genuinely push for the kind of sustainable supply chain which both guarantees quality and that our food will be affordable, though not necessarily dirt cheap. We need to find a way to mate the delicious promise of gastronomic culture with the rather less delicious but equally important demands of hardcore economics. For want of a better word – and there may well be one – we need a New Gastronomics.

So come with me as I show you why the committed locavore, who thinks that buying food produced as close by as possible is always the most sustainable option, has been sold a big fat lie. If what really concerns you is the carbon footprint of your food, then it turns out the stuff shipped halfway round the world may not be the great evil you've always been told it is. And because local does not necessarily mean sustainable, it transpires that seasonality is generally about nothing more than taste. Being concerned about how things taste is lovely. Worrying about that stuff is lovely. I do it all the time. But it's not the same as being good to the planet. I'll explain why 'farmers' markets' can never solve our food supply problems – indeed are a part of the problem – how little the organic movement has to offer a world looking to produce more food in as sustainable a manner as possible, and why growing your own will never be more than a lovely hobby. I'll explain why small is not beautiful and why big is not necessarily bad.

You know all those great sacred cows of ethical foodie-ism? Well, I think the moment has come for you to say your good-byes. Give the old dears a hug. Celebrate how much you've shared together. Then wave them off for ever. Because I'm about to lead most of those sacred cows out into the market square and shoot them dead. I'm so sorry, but it has to be done.

People are occasionally surprised that I give a toss about all this. After all, I earn part of my living as a restaurant critic. I swan around on somebody else's dime, licking the plate clean, trying not to order pork belly too often and writing smartarse things about it all. I have run up three-figure bills for dinner that almost ran to four figures. I have taken plane trips simply to buy a specific brand of vinegar. When my kids want to mock me they recite a tweet – 'The dish had a hint of rose-mary' – that I swear I never sent, but which very efficiently marks me out as some ludicrous, gourmand fop who obsesses over tiny gustatory details. And all of this is, I suppose, true. I do, after all, earn enough money to be able to pay £31.78 for a chicken just for the hell of it.

But none of that precludes an interest in our food chain in general, and the ability of everybody in our society to eat as well as they need to. Indeed, I would argue that to be in such a privileged position and not to have an interest in these things would be not just obscene but contrary. Challenged once on this point by a journalist who was interviewing me, I compared it to issues of reading and writing. There was, I said, nothing contradictory about having a love for, say, the rich, expansive language of William Shakespeare, and having a keen interest in basic literacy standards in our schools. Indeed, without one you couldn't really have the other. I think the same applies to food.

So we need to get real about our food. If we really are to shape a New Gastronomics, we need to be honest and brave. And being those things means saying stuff that some people might find unpalatable. Which is exactly what I'm about to do.

2.

SUPERMARKETS ARE NOT EVIL

Berwick Street in London's Soho. It is the mid-sixties and my dad is striding past market stalls laden with fruit and vegetables and meat and fish and bolts of cloth and a whole bunch of other things besides. There has been a market on this site since 1778 and it remains there to this day, albeit much reduced. In the sixties, though, it was a vital part of Soho's village life, closing the road between the junction with Broadwick Street to the north and Walker's Court to the south, home then to the infamous Raymond's Revue Bar and its special brand of nipple-tasselled stripping. Even to this day Soho manages to cling onto its reputation for debauchery. The 'models' still advertise their availability by placing in the windows of their dingy flats the sort of red tassel-shaded lamps you'd normally find in a B&B in Torquay; places like Walker's Court are still lined with sex shops, even if they are a little more glossy and welcoming than once they were. But in the sixties Soho was the real deal, run by Maltese hoods who had the vice squad of the Metropolitan Police in their pay, so they could continue trading merrily in the glorious triumvirate of prostitution, drugs and gambling. If you were in the market for filth, Soho was where you went.

But it was still a mixed economy. In spite of – or perhaps because of – the loucheness, other industries congregated here. Some of the best Italian delicatessens in town were here (and still are), the British film industry had started occupying the warrens of offices not used by the hookers, and many of the shop units were home to the cheaper tailors, serving the theatres of the West End or the kind of clients who liked their lapels just a little too wide. Many of the narrow alleyways were filled with shops stacked with cloths of myriad weights and hues. And, of course, there was the street market.

My father, Des, fitted in well. Although he started his working life as an actor, he had become bored with unemployment and starvation and moved into the fashion industry, and worked now as a PR for the classy mid-market label Alexon. I like to think of him marching down Berwick Street in the ankle-length black leather coat with the shaggy black fur collar that he liked to wear, a cravat tied at the neck, hair swept back, beard trimmed just so. My old man wasn't in the fashion business for nothing. And so he stops now at one of the fruit stalls to pick up some apples to take to my mother, who is back home looking after my older brother and sister. For we are in the golden age of the local shop and the street market. Self-service supermarkets are burgeoning across the US, but not yet widespread here in the UK. Even the well-known company J. Sainsbury does not generally run supermarkets. They are merely grocers, and when you shop there you must queue at separate counters for meat and dairy and fish and so on.

The fact is that there is nothing much more convenient than this market stall for a man in search of apples. So now

Des points to the pristine fruit on the display that he wants. The stallholder turns and starts filling the bag from an unseen box hidden away somewhere underneath.

'Hang on a moment,' says Des. 'I can't see which apples you're giving me.'

'I'll give you whichever bloody apples I like,' says the man.

'In which case,' Des replies, 'you can keep 'em.' He turns and walks away only to hear the stallholder shout after him: 'Suit yourself, you black-bearded, bollock-faced bastard.'

This is one of the stories with which I grew up; one of those legends that all families have. My dad was a black-bearded, bollock-faced bastard. 'What was it that man called you?' my mother would ask from the opposite end of the dinner table, when she thought he was being difficult. And we would reply in unison: 'A black-bearded, bollock-faced bastard.'

What does this story tell us? Just this: that whatever critics of supermarkets might like to tell you, the alternatives – street markets and local shops – were not, and are not, all run by lovely people, with a genuine interest in and concern for all their customers. They are merely run by people. As they are across the rest of society, some people are lovely. Some of them do genuinely care about the people who shop with them. And some of those shopkeepers and market stallholders are miserable scumbags who are to customer service what napalm is to peace.

Another story, this time from the other side of the debate. I am in the very large Tesco supermarket near my home in Brixton, south London, doing the weekly shop. I am with my son Eddie, who must be 2 or 3 years old; certainly he has not yet started school. Usually he does this shop with my wife, who works part-time, and it quickly becomes clear that he is very comfortable here. For, everywhere we go, the staff say hello to him. It doesn't just happen once or twice during our hour in Tesco. It happens perhaps eight or ten times: from the shelf stackers to the women on the deli counter to those working the checkouts. All of them know Eddie by name and have a few words for him. I am intrigued by this and so begin to notice something. We are not the only people this happens to. There are conversations between staff and customers going on all over the place, and they are not simply about which aisle the dried fruits are located on. The staff here know their customers, which really isn't surprising, because almost all the employees come from the heart of this community.

So what does this second story tell us? Just this: that whatever critics of supermarkets might like to tell you, they are not all bland, anonymous, swollen warehouses disconnected from the neighbourhoods in which they sit. Of course, some of them might be. Some of them might feel like waiting rooms for death, just as some local shopkeepers are not very nice. But the assumptions we make about these enormous shops from which we buy the vast majority of our food simply do not stand up.

We forget very easily just what life was like in the World Before Supermarkets. I am old enough to remember as a small child being taken on the family food shopping expedition to J. Sainsbury's in Kenton, north-west London, and the way we really would move from counter to counter. It was my job to say 'six wings and six legs' to the man at the butchery counter, so he could fill our weekly chicken order. It was cute. It was adorable. It was one of the ways in which my mother made the whole damn experience in some way bearable. The thing at the chicken counter broke up the tedium. Our bread came from the baker's on the corner by our house, our fruit and veg from Robert the Greengrocers across the road, and any tinned goods from a small shop called Walton, Hassle and Port ten minutes' walk away. It sounds lovely, doesn't it, this patronage of local and small businesses, this tight web of interdependent relationships? And we did like the people involved. But gathering everything that the family might need for the week was a tiresome job.

My mother is gone now, but her close friend Carole Shuter, who also had three small kids in the sixties and seventies, remembers it in detail. 'Oh God, it was a whole morning's outing,' she told me. 'You'd have to clear the diary. I remember the Sainsbury's thing very well, the way we had to queue half a dozen times and pay separately at each one. People romanticize things like butter being sold in blocks and you asking for a bit to be cut off, but you wouldn't romanticize it if you had to do it every bloody week. It takes so long.'

Alan Sainsbury, the family-owned firm's head, had come across the notion of self-service supermarkets in the US in the years immediately after the Second World War, and imported the idea. The company opened its first self-service branch in Croydon, just south of London, in 1950. Still, the roll-out didn't begin in earnest until many years later, after Sainsbury's went public in 1973 with what was then the biggest flotation in British stock exchange history. It didn't reach our corner of London until the early seventies. (The last counter store hung on, in Peckham, until 1982.)

'The first proper supermarket was a complete revelation,' Carole says. 'It was bloody marvellous. People are too quick to demean modern developments like that. They have no idea what it was like before. No idea at all.'

The point is that women like my mother and Carole had far better things to do than waste whole mornings of their week just getting the food shopping done. In Felicity Lawrence's highly regarded book *Not on the Label*, a searing critique of Britain's supermarkets, first published in 2004, she writes about the joys of shopping locally; of how it could be a bonding experience for her and her young family; that there was always time for such pleasures.

Really? Many of the generation of women who came before Felicity Lawrence that I talked to about this regarded it as a retrograde step: an attempt to cast women in a role they had fought throughout the second half of the twentieth century to throw off. One went as far as to say to me that buried within the anti-supermarket argument was one that sounded profoundly anti-woman because it was always the women who were burdened with the job of schlepping around the shops, which in turn made the notion of their having a full-time profession all but unsupportable. Whether the arguments around supermarkets really can be cast in these terms – a modern embarrassment about the idea that such things as food shopping should ever be seen as women's work do kick in here – there is no doubt that, by reducing the number of hours needed to get domestic chores done, there was more time for other things. And thank Christ for that, because otherwise the economics of domestic life would have been completely unsustainable.

There are, of course, the economies of scale. Supermarkets make things cheaper. They just do. When you have more than 2,500 stores, as Tesco does, or over 1,000 like Sainsbury's, you have serious buying power. Over 80 per cent of the retail food market spend is concentrated in the hands of the big supermarkets and, whatever the downsides of that, it has, historically, led to cheaper food. In the early post-war years it took over a third of average salary to pay for the food shop. Today it is just under 10 per cent. Or, to put it another way, you had to work until Wednesday morning to pay for the family's weekly shop; now you'll have earned enough by some time just after noon on Monday. And that's not because salaries have increased enormously, compared with all the other costs we face; quite the opposite.

For these are the economic realities within which supermarkets operate. In 1962 average yearly pay was £799. By 2012 it was £26,200. It has increased by a factor of just over thirty. However, the picture with house prices is rather different. In 1962 the average house in Britain cost £2,670. Fifty years later it costs around £245,000. House prices have therefore increased by a factor of over ninety. Just stare at those numbers for a moment. House prices have increased at roughly three times the rate of earnings. Brutal, those figures, aren't they? Faced with these realities, all those interesting historical debates about the fight by women like my mother and her friend Carole for the right to go out to work in the sixties and seventies become completely irrelevant. It's no longer about the *right* to work. It's about the *need* to work. The fact of the matter is that to support and run a household both members of a couple with kids need to be holding down full-time jobs. That makes them hideously time-poor. Ask anybody today to clear a morning of their diary just to go down the road to watch a man cut the butter you need off a huge block and they'd laugh in your face. In that context, supermarkets really are not evil. They are a complete godsend.

They are something else too, something the legions of food obsessives who spend so much of their time bemoaning their dreadful impact on our culture could never bring themselves to admit. Supermarkets are a force for change, good change, the sort of change that makes life worth living. We talk endlessly about food revolutions, about the way our culture has developed over the years; how we have gone from a time when olive oil was something sold in the chemist's for earache, and Parmesan cheese came grated unto dust and smelling lightly of vomit, to a foodie Shangri-La in which we all feast at a national table weighed down with gloriously good things to eat. We go on about this without noticing that in the vanguard of this revolution are the supermarkets. None of the things we take for granted these days – bunches of fresh brassic flat-leaf parsley rather than the dried, friable stuff that looks like the wrong end of a pot-pourri; butter from Brittany with crunchy salt crystals and a slight cheesy edge; cooking chorizos; crisp, green, peppery first-press olive oils; artisan breads; free-range eggs; big, butch sausages made from happy, outdoor-reared pigs; Thai cooking pastes; miso sauce and fish sauce and sesame oil, and so many other things besides – would be as freely and as widely available as they are today without the supermarkets.

I remember the first moment this struck me. It was the mid-nineties and I was on holiday in the Yorkshire Dales. We took a day trip to Blackpool. I'm not sure why. I think we just wanted to feel cheap and dirty for an afternoon. It worked. In a good way. On the way back I decided we should stop off at the big supermarket – I think it was an Asda – on the edge of town to pick up some stuff for dinner. I had a double rack of lamb back at the cottage we were renting and I wanted to stuff it with a mixture of breadcrumbs and basil, olives, anchovies and caramelized onions. In those days my credentials as an urbane young man, who understood the imperatives of a Mediterranean diet, rested on that thing I did with the double rack of lamb. It was something I made quite often at home, but to caramelize the onions I needed a bottle of deep, dark, sour-sweet balsamic vinegar. In London, getting hold of some of that was no problem at all. There was always a well-stocked deli somewhere nearby, ready to do the business. But on the edge of Blackpool? I trudged moodily around the aisles, my face fixed in a sneer of pure metropolitan disdain. In short, I had my normal face on.

Soon the expression was gone. For there, on the shelf, was not just a bottle of balsamic vinegar. There was a choice of balsamics. Oh my.

This story looks ludicrous, doesn't it? It's quite clear that I'm a patronizing schmuck. What's so amazing about balsamic vinegar in a Blackpool supermarket? But that's the thing. In the nineties – less than twenty years ago – everything was amazing about this. I left that Asda clutching my bottle of balsamic – and my fresh basil, and my glistening anchovies – feeling like the country in which I lived was suddenly a better place. And it was suddenly a better place because a supermarket had decided to stock the things I wanted to eat.

Why had this happened? Because food media in Britain, as elsewhere around the world, had exploded.

A SHORT HISTORY OF A FOOD REVOLUTION

Just as we have to acknowledge the part that the supermarkets have played in revolutionizing the way we eat, so we also have to swallow hard and accept that the key people responsible for changing the way we eat in Britain are those renowned gourmands Margaret Thatcher and Rupert Murdoch.

I'll say that again: Margaret Thatcher and Rupert Murdoch. Or, to give them their full job descriptions, arguably Britain's most divisive post-war Prime Minister, and a media mogul now generally regarded as having been at the head of a company whose employees routinely engaged in phone hacking.

Let's go back a bit. Whenever you hear Britain's Dordogne-loving middle classes engage in eye-rolling about the state of food culture in their own country and extolling the virtues and marvels of France, where every small town and village supports a perfect restaurant, and where they do not object to spending reasonable sums of money on food, and a family bonding experience involves slaughtering a whole pig and butchering it down so that everything other than the oink can be eaten, it is worth reminding them of this: during the Second World War the French quickly decided the game was up, laid down their arms and got on with their lives. Or lunch, as they called it.

When that great historian and social commentator Bart Simpson described the French as 'cheese-eating surrender monkeys' he was obviously being shamelessly provocative.

On the other hand, as with all great gags, there was more than a grain of truth in it. The French do eat an awful lot of cheese. Witness General de Gaulle's great gastronomic boast, disguised as despair, about the impossibility of successfully ruling a country that has '246 different kinds of cheese'. And, well, they did actually surrender. Quite a lot.

Britain, meanwhile, locked in a war of national survival, industrialized its food-production system and introduced rationing on a vast scale. (And yes, of course, there was also some rationing in France during the twentieth century, but nothing like on the scale of that in Britain.) It is hard to over-state the damage that this war did to Britain's food culture. A whole generation forgot how to cook. Likewise, a genuine fight for survival, combined with an ingrained Puritanism

which regarded the spending of anything more than necessary on food as plain wrong, made completely redundant any
sort of interest in food beyond its importance for basic
nutrition.

There were, of course, torch-bearers in post-war Britain
who fought the good fight. Raymond Postgate launched *The
Good Food Guide* in 1951, identifying the few places worth
eating in by soliciting reviews from diners around the country;
it was an early example of the kind of crowdsourcing the web
would make *de rigueur* half a century later. A few chefs and
restaurateurs – George Perry-Smith at the Hole in the Wall in
Bath, for example, Joyce Molyneux at the Carved Angel in
Dartmouth, or Brian Sack and Francis Coulson at Sharrow
Bay in the Lake District – worked hard to introduce a select
band of people to a better way of eating. But it was a minority
sport for what was regarded as a decadent, over-indulged
minority. Hell, in the early seventies most people had to live
with the lights going off half the time. Against that a dish of
salmon *en croute* with a sorrel sauce wasn't merely a luxury;
many people thought it was nothing less than an obscenity.

It took Margaret Thatcher's second election victory in 1983,
and the boom that followed, to solve that problem. Suddenly
having money was OK. It was better than OK. In the famous
words of Oliver Stone's creation Gordon Gecko in the movie
Wall Street, greed was good. So we spent money on houses and
on cars and on shares, and on awful double-breasted suits
with big shoulders and sleeves baggy enough so we could roll
them up. Oh, the shame.

Eventually we were going to need something else to spend
our money on, and food was the solution. It is no coincidence
that some of the key restaurants of Britain's first restaurant
boom – Bibendum, Kensington Place, The River Café and

Harvey's, with a young chef called Marco Pierre White at the stove – all opened in 1987.

At the same time something else happened, something absolutely vital. Rupert Murdoch went to war with the print unions, to free himself from the labour restrictions that were stopping the introduction of new technology. Others had been involved in this struggle, most notably Eddie Shah, who finally launched the all-colour *Today* tabloid newspaper in 1986. But it was Murdoch's decision later in the same year to lock out the unions and move production of his papers – the *Sun*, the *News of the World*, *The Times* and the *Sunday Times* – from Fleet Street to a wholly new computerized plant in Wapping which changed everything for the newspaper business. It made the industry cheaper. It made it quicker. And it made the newspapers bigger. Suddenly, printing multiple sections was not only doable. It was necessary. After all, the economy was booming and advertisers were gagging to buy space. There was only one problem: what the hell to put in that space?

The success of glossy magazines like *ID* and *The Face*, launched in the early eighties, alerted older national newspaper editors to something their younger magazine brethren had long known: there was this thing called lifestyle, and it sold copies. These newspaper supplements quickly filled up with pages of property, fashion and, of course, food. There is an assumption that there have been restaurant critics on Britain's national newspapers for decades. It's not so. Jonathan Meades was one of the first to be appointed, to a column on *The Times*, but not until 1986. Likewise, today the profession of restaurant PR is firmly established. However did we get by without them? Presumably restaurants used to just unlock the doors and wait for people to come and be fed.

The first public relations man solely dedicated to the dark arts of promoting restaurants and chefs was a former music business PR with a mop of blond hair, a neat line in patter and a taste for the hard stuff. Alan Crompton-Batt single-handedly invented the restaurant PR industry in 1987 when he began pushing a young Yorkshire-born cook with lots of black hair, piercing eyes and a talent for rock-star antics called Marco Pierre White. If Marco hadn't existed it's entirely possible those acres of newsprint crying out for content would have had to invent him. Indeed, it's arguable they actually did. And quickly this spread from print to television. Where once food on TV was presented by essentially domestically orientated cooks and food writers like Fanny Craddock and Delia Smith, suddenly there was a bunch of intense-looking men in whites emerging from behind their restaurant ranges. *Take Six Cooks*, three series of which ran on the BBC in the mid- to late eighties, introduced the British public to a whole new set of combustible, distinctly uncosy personalities like Raymond Blanc, Nico Ladenis, Marco, and a very young Gary Rhodes.

Witness the birth of the celebrity chef. Britain's food revolution was under way.

Britain's supermarkets were brilliantly placed to cash in on it. A classically Thatcherite relaxation of the planning laws, combined with an abundance of capital on the markets, had enabled the biggest supermarkets to grow and prosper. They abandoned city centres where there was not enough space – many of the original self-service supermarkets were in disused cinemas, the only buildings big enough to accommodate them on the high street – for purpose-built retail sheds on the edges of residential areas. With this expansion came a greater responsiveness. If a big-name cook named a must-have ingredient on TV, the supermarkets could have it on the shelves within days.

Over the years Delia Smith has moved the market in liquid glucose, cranberries, and even something as basic as eggs. In more recent years supermarkets have rushed to stock ingredients as diverse as crab, rabbit, fresh herbs and wild mushrooms in response to recipes from the likes of Hugh Fearnley-Whittingstall, Gordon Ramsay and Nigella Lawson.

But the relationship between big-name chefs and the supermarkets goes much further. Many chefs like Rick Stein or Hugh Fearnley-Whittingstall may well make a point about the imperative to support local food producers and suppliers. Rick Stein has included at the back of some of his books long lists of contact information for these suppliers. The implication – and sometimes the overt message – is that the spread of supermarkets is something that must be resisted. And yet, increasingly, it is the very same supermarkets which are responsible for making these books best-sellers. Publishers are unembarrassed about it. They will tell you this: unless a big, glossy cookbook from a big, glossy Celeb Chef has supermarket support, it simply will not do well. As to the supermarkets, they really don't care what message is being handed out as long as it sells. In 2004 Felicity Lawrence's *Not on the Label*, which took absolutely no prisoners in explaining the evils of supermarkets, began selling so well that Tesco simply couldn't resist. They just had to start stocking it. And so the sales increased even further.

This is the reality. It is fashionable to slag off supermarkets (even as, sheepishly, we slope off to them to do our weekly shop). It seems no discussion of British food culture can ever

29

be complete unless it includes a complete trashing of the awfulness of these food retail leviathans. And yet, if they did not exist, if they were not such sophisticated, complex, customer-focused businesses, the food revolution of which this whole discussion is a part simply wouldn't have happened. They have become a vital part of our national life, and have benefited us hugely.

And all of this would be a glorious and marvellous thing. We should be moved to write prose poems about our supermarket sector, compose rousing anthems, erect monuments in its honour. We should, at the very least, be hugely thankful for what we have and its impact on the modern way of life. Were it not for one thing, which is …

3.
SUPERMARKETS ARE EVIL

The spring of 2011 in Britain was marked by an unusually warm, sunny spell of blue skies and soft breezes, and in the plum orchards of Kent the white blossoms bloomed full and heavy. It promised a solid harvest with yields up on the year before. There would, as there had so often been, be lots of domestic plums to meet demand. Britain is good at growing plums. Which is not really surprising. We have been growing them for a very long time. There is evidence of plums being used in cookery during the Roman occupation. By the medieval era they were so dominant that the word 'plum' had become a synonym for all sorts of dried fruits, the famed plum pudding served at the Victorian Christmas a mark of its lasting popularity.

Certainly when the technologists for the major supermarkets began talking to plum farmer Peter Kedge early in 2011, he was able to reassure them that he would have lots and lots of fruit for them to buy, punnet after punnet of Marjorie's Seedling, Reeves and Victoria, as much as 260 tonnes. The technologists monitor the levels of produce supply, to ensure the big multiples can keep their shelves stocked. 'The message I was getting back from the supermarkets was that they could take everything we would grow,' says Kedge, who has been a farmer of apples and plums since 1988, when he joined his wife's family business. 'Mind you,' he says with a weary air, 'they always say that.' Even so, early in 2011 Kedge had no reason to think the harvest would be anything other than a roaring success.

And it might have been were it not for an 83-year-old woman, who was admitted to hospital in the north-west German state of Lower Saxony on 15 May, suffering from bloody diarrhoea. On Saturday 21 May she died, becoming the first of fifty people across Europe – more than forty of them in Germany – to lose their lives to a virulent strain of shiga toxin-producing E. Coli. It's a complicated name for a vicious bug that shreds your kidneys and turns your blood poisonous. As well as the fifty deaths there would be 4,000 other serious cases across Europe, an outbreak that initiated the scientific version of a manhunt for a serial killer. Like all proper detective stories the search came complete with blind alleys, false leads and undeserving suspects. Prime among the innocent were cucumbers from Spain which, on 26 May, were fingered as the cause by German health officials. The next day a Europe-wide alert was issued calling for the withdrawal from sale of all organic Spanish cucumbers. Shortly afterwards the Robert Koch Institute, the German state body with respon-sibility for disease control and prevention, issued guidance warning against the consumption of not just cucumbers but also raw tomatoes and lettuce. It was a bad month for salad.

The consumer response was all but instantaneous. Even in Britain, where nobody had died, and where the only people who had contracted the illness had visited Germany, sales of cucumbers simply halted, regardless of where they had come from. Health officials in Britain tried to reassure the public that the cucumbers on sale here were safe; even so a glut built up and tonnes had to be dumped. (So much so that on Friday 10 June I found myself interviewing chef Jamie Oliver live on BBC1's *The One Show* about the best way to use up cucumbers. He demonstrated a killer twelve-hour pickling recipe.)

In time the German authorities would absolve the innocent cucumbers of blame. Attention would shift swiftly to a bean-sprout farm in Lower Saxony, and from there back down the food chain to a 15,000-kilogram consignment of seeds that had left the port of Damietta in Egypt almost two years earlier on 24 November 2009. But by then the damage had been done. German consumers hadn't simply turned against cucumbers or even just salad vegetables in general. They had pretty much started boycotting all produce from Spain. What had begun with the death of one octogenarian German lady would, by the middle of that summer, have become a full-blown political and economic crisis, with the Spanish authorities estimating that it had cost Spain's agriculture sector over a quarter of a billion dollars.

And that's where it became a problem for Peter Kedge.

Because among the produce Spanish farmers could no longer sell to the Germans were plums. An enormous number of cricket-ball-sized, blemish-free, sun-ripened plums. For the Spanish farmers this was, as it happened, not much of a problem. In Britain farmers generally don't get paid in full for their produce until the supermarkets take delivery, a major issue we will come to later. In Spain, however, the agents, who act as middlemen, pay for the plums before they're harvested, and then profit when they finally sell on. In Spain there was now a major glut of plums which the agents had to find some way to sell, in a manner which might literally cut their losses. What they needed were customers, and in the British supermarkets that was exactly what they found.

'It was just as we were about to harvest,' Peter Kedge says. 'All of a sudden we got a message from our agents telling us the supermarkets we normally supply had decided to bring in foreign plums.' It didn't matter that the orchards of Kent were bulging with the things, that Britain has an ancient and venerable plum-growing history, or that for years a debate had been growing around the importance of sourcing local produce where possible to cut down on food miles. The supermarkets were going to follow the money. British growers estimated that they had to sell each punnet of plums to the supermarkets at 65p to break even. Spanish agents were offering their plums at 45p a punnet, simply to get them moving. 'We couldn't pick and pack our plums for that money.'

And so Kedge did the one thing which to him made any economic sense. 'We decided not to pick them all, to just leave a significant amount to rot in the orchards.' Dozens of tonnes of perfect British plums fell from the trees and decayed where they lay, until the air in the orchards was heavy with the boozy smell of rotting fruit and they buzzed with the sound of happy fruit flies. 'It's hard to describe what it's like watching your harvest literally go to waste,' Kedge said. 'It's horrible. There's nothing worse.'

Peter Kedge's family originally planted fifty acres of plum orchards back in 1999. Over the years, as supermarkets' buying policies had bitten hard, that had been reduced to thirty-five acres, as trees were 'grubbed out'. In the wake of the disaster of 2011 the farmer once again made plans to grub out trees – to destroy the capacity of his orchards. It was, according to the National Farmers Union (NFU), a story repeated across Britain: tonne after tonne of perfect plums left to rot, prime trees cut down, orchards emptied.

This is one of the complications of the fruit-growing business. If you are in arable crops – wheat or barley or maize or rapeseed – you can follow the ups and downs of supply and demand, changing your crop from one year to the next depending upon who wants what. Fruit farmers can't do that. 'Planting a plum tree is a major investment,' Kedge says. 'It takes about six years from initial planting to recoup the investment. And after that you might have another ten years in which to make money.' The killing of trees simply ends that story. A little bit more of Britain's ability to feed itself also dies.

The brutal, clear-eyed, wake up and smell the prime, Grade A, dark roast Taste the Extra Special Finest Difference coffee is: this is just business. This is what supermarkets do. Complaining about a supermarket chasing the cheapest price is like wandering into a brothel and complaining about all the shagging going on in there. And it's true, up to a point. These corporate behemoths have shareholders to think about and profits to make. In the short term that is exactly what they do, and they do it extraordinarily well. Tesco made £1.9 billion in the first six months of 2011, up 12.1 per cent on the previous year. Sainsbury's made £395 million, up 6.6 per cent. Asda made £803 million, and that was a drop of over 10 per cent. But there is a bigger, dirtier picture. The business of food supply is full of consequences, and some of them are very serious indeed.

Consider the dodo. A butcher trading in prime dodo meat – such lovely animals, all free-range, look at the drumsticks on that – would have been laughing all the way to the bank in 1620. He would have had access to all the dodo he could possibly want. By 1681, however, when the last dodo was killed by the last scurvy-ridden Dutch sailor to feed himself, it might not have looked like such a smart business model. Right now it feels like the big supermarkets are in the dodo extinction business.

The buyers drive such hard bargains, under such extraordinarily unfair terms, that British farming is being decimated. (And the way is being opened to fraud. The scandal around horsemeat being found in processed food products labelled as beef, which first broke across Britain and then Europe in January of 2013, was attributed by many to pressures on price. With beef at an all time high of £2.75 a kilo deadweight on the international markets and horsemeat at around £1.85, the substitution by unscrupulous traders made economic sense in the face of profit margins cut to the bone by supermarket buyers.) In the summer of 2011 food journalist Alex Renton tried to get farmers to talk, on the record, about their dealings with the supermarkets. Most of them refused. They demanded anonymity. They insisted upon off-the-record briefings. Whilst they are obviously lawful companies, the supermarkets did come across less as food retailers and more like mafias, hell-bent on extortion. Anybody who has done business with them might not think the comparison overblown: the supermarkets would insist upon legally binding contracts that would tie producers into supplying them, but without a specified price. The supermarkets could, with little or no warning, simply reject a consignment of produce, insisting it didn't hit quality thresholds. The producers would be required to carry the cost of any two-for-one and discounting offers. They would have to get their harvests packaged at plants designated by the supermarkets, often at twice the price it might cost to get the job done independently. (In June 2011 Peter Kendall, chairman of the NFU, told a parliamentary committee that some of these packers and processors pay a portion of the premium extracted from the farmers to the very supermarkets who had enforced the extra charge, as a kind of kickback.)

Most of all there is the issue of price. The best-known sector of British farming to suffer is dairy. Not long ago I spent a day working on a dairy farm in Cornwall. It's not easy. I got up at four o'clock in the morning, which surely must be regarded as cruel and unusual punishment in itself. I did so, merely so I could stand in a cow shed and dodge plumes of steaming shite being fired out of big animals under pressure. A lot of the job seems to involve shit – dodging it, hosing it off, scraping it up. I weaved my way around the stamping, clanking hooves to wipe down teats with disinfectant. I felt the suck and pull of the automated milking system as the rubber plugs went on. I washed floors, scraped yards, piled hay, interacted with more shit, and then gave thanks to the gods that my day job mostly involves sitting at tables, either eating or writing about what I've eaten or feeling smug about what I've written about what I've eaten while wondering what I'll eat next.

For all this – the brutal, grinding hard labour of milk production – the supermarkets were at that point willing to pay, through their intermediaries, the princely sum of 25p a litre. The cost of producing milk is around 27p a litre. It's not a brilliant business model, is it? It's not even on nodding terms with a brilliant business model. The majority of dairy farmers had, courtesy of supermarket buying policies, been sentenced to make a loss on every litre of milk they sold. The farmer who let me onto his farm as the worst work-experience student in world history said he hoped they might make enough to keep their heads above water by renting out holiday accommodation or selling the calves from their herd for beef. In short, the only way he might make money as a producer of milk was not by producing milk at all, but from other things.

Having spent that day working on a traditional dairy farm, to me it was no surprise at all that one dairy farmer was leaving the industry every week, simply because they couldn't make it pay. Obviously, a lot of farmers do what they do because they love it. There are easier ways to make money, most of which don't involve close proximity to animal faeces. But eventually even that sort of loving relationship can get dysfunctional, especially when it occurs to you that you're not making money any more. Britain, a country full of green grassy fields, a place that could hardly have been more expertly engineered for grazing cows and producing milk, was losing its capacity to do so. At the peak of milk production in Britain, in 2001, there were, according to DairyCo, which represents British dairy farmers, 2.25 million cows producing five billion litres of milk a year, but their numbers were dwindling, down to 1.8 million cows in 2012. We had always been self-sufficient in liquid milk and yet by 2010 we were finally having to import the stuff from elsewhere to top up our own supply.

It's the same story in a branch of farming which is close to my animal-fat-drenched heart: pigs. It's close to my heart because I very much like eating them. A couple of years ago, pig farmers took out full-page newspaper adverts announcing that they were being paid less by the supermarkets than the cost of production for their animals. As a result, like dairy farmers, pig farmers were simply giving up. Jamie Oliver dedicated a whole hour of (distinctly unsexy) television to the problem. It had a snappy title, *Save Our Bacon*, but came down to sixty minutes of stolid, grumpy, whingeing farmers. And who wants to watch that? In any case the supermarkets really didn't regard this as such a huge problem because they could buy in from elsewhere – Denmark, for example, or the Netherlands – where animal welfare standards are much lower. In this country it's illegal to put sows in tightly confined stalls, which make it impossible for them to move around while they wean their litters. On the continent the practices continue. BPEX, the body which represents British pig producers, estimates that two-thirds of the imported pork and pork products consumed in Britain are produced in conditions that would be illegal in this country.

And yet, because of the power of the supermarkets, the industry seems incapable of mounting anything other than the most feeble of fightbacks. In the autumn of 2011 I was approached by BPEX to see if I would front a campaign for them. They wanted consumers to sign up to take a pledge, committing themselves only to buying pork which carried the British red tractor label. If you stick to that simple rule then you know that the meat you are eating has been raised under higher welfare standards. It sounded like a good campaign. After all, I had been arguing for exactly this for a while. Plus the campaign was on behalf of a trade body rather than a specific producer, so it wasn't a product endorsement. We agreed a fee. We discussed what they wanted me to do: photo calls, a series of media interviews, lending my name and image to the campaign. All fine and dandy. It's rather agreeable to be paid to say what you have already been saying for free.

There was just one thing. Obviously, getting consumers to buy the right kind of pork is important. It's vital. But I had to be able to say during the interviews that the supermarkets also had a massive responsibility to pay British pork producers a viable price for their meat, and to support British producers so that they stopped going out of business. So that, in turn, the supermarkets didn't have an excuse to import the stuff from animals tortured on the continent.

The PR company started wringing their hands. 'You are right,' they said, in response to my email, 'supermarkets are part of the issue because the price paid to farmers is not reflective of the conditions in which farmers work and the cost of raising pigs in the UK versus abroad because of the higher welfare standards. However, BPEX is working with the supermarkets to lobby on the issues and we can't be seen to rock the boat. Therefore we are utilizing customers to create demand.' Great. Put it all back on the punters and let the supermarkets off the hook.

I said it was a deal breaker. I said that I had to be able to talk about the supermarkets. The PR people went silent for twenty-four hours and then announced that they had, after much thought, decided to go with a different person altogether. Funny that.

Witness the power of the supermarkets.

Witness it in numbers. By the mid-nineties, if you added up everything Britain grew and exported – British seafood and beef have always been big sellers, for example – against everything the country imported, it was over 70 per cent self-sufficient in food. By 2011 British self-sufficiency had dropped, according to figures from the Department for Environment, Food and Rural Affairs (Defra), to around 58 per cent and there were many in the food policy world who believed that it was much lower than that; that we were slipping inexorably towards a point where we could supply barely 50 per cent of our food needs. And all because the damned evil supermarkets had undermined the British agricultural base.

What's more, they had been given British government encouragement to do so. In a Defra paper published in December 2006, the government's position on food security was articulated thus: 'Poverty and subsistence agriculture are root causes of national food insecurity. National food security is hugely more relevant for developing countries than the rich countries of Western Europe.' In short, all that really mattered was free trade, and access to foodstuffs from wherever they might be available across our fecund globe.

In academic food policy circles, within universities and institutes, this paper was nicknamed the 'Leave it to Tesco' report. Food security wasn't an issue for the rich, industrialized nations. We had big fat wallets. We could always buy our way out of trouble. So stop whining and whingeing, and crack open another Chicken Jalfrezi ready meal made with hen from Brazil, tomatoes from Morocco and palm oil from some poor benighted orang-utan's last remaining bit of virgin forest. And how about an apple pie to finish, made with pristine apples from China, each individually picked and wrapped by a Chinese peasant with their eyes on the main prize of a Western-style industrialized, urban lifestyle?

Then 2008 happened. It happened like one of those awful slow-motion car crashes, with screeching tyres and the smell of burning brakes and the knowledge even as you watched it that nothing would ever be quite the same again. The causes were obvious and predictable, but still it took people by surprise: a bad harvest in Australia, a cyclone in the Bay of Bengal, a set of bizarre US government policies which then saw 20 per cent of the perfectly edible corn harvest being directed towards the manufacture of bioethanol (a policy which was meant to be impeccably green, but really wasn't), those damn Chinese peasants getting a taste for beef that required seven kilos of grain for every kilo of meat produced, a hike in oil prices which, in turn, made petrochemical-based fertilizers much more expensive, the rise and rise of commodity trading. And then there was a failure to keep reserves of basic foodstuffs. Where once a nation might have four months of wheat backed up, in our just-in-time culture, meaning it is delivered only when needed, reserves have fallen to only a matter of a few days. All of these factors we will come back to in detail. What matters is the impact they had on food prices: they went up.

And up.

Between 2006 and 2008 the price of rice rose 217 per cent. Wheat went up by 136 per cent, corn by 125 per cent and soya beans by 107 per cent. Countries like Brazil, Thailand and India temporarily banned the export of certain varieties of rice. There were food riots all over the world, including in Bangladesh, Cameroon and Ivory Coast – and those are only the countries in the first part of the alphabet where there was civil unrest. In Mozambique people were killed in riots over the cost of food. Food prices would later be blamed for a second wave of civil unrest that started in Tunisia on 18 December 2010 and soon spread across the region in what was to become known as the Arab Spring. While events like the downfall of Colonel Gaddafi in Libya, the end of Hosni Mubarak's thirty-year reign in Egypt, and the strife in Yemen and the civil war in Syria were clearly caused by a multitude of different competing pressures, there is a growing body of opinion that the one thing which united them was societal outrage over food prices.

Countries across the Middle East and North Africa had long suffered from low agricultural productivity and a huge reliance on imports, with governments attempting to placate their populace through endless unsustainable subsidies. The food price rises of 2007–8 simply pushed the situation over the edge. As David Rosenberg, a Senior Fellow on Economic Issues at the GLORIA Center, a foreign affairs think-tank based in Jerusalem, put it in a paper on the Arab Spring, 'virtually all the countries of the region are contending with a food crisis of one kind or another'. It was a crisis so deep and intense and severe that it caused civil wars and overthrew governments.

And in Britain in 2008? That rich, Westernized, mine's-a-prawn-ring-from-Iceland-for-£5.99-thank-you-very-much Britain? We felt it. We felt it like footballers feel a blown Achilles tendon. By August 2008 food price inflation was running at nearly 14 per cent. The cost of fat and oil had risen by 29 per cent, of meat by 16.3 per cent. This had begun to hurt. Finally the government began to wake up. New reports on food security were being published, declaring the challenges posed by a rising global population – expected to reach nine billion by 2050 – and by climate change potentially taking once productive slabs of land out of use. Suddenly Defra, a ministry which actually had the word 'Food' in its title, seemed to think that food production was important.

There was one issue, however, that they didn't want to deal with: the bastard supermarkets. They didn't appear anywhere in the equation. For years pressure groups and farmers' representatives had been campaigning for some sort of ombudsman with real powers who could intervene in the relationship between the supermarkets and the producers to ensure a fair price was achieved, so that plum farmers didn't grub up their trees. For years successive governments dragged their feet. The market was the thing. The market would see us right. A code of conduct was introduced, and yet there was no one to oversee it. In the run-up to the 2010 General Election the

Liberal Democrats suddenly announced a policy for a grocery ombudsman, if they should win the vote. In what was looking like an increasingly close race, both Labour and the Conservatives followed suit, announcing various plans for a new body which would have some ill-defined powers.

After the Conservative–Liberal Democrat coalition came to power in May 2010, nothing happened. And then a lot more of nothing happened. The agriculture ministers in Defra made noises, said there would be a paper proposing a new ombudsman, just as soon as they had cleaned the oven and sorted through their sock drawer, or whatever else it is government departments do when they are stalling for time. In February 2011 I was invited to sit on a panel at the NFU's annual conference, alongside Jim Paice MP, himself a one-time farmer and now agriculture minister. Asked to make some opening comments to the 750-strong audience, I pointed out that we were still waiting for news of a supermarket ombudsman, that the way things were going the bill wouldn't be before Parliament for at least a year, which would mean it would be at least two or three years before any such office would be established.

Paice attacked me. He shouted me down like I was a stupid schoolboy, said the bill would be along within a few weeks, that frankly I didn't know what the hell I was talking about. I was baffled. I hadn't made it up: I had been talking to reporters on *Farmers Weekly*. I had been having off-the-record discussions with officials within the NFU who liaised with Parliament. Now it appeared I had got it wrong. It was a humiliating experience.

I hadn't got it wrong. The first paper proposing a new ombudsman did not appear until late autumn of that year, and even then it was roundly attacked by everybody in the farming world for being nowhere near robust enough. As I prepared to address the NFU conference again in February 2012 there was still no news of when the bill would come before Parliament. And if the bill still hadn't come before the House there was no way an ombudsman to oversee the supermarkets and make sure they didn't screw the farmers could be established before 2013 at the very earliest. The supermarkets were free to carry on destroying the dairy, pig and plum industries. They were free to carry on undermining the agricultural base. They were free to carry on making Britain less and less self-sufficient.

Result!

A dull weekday afternoon, and I am running for my life. This is what I tell myself as my feet thud, like slimy, dead fish, on the treadmill. I am in the gym running to stay alive; or, more to the point, so that I can carry on living in a way which makes me happy. Lunch makes me happy. So does dinner. Being hugely overweight does not. As a result, three, four or sometimes even five times a week I am on the treadmill in my local gym beating out the miles. Or I'm in a brightly lit, reconditioned railway arch, being ordered to do strenuous things by an irritatingly cheerful personal trainer called Jonny. I pay to experience this pain. But then I am motivated. For good or ill, some of my working life now takes place in front of television cameras. I do not want to have to watch these appearances from behind a cushion, or feel the stab of childish hurt when somebody tweets about my 'generous moobs'. As they have.

Run, fat boy, run.

There is one way of telling this tale which positions me less as culprit than as victim. In this version of the story it is the supermarkets, with their endless largesse, which have made me fat. It's all their fault for being stocked with so much irresistible fat and sugar and general starchy carbs. In my case it's simply not true. I have always been fat. I was a fat little boy and a fat adolescent and a fat twenty-something. In my house, when I was growing up, diets – as against diet – were a regular feature. There was one which required the eating of nine eggs a day and not much else. It made my breath smell of the entire world's farts. I was 8 years old. There was another which applied units to foodstuffs and demanded endless counting and calculation so you didn't exceed a daily total. I dieted in my teens and again in my twenties and thirties. Becoming a restaurant critic was not a turning point in my life. It was simply a coming together of greed and earning potential. I had always spent my own money in restaurants. I had always read restaurant reviews. Now I could write them too.

This did have consequences, most of them measurable in inches. A few years ago I wrote a book about the growth of the global luxury restaurant industry. I travelled the world, telling the stories of seven great cities – Las Vegas, Moscow, Dubai, Tokyo, and so on – through their gastro palaces. In the last chapter, as my doubts about the whole business of big-ticket dining began to grow, I went to Paris to experience the high-end version of Morgan Spurlock's film *Supersize Me*. In this, Spurlock ate at McDonald's every day for a month, and if asked whether he wished to supersize his meal, he had to say yes. Doctors monitored his progress and at the end he had the fatty liver of a foie gras goose.

In the luxury version I went to Paris and ate in a Michelin three-star restaurant every day for a week; if they offered me the tasting menu I had to say yes.

I too received the once-over from a doctor. Although I managed not to put on any weight – I tended to eat just the fancy restaurant meal and nothing else each day – it didn't much matter. My weight was already out of control. My waist was north of forty-four inches much as Edinburgh is north of Madrid. My chest was beyond fifty-two inches and I was well over twenty stone. I had avoided checking my weight. I didn't want to know. Now, courtesy of the experiment, I knew. I was so large I had my own gravitational pull; planets were slipping out of alignment because of me. Something had to be done. I had always worked out, but only a couple of times a week; now I went five or six times a week. I dropped a lot of the carbohydrate from my diet and the weight did begin to come off. A woman working at the gym told me one day that they had nicknamed me 'Candle Man' because I was melting. Eventually I would shift nearly four stone. Hurrah for me.

The change didn't go unnoticed. One of my editors at the *Observer* saw there was less of me and, convinced that all personal experiences could be processed into good copy, asked me to write about my gym habit and what had motivated it. I resisted. She asked again. I still said no. I hate self-congratulatory diet pieces. After all, nobody had forced me to eat the pork belly–langoustine combo. Or the truffled pommes purées. Or the millefeuilles of chestnuts and Chantilly cream. I did it all to myself. I was my own special creation. Plus there was always the risk that I wouldn't keep the weight off. I had done the job, but for how long exactly? Inside this newly thinner man was that old fat bloke desperate to get out again. (A reasonable fear: some, though by no means all, has indeed crept back on.) But my editor was persistent and wore me down. I finally agreed to write the article on one condition: that she hire the most expensive photographer she could afford, so that I would have a killer set of pictures to look back on when my body had degenerated into a garish flesh atrocity of the sort Francis Bacon liked to paint. Gazing at those pictures – me, in the gym, lifting weights – I could say, 'There was a moment, perhaps just an afternoon, when I looked OK.' I posed for those pictures only for me. The fact that they were published in a national newspaper with a circulation of hundreds of thousands was neither here nor there.

After the article appeared I was told by a number of my female friends that my behaviour was curiously feminized; that by having focused so tightly on food and body image in this way I was heading more into the chromosomal column marked xx than xy. I didn't take offence. For all the big hair and the beard and the moustache, I accept I am indeed a feminized male. My hands may be large but they are bizarrely smooth and soft. I always say I have the hands of a male-to-female transsexual, after the hormones have kicked in. My chest is so hairless I have been accused of waxing. I don't. (I did once, but only for money; it was for a piece of journalism. It seriously bloody hurt.) I hate football. Actually, I have no interest in any sports. I like musicals. I work out to them. I prefer wine to beer and will nurse a glass of rosé without embarrassment. My wife once called me the gayest straight man in London. A very gay male friend of mine once called me a male lesbian. I said: a what? He said: 'You'd make a great gay man if it wasn't for the fact you're so obviously into women.' I wear all of this as a badge of honour. I can't do bloke and I'm proud of the fact.

Still, I was bemused to hear that there might be anything about my relationship with food which was especially female. Because there is a particular kind of female response to food which, to me, has always looked at best exhausting and at worst completely dysfunctional; a desperate mixture of fear, guilt and shame for which I have neither time nor understanding. There is an industry to serve it. Put the words 'healthy eating' into amazon.com and you will get over 25,000 references. There are more than 170 books with the word 'skinny' in the title and 129 using that filthy four-letter word 'thin'. There's *Cook Yourself Thin*, *Cook Yourself Thin, Faster* and *Soup Can Make You Thin*. There's *The Skinny Rules, Naturally Thin: Unleash Your Skinnygirl and Free Yourself from a Lifetime of Dieting*, not forgetting *The French Don't Diet Plan: 10 Simple Steps to Stay Thin for Life*. There's *Hungry Girl to the Max!: The Ultimate Guilt-Free Cookbook*. Pitch: 'In *Hungry Girl to the Max!*, Lisa Lillien has created a book that is a must-have for anyone who craves insanely delicious food without the high-calorie price tag!' Beware any book with exclamation marks in the title.

Over the years, of course, many of these books, and others like them, have been sold in supermarkets, alongside racks of magazines promising to show you how to 'Slim Down in Just 24 hours' (*Women's Fitness*) 'Eat, Drink and Still Shrink' (*Women's Health*) and 'How to Spot a Healthy Canapé' (*Zest*). It's clear that for a certain type of woman the supermarket has become a one-stop shop, not merely for their groceries but also for desperate self-loathing. You can buy both the foods to make you hate yourself, and the holy texts through which, with enough commitment and devotion, you can atone for that sinful behaviour. Quite so: after all, supermarkets are built for convenience.

It all plays to a strongly held notion that the supermarket is part of a new-fangled modern way of living which, slowly but surely, is killing us. We are, it seems, the victims of a massively over-processed, fat-saturated, sugar-coated, super-sized, under-exercised food conspiracy. And this is where it gets very complicated indeed. Because there are many statistics you can deploy to show that modern life is not actually killing us at all. Indeed, you can prove it is doing precisely the opposite. It is making us live much, much longer very fast. Between 1991 and 2009 male life expectancy in the UK rose from 73.37 to 77.85 years. Female life expectancy rose from 78.86 to just over 82 years. Those are significant rises. Life expectancy in the US has risen by roughly similar amounts. At the same time, while the incidence of cancers in the UK has risen by a third since the seventies, the figure has actually been fairly stable since the late nineties, which is remarkable given that an increasingly ageing population should present more in the way of cancers. In the US the rates of a number of key cancers have been falling (especially bowel cancer, which has dropped from just over 63 cases per 100,000 men in 1995 to just over 48 per 100,000 men now.)

That, however, is not the full story, for there are other key indicators which matter here and they are around obesity and, even more importantly, the lifestyle-related incidence of Type 2 diabetes. There the story is bleak. Nobody publishes zappy self-help books about that; glossy magazines don't have shouty, cheery cover-lines drawing you into stories on the subject. Between 1996 and 2012 the number of people in the UK with Type 2 diabetes rose from 1.4 million to 2.9 million. (In the US the picture is, if anything, worse. Between 1980 and 2008 the number of people with the disease rose from 5.6 million to 18.1 million.) Funnily enough, all those fretting, guilt-ridden young women with the money to buy copies of *Soup Can Make You Thin* and *The Skinny Rules* – and, according to the publishing industry, these books generally are aimed at those young women – are unlikely to be the ones developing

Type 2 diabetes. For it is a disease both of age – the older the population the more diabetes there will be – and of poverty.

And it is where the most dire poverty is concerned that the supermarkets score the most badly. A few years ago I sat down with Heston Blumenthal of the Fat Duck to taste-test products from the supermarket value ranges, the very cheapest of the cheap, the lowest of the low. It was a truly humbling experience. As we studied the prices, all of them measured in pence rather than pounds, we swiftly concluded that whatever aesthetic considerations we might want to bring to bear – Did this stuff taste nice? Was it well made? – were irrelevant. Nobody bought these products because they liked them: they bought them because economic circumstance forced them to do so. And as the banking crisis of 2007 turned into a deep, lengthy recession, more and more people found themselves having to do the same. The big supermarkets were quickly reporting that, while the sales of their premium ranges were dropping, sales of their own-brand budget ranges were rising by over 40 per cent.

So what do you get for your money? Not an awful lot. For a TV investigation I did a forensic job on the cheapest supermarket products. What would you say to a beef pie that was only 18 per cent beef, and a few more per cent 'beef connective tissue' – or gristle, collagen and fat, as it's more commonly known? How about a pork sausage that's just 40 per cent pork, with a slab of pig skin chucked in for bulk? Or an apple pie with so little apple – a mere 14 per cent – that you can't help but wonder whether it really deserves the name? I suspect, like me, you would say 'No thanks' and pull a 'What do you take me for?' face. Then again, I have a choice. I don't have to buy cheese slices with half the levels of calcium of the more expensive variety or chicken breasts that have been bulked up with 40 per cent water to give you the impression you are getting more for less. The people who are buying these products generally don't have that choice. They have to take what the supermarkets deign to give them. Which raises the question: is what the supermarkets give them good enough?

Only the most callous could argue that it is. Across the world the big supermarkets have been given all but unfettered access to the massive food retail market. But with that unfettered access must come responsibilities – and surely that should include improving the quality of the food sold to the very poorest in society? We can fight long and hard about what the word 'quality' means. The supermarkets will argue that their budget ranges aren't in any way harmful and point out – rightly – that in recent years great efforts have been made to reduce the levels of salt and sugar in very cheap bread. The age of rickets is over. But that still leaves them selling products that contain animal products that the vast majority of us would actually throw away rather than cook with. Pig skin is apparently quite high in protein, but would you really choose to have it minced up and put in your sausages simply because it's cheap?

As part of the TV show I worked on, I asked food technologist David Harrison to re-engineer some standard value-range products. I didn't want him to make a gourmet beef pie. That would be easy. Just throw money and some quality sirloin at the problem. I wanted Harrison to make a better pie, keeping within reasonable financial parameters. He started by analysing all the cheapest pies on the market and found that, on average, they had just 18 per cent beef plus a few more percentage points of that connective tissue. (It can go much lower: I came across a minced beef and onion pie that declared a beef content on the label of just 7 per cent.) Harrison upgraded our generic recipe to produce one that had no connective tissue and 25 per cent beef. The extra cost, to increase the meat content by 38 per cent? A penny a pie. To remove the pig skin from a budget pork sausage and lift the meat content from 40 per cent to 54 per cent cost 0.7p per sausage. To increase the amount of apple in an apple pie by more than 40 per cent cost 0.8p. As the cost of raw ingredients is only a quarter of the finished product's retail price, these really are tiny amounts. All of these improvements, even represented as double-digit percentages, may look marginal, but the differences in the finished product were discernible. We did a series of blind taste tests and the overwhelming majority of people identified our new improved products and preferred them. And if that sounds like banal advertising patter, so be it.

Obviously companies need to make money, or they wouldn't be able to invest in their business, which in turn means they wouldn't be able to serve their customers. But if absorbing the expense to make these improvements meant Tesco's 2011 half-yearly profits went from £1.95 billion to, say, £1.85 billion, and if Sainsbury's made not £395 million but £390 million, who exactly would weep? Not me.

Let's be clear. A 25 per cent meat pie is still not a fabulous item. Nor would Blumenthal and I have swooned over a 54 per cent pork sausage. Likewise, we can lecture those in dire straits on the need to eat more fresh fruit and vegetables – where the value ranges happen to score well – though patronizing people who are struggling to make ends meet has always left me with a nasty taste in the mouth. The fact is that the items I looked at are invariably going to be a part of the diet, and that leads to simple questions of respect; of the supermarkets, which do so well out of us in good times, not forcing the very poorest to eat dross when the bad times come.

Because that's what we have been living through recently. A survey in late 2012 by the market research company Kantar Worldpanel found that the households on the lowest incomes in Britain were spending more and more money on the very cheapest processed foods, because they were perceived to be more filling. They were buying exactly the grim products that we had trawled through, shoving the country into what was being described as a 'nutritional recession'. It was presented as a trend, a function of short-term food price rises and falling incomes.

But what happens to the total crap pedalled by the supermarkets to the people with the least choice when, as a result of their own brutal buying policies, the supply chain breaks down? When the prices for absolutely everything go through the roof? When producers from abroad no longer wish to supply the supermarkets and there isn't enough agricultural production left at home to pick up the slack?

What happens then?

One evening late in 2011 I found myself at a private dinner, sitting next to a very senior board-level executive from one of the big supermarkets. Although I had written positive pieces about the supermarkets in the past, and had explained patiently why they weren't necessarily evil, my relationships with the big multiples had become increasingly strained. I rarely got an answer from them when, as a journalist, I asked questions. And yet, here I was, sitting next to one of the big beasts. It was an opportunity.

And so, very intently, while filling up the exec's wine glass, I began to explain my over-arching theory of everything: that by giving the big supermarkets unfettered access to the retail food market we had allowed them to completely destroy farming; that we were becoming increasingly less self-sufficient in food because so many farmers were quitting in the face of horrible business practices. All of this mattered, I said, because of the global food security situation. Some of the price spikes of 2008 might have eased, but it was only a moment's respite. Those issues would come back to haunt us. Countries like China, India and Brazil would be competing for the resources we wanted and when prices spiked again we would no longer be able to afford them. And when we turned back to Britain for our food needs the supply simply wouldn't be there. In short, I said, supermarkets had to start paying producers more so they could invest in agriculture and reinforce our food supply system.

I said it all very cleverly with my special, non-patronizing explaining face.

There was a pause. The executive looked at me. The big beast of the supermarket world said, 'Is this off the record?' I said yes. (Look how I'm not even giving them a gender to protect their identity. It could be a woman. It could be a man. It could be a man dressed as a woman. It isn't. But it could be.)

The executive nodded slowly and said, 'I entirely agree with you.'

I opened my mouth and closed it again. That, I hadn't expected.

My dining companion did go on to say that it was their life's mission to secure a means of food supply so that the supermarket they worked for could source everything they need for decades to come, but still, the point had been made. We are facing a very serious crisis. A global crisis, one in which the supermarkets are complicit.

And to fully understand it, we need to get out a bit. We need to travel. So let's start in Rwanda, a country in central East Africa with a dark history and a complicated present, which also happens to have a lot to tell us about global food supply. And perhaps even more to tell me about the knotty business of being a greedy man in a hungry world.

4.
FINDING THE CHINESE IN KIGALI

I like eating Chinese food in odd places. Anybody can go out for a Chinese in a place where lots of Chinese people live, like central London or Toronto or perhaps even China. But eating Chinese food on a Greek island or in Turkey or in Paris, where Chinese food is famous for being bone-numbingly awful, has a certain cachet. Other people try to make themselves sound like gastronomic adventurers by sucking fat-thick milk straight from the hot teats of yaks, while being watched by baffled Mongolian herdsmen, or by scarfing fermented shark meat which has been preserved in the urine of the fishermen who caught it. I'm sure the shark-in-wee thing is an interesting experience, and one of the many reasons for visiting Iceland, but interesting is not always the same as good. To me it just sounds like the waste of a perfectly good mealtime.

So instead I express my gastronomic adventurism through Chinese food in peculiar places. It's intriguing to see how a set of dishes you know from one setting is shaped and changed by another, depending on the size of the Chinese population and the availability of ingredients. Plus it gives you something to say when you get home from a holiday during which you did nothing other than lie on the beach and read. Chinese food on the Greek island of Zakynthos, for example, is generally very poor: too many gloopy sauces thickened with cornflour; too many gnarly spare ribs coated in sugar and bright orange food dye the colour of an American daytime TV host. By contrast, the food at the Peking Garden in Ovacik, a small, trashy Turkish holiday resort just over the hills to the south of Fethiye, was, for a while, surprisingly good. Their hot and sour soup had a proper punch and they made their own pancakes to go with the crispy duck, pressing a local wheat-heavy crepe recipe into the service of this famous British suburban Saturday-night favourite. Then we went back one year and it was awful. Perhaps the chef had gone home. Perhaps they couldn't get the ingredients any more. Perhaps they had simply lost interest. It was practically Zakynthos standard. Yes, that bad.

So now I was in Kigali, the capital of Rwanda, there was a Chinese restaurant called The Great Wall opposite my hotel, and I knew what I had to do. I had to eat there.

Rwanda is, of course, less famous these days as a place for dinner and more as the country where, in 1994, 800,000 or more souls were slaughtered in a furious genocide executed in a matter of months and, for the most part, using machetes. Nazi Germany industrialized its genocide of the Jews and the Gypsies, the disabled and the gays. It built gas chambers and crematoriums and did serious systems analysis to make it all function with as much Teutonic efficiency as possible. By contrast the Rwandan genocide – inspired in the main by long-held inter-tribal enmities – was a bespoke, hand-tooled affair. It was neighbour on neighbour. It was townsfolk on townsfolk. It was embedded into the very weft and warp of society. Rwanda has done an impressive job of reconstructing and reconfiguring itself in the years since. It has both confronted the issue and not confronted the issue. There is a museum in the centre of Kigali to the genocide. But there are also laws in place to prohibit discussion in the workplace of which tribe – Hutu or Tutsi – people happen to be from. It is the great undiscussable, mentioned more in whispers than shouts. Spending time in Rwanda is like hanging out with a huge extended family with a big, dark secret that is so terrible and so exhausting and so completely known that nobody has the energy to discuss it any more. Just move on. Nothing to see here.

I was in Rwanda with the charity Save the Children, helping to launch a campaign on chronic child malnourishment. We know about acute hunger. We know about famines that emaciate; food supply crises that fill the nightly news with shots of cargo planes unloading sacks of aid onto dusty runways at the very end of the world. Rock stars hold gigs in stadiums to ease acute hunger. Comedians swim the Channel to raise funds. Chronic malnutrition does not make the nightly news in the same way, because it rarely comes with pictures, and nobody swims anything to raise money to deal with the problem. Save the Children estimates that if affects 170 million children worldwide and could blight the lives of half a billion kids in the next fifteen years. It is the hidden underlying cause of 2.6 million child deaths a year as their malnourished bodies give in to diseases like malaria or pneumonia they might otherwise have been able to survive. Malnourishment never appears on death certificates in these cases. It is just there, a fact of life and a bigger fact of death. The children have food to eat but not enough. Or if they have what looks like enough, it lacks the basic nutrients they need for healthy development.

Chronically malnourished children can be 15 per cent smaller than they should be for their age. Their intellectual development is also held back. Malnourishment can knock off IQ points, a blunt measure of smartness, but in these circumstances a valuable one. They are, in the brutal language of child malnourishment, stunted. And all of that affects the population as a whole, because if malnourished, stunted kids make it to adulthood they are unlikely to achieve their full economic potential. In a country like Rwanda, where over 40 per cent of children are malnourished, that can have a massive impact on the ability of society to prosper, develop, and pull itself out of the mire of poverty.

That was why I was there: to see the situation for myself, to write and broadcast about it.

It was also why I suggested to some of the team I was travelling with that we should go for a Chinese at the restaurant across the road. I told them my story about eating Chinese food in odd places, and about how I'd eaten awful Chinese meals in Greece and Turkey and France. And I laughed and said what we needed was a totally surreal experience, so let's go to that dimly lit place across the road, the one with the hanging Chinese lanterns and the open walls with its views out over the city.

But it wasn't true. What I actually needed, what I craved, was a bit of normality, and in the flavours of Chinese food that I knew so well I felt I could locate that.

Because what I was seeing during my trip wasn't normal. It felt a very long way beyond normal. I was wrong, of course. It was only not normal for *me*. For the people I was meeting in Rwanda who were living these lives it was entirely normal. That was the real tragedy.

* * *

Rwanda has food. The place looks like it is built of the stuff, the deep red earth heavy with fruit and grain and leaf. It is called 'the country of a thousand hills' – a gross underestimate – and it looks like every inch of those hills is under cultivation, from the prime plots at the bottom of the valleys to the very peaks for the poorer landowners, who must exhaust themselves climbing up there before they can even start work. The land is laid out in a tight patchwork of fields which, to the average grow-your-own fanatic in the West, must be a unique kind of gastro-porn. Look at the hand-tilled land! Gawp at the rows of beans, the tall stalks of maize, the cassava and sorghum and groundnut crops! Gasp at the yams, the tomatoes ripened to the deep red of a postbox. Oh my! What a perfect small-is-beautiful world. If only Kentish Town could look like this. If only we all grew our own and abandoned supermarkets and fed ourselves like the Rwandans, who are so much closer to the earth.

Or not quite. There is an ugly reality hidden by all this verdant loveliness. Rwanda may be very fertile but it also has lots of people. It is the most densely populated country in Sub-Saharan Africa, with over 400 souls per square kilometre (and, in places, over 700). By contrast, the UK has a population density of just over 250 per square kilometre, while the United States has a mere 32. Although the inter-tribal hatreds behind the genocide are well known, some theorists, most prominent among them the Pulitzer Prize-winning academic and writer Jared Diamond, have described the events in Rwanda as proof positive of Thomas Malthus's theory that lack of resources would keep the human population in check. In short, they say, underlying the genocide was a scarcity of food and land to grow it on. If true, it's further cause for concern: the population of Rwanda is now higher than it was before the genocide. Certainly the battle for those resources is fierce. Nearly 60 per cent of the population have less than half a hectare to cultivate.

According to figures from the Food and Agriculture Organization of the United Nations, the average Rwandan gets by on 2,090 calories a day. The average British person consumes 3,450 and the average American 3,750. Around 9.5 per cent of the Rwandan diet is protein, of which just 0.9 per cent comes from animals. In both the UK and US, 12.1 per cent of the diet is protein and more than half of that comes from animals. Around 38 per cent of the diet in the UK and US is fat; in Rwanda it's just over 20 per cent. Rwanda does not have an obesity problem. Instead it has a population problem.

Not that you need to be bombarded with facts and figures to get to grips with Rwanda's challenges. You can see it everywhere. One day we drove out from Kigali in our Save the Children 4x4s, the vehicle of choice for celebrity poverty tours. At first we were on solid, metalled roads paid for with international aid – half the country's budget comes from donors – and then on roads of rutted earth. There were the hills to look at and the fields to admire, for it is a jewel of a place. But most of all there are the people, and so many of them so young. Half the population is under 18 years old, and while there are efforts to get them into school many are still not in full-time education. They were hanging out on the grass verges watching the world go by, or waving furiously at our cars as they passed. There was an overwhelming sense of a horde of humanity at rest (though across the fields we could also see the silhouettes of women, stooped over their crops as they worked. It was almost always the women, not the men).

We visited a new health centre, built by the charity, on land punctuated by outcrops of black volcanic rock from the smouldering volcanoes that ring this part of the country. Mothers sat with their tiny babies, waiting patiently for their children to be weighed, part of a project to monitor their progress since being identified as malnourished. Measuring bands were wrapped around the kids' spindly arms to check if they were filling out. If their arms were found to be in the green area of the scale they were fine. If they were in yellow, as many were, they were chronically malnourished; if in the red, the situation was acute. Rain battered down on the veranda roofs and the air smelt heavily of vegetation on the turn.

I talked to 23-year-old Josephine, who was sitting with a 2-year-old and a 1-year-old on her lap, the two fighting over her breasts for feeding rights as she talked. She seemed oblivious to the lifelong sibling rivalry being born on her knees. She was small and thin with high cheekbones and a long slender neck and dressed in vivid wraps of fabulous prints; these were, I was told by my guides, probably her Sunday best, put on because she knew we were coming. I was wearing tired linen trousers and a saggy jacket. I felt I should have made more of an effort.

A health visitor had come to her house a kilometre or two away to tell her there was a problem with her kids, Josephine said. I asked if it was upsetting. 'Not really. They gave me the supplements.' They were fed on Plumpy Nut, a protein and fat-rich peanut paste, fortified with vitamins, foil-wrapped packs of which she received at each visit. Gathering enough food for her family – she had other children at home – was tough. 'I have no land and I am the only one who gathers food. I get it by working in other people's fields.' So why did her children become malnourished? I asked.

It was a stupid question, but I was flailing around, trying to find the right way to talk about what sounded to me like any parent's worst nightmare. Before becoming a restaurant critic I was another sort of journalist, one who spent too much time writing about the evil that men do. I covered murders and terrorism and politics and poverty. Worst of all were the child abuse cases, for I found in myself the ability to project the stories I was hearing onto my own children, to swap one set of faces for another. One night after a day spent sitting in court listening to the wretched and banal details of acute neglect, of small children left to rest in their own faeces, ignored despite their calls for help, I went home and washed my own eighteen-month-old so fiercely in the bath I gave him a rash. My child would be clean. My child would be cared for. I needed to wash out the dark stain of those stories.

This felt similar, and yet I was required to engage. I was required to find a language. So then, why did Josephine's children become malnourished? She looked at me blankly and, through the translator, said, 'Because I cannot get enough food.' I nodded solemnly and wrote the words down in my notebook – 'cannot get enough food' – knowing they were the answer to a very stupid question.

In another part of the centre we met a mother who had only given birth a couple of days before, her newborn son in her arms, tightly swaddled. He stared up at us, wide eyed and baffled, and we made the right noises about how beautiful he was and how I hoped the delivery had been OK and how helpful a health centre like this must be to mothers like her. Then I asked his name. She smiled thinly and said something to my translator. By tradition, he told me in turn, they did not give babies names until they were eight days old, 'because they need to see if the baby will live'. I scratched more notes on the bloody obvious in my notebook. It was all part of the same story. It was all about maternal malnutrition as much as it was about child malnutrition. It was about the creaking arithmetic of life and death here on Rwanda's fecund, pulsing earth.

The problem was not simply lack of land, though that was a big part of it. The price of staple foods in the markets here had, as everywhere else around the world, shot up. There didn't appear to be a shortage of food to buy. In the central covered market in Kigali I saw heaps of flour and potatoes, and piles of shiny aubergines of a quality that would make a London restaurateur weep. It was all there. It just cost too much. The impact was twofold. First, there was the obvious problem that those right at the bottom of the economic heap simply couldn't afford to supplement their diets with extras from the market because of the global price rise. And then there was a curious impact: instead of feeding all their crops to their kids some subsistence farmers had a price incentive to sell them for money, because of those price rises, earning cash which they might then use to buy things other than food, often for the best of reasons. A farmer might choose to buy a kerosene lamp, I was told, so his kids could carry on with their homework once the sun had gone down, education being seen as a route to a better life. Poor families in Rwanda, I learned, were likely to fall back on a staple like cassava, a starchy root that could be ground down into a flour to make a dry doughy paste. It's about as bland nutritionally as it tastes. Imagine a soft dough made from cardboard. Then remove any of cardboard's grace notes. Cassava does boast calories but it is almost completely nutrient free. Eat too much of that and you would soon have a vitamin deficit. The Rwandan diet is in need of a serious overhaul.

We moved on to a village where the houses had mud walls and mud floors and most of the cooking was done inside, over open fires so that the high tang of soot hung over the room. Outside the house representatives from the Rwandan health ministry, the health centre and Save the Children, the standard entourage for a visitor to the country with a media profile they might be able to work to their advantage, stood around tapping away on smartphones and making calls. Here, as elsewhere in Africa, the mobile phone network has revolutionized communication.

Outside the house we were firmly in the twenty-first century. Inside we had slipped backwards into what felt like a pre-industrial age. I was introduced to Leonie and Immaculate, both widows, both mothers of six, each of whom had children displaying the most acute symptoms of stunting. Immaculate's 9-year-old daughter, Claudine, was particularly affected. She had learning difficulties and was very small for her age, and stood curled into the folds of her mother's long skirt, staring out at me from a domed, slightly swollen head. She had scant hair, a classic sign of malnutrition. 'I was surprised when they told me,' Immaculate said, 'because I did my best to feed my children. I thought it was some other form of disease.'

At another home I met Vestine, who had lost three pregnancies because she was malnourished and forced to work in the fields too close to her due date. She and her husband, Claver, had a daughter who was 8, plus eighteen-month-old twins. Their daughter in particular was showing symptoms of malnourishment. When Vestine led me into the house to show me what she had to feed them with, it was easy to see why. She was doing her best, but the pile of beans, potatoes and green leaves defined the word meagre.

I was accompanied by a producer from Save the Children and a cameraman, who had passed most of his career in war zones – Bosnia, Afghanistan, Iraq – and now liked to spend some of his time working for charities. We were shooting a short film about my trip that would go up on the web and they asked me now to do a piece to camera about the situation in which Vestine found herself. I knew the film would be seen by lots of people. I knew I was doing what the charity asked of me. I knew that it would highlight a vital and important issue. I knew an awful lot of very obvious things.

But as I squatted down by Vestine's open fire, and felt my knees creak and saw my linen trousers stretch tight across my bulked-out, varicose thighs, I couldn't help but feel a certain impotency. What in God's name did I think I was doing here?

I have experienced poverty, but only once and only then for about thirty-six hours. It's not to be recommended. It was at the end of a solo back-packing holiday across Greece and Turkey. I returned to Athens, where the trip had started, with a couple of days left until my flight home and barely enough cash for anything more than a plot for my sleeping bag on the roof of a hostel, and the bus fare to the airport. I passed the time lying in the shade on a bench in a park, reading a book I had already read and trying not to think about how hungry I was. When I finally boarded my flight home, I fell upon the tray of airline food with a genuine enthusiasm, the one and only time that has ever happened.

In short, I have never experienced poverty. I have never gone without, not really. My parents, however, both really did have meagre beginnings, a Jewish working-class background in a time when many Jews in Britain were still at the bottom of the heap. My paternal grandfather was a hairdresser with a gambling habit who managed to lose whatever money he might have made; my mother's parents, whom I never met – she said I wasn't missing anything and I took her word for it – were mostly feckless and on the run. My mother told me that if she ever came into any cash as a child – say an aunt had given her a ten-shilling note – her mother would use emotional blackmail to talk it off her, or her dad would nick it. Either way they would get their hands on the money.

My late mother Claire eventually met and married my father Des Rayner and became nationally famous as the agony aunt, broadcaster and novelist Claire Rayner. She made that journey by lying about her age and, at 15, enlisting as a trainee nurse. In nursing she found an escape from the parents she'd come to hate, and a new kind of family. Because her parents kept moving the kids around she had never been able to complete formal education but found a capacity for learning that saw her advance in nursing exams, though it was not a route to riches. When we were kids Claire told us that as a student nurse she was so poor she couldn't afford both bits of underwear. Being a big girl she decided a bra was more impor-tant. It was a troubling image, one I never thanked her for, though the point about money being tight was well made. Still, by the time I was born, in 1966, that was all history. My father had abandoned a less than rewarding career as an actor for fashion PR and my mother was a successful freelance journalist.

Then in 1972 we fell rich. That was the year my mother became famous. She had already published a number of novels but in 1972 one of them, the first in an historical series called 'The Performers', sold paperback rights in the US for $250,000 – a big sum now, a huge one then. In the same year she landed a weekly agony column on the *Sun* newspaper and a regular slot on *Pebble Mill at One*, a BBC daytime show broadcast daily from Birmingham. With the money my parents bought two rings. One was my dad's freedom from that PR job he had come to hate. He became my mother's agent and manager, bringing the 10 per cent in-house, and was able to concentrate on his career as an artist which up to then had been a sideline. The other thing they bought was duvets. We were one of the first families in north-west London to chuck out the sheets and blankets. We felt very modern. Plus making the beds was quicker. One night, lying beneath his crisp, brand-new duvet as my mother came to say goodnight, my brother Adam asked if, when she died, she would be buried in a diamond coffin. She laughed, and said, no, darling. (She was, for the record, cremated in an eco-friendly wicker basket affair.) The fact was we were well off and we knew it.

So now we took our places in the self-made upper middle classes. It came with many things: a series of au pairs, various extensions to our suburban semi, expensive summer holidays down on the Dorset coast in a hotel patronized by the fading aristocracy. And then there was all that food. I have always wondered about my mother's instinct to over-cater. It could be seen as a reaction against a childhood of poverty and not having enough. She told me once that, during a period as a neglected evacuee to the country, she was taught by the local kids how to nick swedes from the fields, which they ate raw, cutting the pieces up with pocket knives. 'You could fill yourself up quite well from one of those.' I think she liked the image of herself when young, stealing crops from wealthy farmers just to keep herself fed.

Certainly she was in a position to make sure none of that was visited on her children, and so the table was always full.

She never simply prepared enough, because enough to her felt like the exact opposite. She made meals with emergency guests and seconds in mind. She cooked as though we were limbering up to be an emergency shelter in a storm. Of course, despite her antipathy to organized religion, this could all have been as a result of a genetic marker. Jews over-cater. It's what we do. After all, the Cossacks may be coming, and you'd better eat now, in case tomorrow you are on the run across the Russian steppe. I grant you it would take a vivid imagination to get you from our home in the cherry-blossomed streets of suburban London to the cold wastes of Russia, but the collective memory was there.

Claire fed us as if food was a defence against the brutal realities of the world. Despite a busy working life she found a way to build chicken casseroles in the morning for a long, slow cook before hitting the typewriter. She roasted lamb breasts and grilled chops and when she had people round for dinner she made coulibiac, that seventies party piece of salmon and rice wrapped in flaky pastry and baked in the oven. At lunchtimes on Saturday, after they had been out doing the weekly shop, a buffet of cold cuts and salads and bread and cheese and pastries would be laid out, with the expectation that friends would drop by, and they did for they knew the drill. Saturday lunch was known as fick and porridge, a spoonerism of 'pick and forage', a wordplay Claire loved a little more than it deserved.

We ate in restaurants like Stone's Chop House, a grand place behind Piccadilly Circus, where almost everything seemed to be flamed tableside in brandy before you were allowed to eat it. And we became regulars at Joe Allen, a New York-style bistro behind the Strand that was so smart and fashionable its entrance was marked by nothing other than a shiny brass plaque. Either you knew about it or you didn't. That was what gained you entrance to this non-membership members-only club. We were members. There we ate proper Caesar salads and plates of sticky ribs with black-eyed peas and a brownie à la mode, which was a fancy name for 'with ice cream'.

Why I should, from childhood, have had those weight issues remains a mystery to me, as it must to you. To be fair, there must be something deep in the genes, a metabolism engineered for those winters on the run across Mother Russia. I am a man built to survive a pogrom, only without a pogrom to survive. I don't think the rest of my family would be too hurt if I were to say that applied to them too. Each of us has at one point or another struggled with our size. Claire eventually found a solution, but it involved surviving a five-week stint in an Intensive Care Unit, during which she lost half her body weight. As weight loss programmes go it's probably not the best. In this narrative greed is learned behaviour, part of a family culture, but it is also an obvious mark of affluence. I became greedy because I was in a position to be so. Greed was presented to me as a lifestyle choice. I decided it was one that would suit me very well.

The food at the Great Wall Chinese restaurant in Kigali was not great, much as a car crash is not great and herpes simplex is not great. There was a plate of deep fried chicken wings which were edible, but otherwise it was all slippery, gloopy things, their ugliness hidden by the ill-lit gloom. Rice steamed inside thick tubes of bamboo is not a wonderful idea; it tastes like new bamboo furniture smells.

It's tempting to argue that this was exactly what I deserved. What the hell was I thinking? Going to Rwanda to investigate the realities of chronic child malnourishment, and hanging out at day's end in a Chinese restaurant just because I thought it would be amusing? Shame on me.

Except the argument doesn't stack up. It's not like I was alone in the restaurant or that there was only one restaurant for me to be alone in. Kigali is full of restaurants, not just Chinese, but Italian, Greek and Indian too. (Apparently African food doesn't work outside the home so well.) Kigali even has a readable restaurant blog. It is a quiet, safe city in a country which is undergoing an economic boom – think yearly growth of around 8 per cent – albeit from a very low base. In the five years before my visit, one million people had been lifted out of abject poverty. Things are changing. These restaurants weren't just full of big-haired food critics from Britain, out on a jolly after a little light, self-serving charity work. Everyone was visiting them. It was a normal thing to do; as normal for a modestly middle-class section of the population as it might be to go out to dinner in London, New York or Paris.

The more time I spent with the aid community in Rwanda, discussing the issues, trying to reconcile what I was seeing with what I did for a living, the more that seemed to be the point. Nobody – or at least very few people, other than the achingly self-righteous and the compulsively bleeding-heart – hesitates to go out for dinner if they can afford to do so in London or New York or Paris just because, in Rwanda, there are kids whose diet is not giving them enough of what they need to eat. Perhaps you think about the issues. Perhaps you give money to charity. You do something to raise awareness. But you also get on with your life.

Or to put it another way, just because one way of living in Rwanda is bad – chronic child malnourishment, leading to higher mortality rates, holding back economic development –

does not necessarily mean that another lifestyle in the developed world is also bad. Sure, if you're a gun-runner or a pimp, a drug dealer or the former CEO of the Royal Bank of Scotland, you may well have grounds to think carefully about your personal morality. Perhaps you should give up a few pension entitlements. But most of us, even those of us who write a newspaper column which seems to be about nothing other than indulging our appetites, lie within the normal spectrum.

A child in Rwanda does not have less to eat because I order the lunch menu at Le Gavroche in London. And thank God for it, because the lunch menu at Le Gavroche – around fifty quid per head for three courses plus half a bottle of really good wine – is bloody lovely. If it was as simple as that, if my greed genuinely was the cause of someone else's hunger, well, then the solution would be simple. Just stop it. Get a grip. And yes, there are some issues where a simple formula does begin to apply (most notably around the consumption of meat; we'll get there.) But for the most part situations like those I saw in Rwanda are to do with failures of good governance, economic mismanagement and lack of infrastructure. Of course, a global population of nine billion poses major challenges, but time and again as I travelled the landscape of food security I was told there were many ways to feed people and keep them fed. Me going on a diet was not one of them. What was needed was investment. And biotechnology. And a whole bunch of other things that countries in the West might find less than appetizing. And the Chinese were already doing it.

One night shortly before my trip to Rwanda I went to a small market town in the north of England to meet a man who works in the wholesale fruit and vegetable business. He trades with supermarkets. He works with distributors. He's deep inside the British food machine, so deep inside that he demanded complete anonymity. I had no idea how brutal and cutthroat a world this was, he said. No one could know we were talking. I said he made it sound like a mafia. He narrowed his eyes and nodded slowly.

Nor, he said, did I realize what a state of flux it was in; how the big British supermarkets were being forced onto the back foot by changes beyond our shores which they had completely failed to anticipate. They were desperately fighting to take costs out of the system. Until now they had done all their buying through middlemen, but those middlemen were being cut out. Some of the supermarkets were trying to buy direct because it helped them save money, and all of them would be doing it in time. The key, he told me, was the Chinese. And the Indians. And the Brazilians. And the Indonesians. The map of global consumption was changing.

He leaned into me conspiratorially, and said, 'Did you know that the price the Chinese are willing to pay for unpacked, ungraded apples is now close to what the British supermarkets are willing to pay for graded and packed?'

I said I didn't.

'Well, it's true. The only issue is that the Chinese haven't got their act together on paying on time.'

So the British supermarkets are still a better customer?

He shrugged. 'Not for long. The Chinese are very quick at adapting to the market. And they will adapt. They'll start paying quickly soon.'

Hang on, I said. I thought the Chinese were an exporter of apples.

'They were. But demand in China is now huge.' For fruit growers in the southern hemisphere the lure of the great

British retail food market was no longer so great, because there were alternatives. He told me about fruit growers from South Africa who had recently abandoned trading with one of the big four supermarkets in Britain because 'it wasn't worth the hassle'. You could no longer leave it to Tesco.

'Go look at the stats,' he said. 'Another glass of wine?'

I did as I was told. I went to look at the statistics on food consumption by the emerging economies. Between 1992 and 2008 animal protein consumption in Indonesia rose 47 per cent. In 1992 the Brazilians were already eating three times as much animal protein as the Indonesians. By 2008 their consumption had risen by another 30 per cent.

China's story, though, is the most extraordinary. It's so extraordinary you may feel you already know it: that there are loads of Chinese people and they are all attempting to join the middle classes like my parents did in the sixties, which means eating big hunks of steak and cooking coulibiac for dinner parties. Or something like that. But you have to see the numbers to grasp the reality. In the mid-seventies Chinese meat consumption was ten kilos per person per year. By 2010 that had more than quadrupled to forty-five kilos per person per year. The UN's Food and Agriculture Organization predicts it will reach sixty kilos per person by 2015 and sixty-nine by 2030, though this may be a gross underestimate. Recently two economists at Nomura Bank studied Taiwan's eating habits. In 1980 Taiwan's annual meat consumption was forty-three kilos per head, roughly the same as China's today, and average incomes were around $3,500, again around the same as China today. By 1995 meat consumption in Taiwan was at seventy-three kilos. That's a massive leap. And Taiwan has a population of under twenty-five million. The impact of that in a country like China with a population that accounts for 20 per cent of all the people on the planet would be enormous.

In 1978 Chinese meat consumption was a third of US meat consumption. China overtook the US as a consumer of meat in 1992, and by 2012 was eating more than double the US. Obviously the Chinese population at 1.35 billion is much higher than the US population of 315 million. Per head the Americans still eat more, at seventy-five kilos a year, though US meat consumption has dropped from its 2004 peak of eighty-four kilos and is expected to carry on falling. But China's sudden affluence and the leap in its appetite for things with a pulse has completely altered the entire functioning of the world's food production system. In 2011 China harvested the largest crop of any country in human history, and a third of that went straight to feeding animals to satisfy the growing hunger for meat, milk, eggs and farmed fish. Between 2006 and 2012 Chinese consumer spending on dairy products as a proportion of their budget leaped 40 per cent. Which is remarkable for a population generally understood to have high levels of lactose intolerance, as much as 30 per cent among children. Since 1978 China's use of grain as an animal feed has increased ninefold.

'The thing is, the Chinese can't produce all this food them-selves,' my friend in the bar told me. 'At least not yet.'

So what are they doing?

'They're buying Africa.'

How do you mean?

'Just as I say. They are buying up huge plots of Africa, offer-ing to build infrastructure in return for farming rights to vast tracts of land.' The West, he said, was hooked to an aid model in Africa. Send them money. Send them skills. Teach them. It was an old-fashioned model built on the blood-stained guilt of a history of colonialism. The Chinese, meanwhile, were taking a totally different tack. Western governments might find many regimes in Africa too obnoxious, too repressive, too corrupt, too dysfunctional to trade with. Giving them hand-outs was more palatable. The Chinese meanwhile just don't care. They are in there. 'Look at Zimbabwe. The Chinese are all over it, farming the land, building power stations. They don't care about crap governance. They're just getting on with it.'

As are countries of the Middle East, which also have their own food security issues. Since 2000 around 5 per cent of Africa's agricultural land has been bought or leased by those foreign interests. China's ZTE Agribusiness did the second biggest of these deals, for at least 100,000 hectares of Democratic Republic of Congo on which to farm palm oil. It may be as much as 280,000 hectares, depending on the figure's source. In truth China's interests in African agriculture are dwarfed by their interests in oil, gas and minerals but still amount to many billions of dollars. The Chinese have pledged to train up thousands of agricultural experts and technicians and fund the building of more than a dozen major technology centres. Some of the Chinese-controlled land is already being farmed; it's believed that the rest of it is being held for a time in the future when long-term food security issues begin to bite.

In October 2012 Oxfam issued a major report on the way land was being bought up by foreign powers. 'In the past decade an area of land eight times the size of the UK has been sold off globally as land sales accelerate,' it said. 'This land could feed a billion people, equivalent to the number of people who go to bed hungry each night. In poor countries, foreign investors have been buying an area of land the size of London every six days.' Thirty per cent of Liberia had been flogged off, the report said. Indeed, in just ten years an area the size of Kenya had gone from Africa. Where it was being used for food crops it was almost always for export from the country where the land was situated. With growing economic and population pressures Oxfam expected the situation only to get worse unless the international community acted now to do something about it.

I wondered if this was having an impact on little Rwanda. I wasn't quite sure how it could. There is some commercial coffee farming in the country – Rwandan coffee is fabulous: rich and intense and fragrant – but most of the agriculture there is built around a subsistence model. What would the Chinese get out of that?

But that, it turned out, was to misunderstand the sophistication of the Chinese approach to securing the resources they need for their population, which some have branded a form of neo-colonialism. From the moment I landed in Kigali and started reading the *East African*, the highly impressive English-language newspaper of the area published in Kenya, it became clear the Chinese were thinking less in terms of nation states and more in terms of the entire region. Everywhere was interconnected to everywhere else (and literally so: attempts to create an East African Union along the lines of the European Union continue apace). Infrastructure work in Rwanda fed in to other contracts with Kenya or Tanzania or Uganda.

'I'm sure the Chinese will be in Rwanda,' my drinking partner said. 'They're everywhere.'

The curious thing was that, while there was a lousy Chinese restaurant opposite my hotel, I hadn't seen any actual Chinese people in Kigali, which might have explained why the food was so dismal. Then one night I found them. My hotel was like something out of a bad David Lynch movie. Outside my room, in the huge, echoey corridors, Ella Fitzgerald was on a constant loop singing 'Stormy Weather'. Some of the rooms had been built with no outside windows. Instead they looked out, into a corridor along the side of the building, as if the architects had got their maths wrong. On the top floor was a circular bar, with a panoramic view of the city, that was almost entirely pitch-black save for pinpricks of light in the ceiling that throbbed on and off.

And on the second floor was Kigali's one and only casino. Through the metal detector, manned with very little enthusiasm by a young man in a suit two sizes too big for him, and there I was in a smoke-filled room full of roulette tables and high-paying one-armed bandits, and dealers in blood-red waistcoats and crisp white shorts, shuffling cards out of horseshoes just as quickly as their fingers would allow. There were 'no smoking' signs all over the walls. But that didn't seem to trouble the clientele, who were almost entirely Chinese. It was like this every night, I was told by a barman. There must have been around a hundred people in the relatively small space and all but about five of them were from China: big, round-cheeked men – there were only men – in white, short-sleeved shirts bulging at the belly, perched side on at the tables, fags grasped hard between the knuckles. Winding down after a hard day's work pouring money into Africa. Trusting to lady luck.

Curiously it was that moment, standing on the casino floor, watching the Chinese expats in Kigali ruling the world from the blackjack tables, that made me realize just how few of those debating food consumption at home had really grasped what was going on. We talked earnestly about food miles, about supermarkets' buying policies, two-for-one offers and the virtues of localism. We cheered when the asparagus season kicked off each spring and booed when retailers filled their shelves with out-of-season stock from Peru, as a sign that something terrible and malignant was eating away at the heart of our long-fought-for food culture.

And yet, beyond our shores, something so much bigger was going on, which too many of us had failed to recognize. It was something which was going to have a vast impact on how and what we ate.

At the same time I also knew that it was only a part of the story; that there was more to tell beyond the narrative of Chinese neo-colonialism in Africa and chronic child malnutrition in Rwanda. I knew that if I was genuinely to get to grips with what was going on I had to carry on travelling. I had to head west to the one country which per head of population has managed to consume more than any other in human history, and which is responsible for feeding a huge swath of the world.

I had to go to America.

5.

SLOW BOAT TO ELLIS ISLAND

Growing up in a north-west London Jewish family, I was haunted by a thought: that if my great grandfather, Josef Burochowiz, had just been blessed with a little more stamina, and had stayed on the boat a few days longer, I wouldn't have grown up in London at all but instead in New York. I would have been one of those noisy American Jews, raised in the land of salt beef and bagels, where the buildings were taller, the skies bigger, and everybody was from somewhere else. I liked my foreign-ness but wanted everyone else to be foreign too. It may explain why, in adulthood, I moved to Brixton in south London, one of the most ethnically diverse areas in Western Europe.

Then, one Saturday lunchtime in 1977, a little bit of America came to me. My mother had been invited to an event at the American Embassy. I have no idea why; it was just the sort of thing that happened to her. All I do recall was that it was odd because Saturday mornings was when my parents did the family food shop. Nothing got in the way of that because if they hadn't been shopping how could we do fick and porridge at lunchtime? And yet, for the American Embassy, Claire would make an exception.

Lunchtime came and she was back and carrying with her the solution to this lack of anything worth ficking or porridging: a shallow cardboard box containing a couple of dozen soft, round packages wrapped in thin, glossy greaseproof paper, dressed with the mammarian curve of golden 'M's. She had brought us hamburgers. A lot of them.

With hindsight, this could be viewed as a blatant act of cultural imperialism. The first branch of McDonald's had opened in Woolwich, south-east London, in 1974, though it had yet to impact upon me. I hadn't been to one. Now here was the US Embassy – the US government itself, on UK soil – handing out McDonald's hamburgers to a woman who, as a high-profile journalist, could influence opinion. Perhaps there was a CIA briefing document somewhere outlining how the American version of freedom could be spread about the world by the judicious distribution of free McDonald's hamburgers to opinion formers. It's not an entirely far-fetched idea. In his book *The Lexus and the Olive Tree*, published in 1999, the *New York Times* columnist Thomas L. Friedman proposed the 'Golden arches theory of conflict prevention' as part of a discourse on Democratic Peace Theory. The latter argues that no two countries which are true democracies will ever go to war against each other, because of shared and mutual interests. Friedman argued that the presence of McDonald's in a country was a similar example of a particularly advanced level of economic and social development, and that no two countries which had outposts of the fast-food giant would ever attack each other. It proved to be a remarkably robust theory until, later that year, when the Kosovo war broke out and NATO bombed Belgrade, already home to the golden arches.

The truth of our hamburger windfall was, I think, a little more prosaic. The embassy had got McDonald's to cater the event and, at the end, seeing a number left over and being appalled by the waste, my mother had offered to take them home, thereby dealing with the lunch issue. Whatever the cause, I was delighted. Even cold, I had never eaten hamburgers like them: there was the intense sweetness of the bun and the juicy meat of the patty and the punch of the pickles. It was a sugar-fat-protein party in my mouth. I bloody loved it.

This was what America meant to me: food with a certain shamelessness; lunch with its knickers around its ankles. Around this time an expatriate American called Gabriel Gutman launched the Dayville chain of ice-cream parlours in Britain. 'There is superb cream in England and excellent chocolate,' he told the *New York Times*, who were so excited by the arrival of American ice cream in Britain they gave it 1,000 words. 'Nobody ever married the two together. It's been driving me crazy for years,' Gutman said. The actress Lee Remick, who had just starred in *The Omen* and was living in London, was more savage. 'They don't know from ice cream in this country,' she said, as if she had identified the very heart of Britain's famed malaise. Remick had a point. Until Dayville arrived you could have any flavour you liked here as long as it was strawberry, chocolate or vanilla. Or maybe, at a push, tutti frutti, but nobody had a clue what tutti frutti really was; it looked like vanilla into which someone had stirred lumps of Lego. Plus the ice cream itself was hard and, well, icy. British ice cream was a beautiful promise, broken. The only alternative was the vegetable-fat-heavy Mr Whippy stuff, served by ice-cream vans which announced their arrival on your street by playing jangly tunes that sounded like a cat being strangled in a bath. The process to inflate the vegetable oil–dairy fat mix with air had partly been invented by a young research chemist called Margaret Hilda Roberts who would, as Margaret Thatcher, soon become Prime Minister. That didn't make the stuff taste any better.

And now here, praise the gods of greed, was Dayville, who proclaimed thirty-two flavours, but seemed to offer many more. There was banana split or bubblegum-flavoured ice cream. There was toffee nut crunch, key lime sorbet, and something called peppermint fudge ripple, which, to a fat boy yet to navigate the hormonal rapids of puberty, sounded seriously rude. This was what America meant to me: it was a place where you could get thirty-two flavours of ice cream, and one of them was called peppermint fudge ripple.

It didn't end there. In 1977 another expatriate American, Bob Payton, opened the Chicago Pizza Pie Factory off St James's, complete with mezuzah on the doorpost; Payton was quiet about his Jewishness, but still closed the joint on Yom Kippur. Not that he was exactly that Jewish. After all, his Rib Shacks were hardly short on pork products. He was my kind of greedy, godless Jew. In these places, and at the chain Maxwell's, music blared, everything came slathered in a sticky vinegary barbecue sauce, and cutlery was optional. Us over-privileged Jewish kids – was there any other kind? – would go to these restaurants without our parents, aged 13 or 14, and play at being grown up, while really we were just getting a big sugary, salty hit. Sod that lazy swine Josef Burochowiz. For an hour or two we were finally American and we had become American through food. It felt good.

*   *   *

I arrived in America for the first time in January 1989, a young journalist on the make, and nothing about my first encounter with New York made me feel I was very far off the mark in my understanding that the American sense of self was intimately tied up with the way it ate. As an immigrant nation it grasped at what that irritating university contemporary of mine Eugene would still have insisted upon calling the 'cultural signifiers' and which I shall instead call 'dinner': at the things which made each ethnic group identifiable. It hunted down those things which held most tightly the symbols of where they had begun. Food is very good at doing that. I was once told by Jonathan Gold, the famed restaurant critic of the *LA Weekly*, that the most traditional Korean restaurants were to be found not in Korea but in Los Angeles. 'In Seoul they are too busy looking forward and reinventing themselves to worry about the past,' he said. 'Here in LA all the Korean restaurants are about remembering.' This is combined with a frontiersman spirit, a sense of pushing at the boundaries to make a better life; it's a characteristic which still underpins the American sensibility. In that narrative having more than enough to eat has always been a mark of having succeeded. Look at how I have prospered: the table is full.

That first night, pissed on jet lag, nervous with adrenalin, I sat on the end of my hotel bed and watched endless adverts for a restaurant chain called Red Lobster. Which served lobster. Proper, big-clawed, snappy, red lobster. This was baffling. In London eating lobster was something you did while being carried about in your very own sedan chair by bare-chested dwarves, while lolling on cushions stuffed with swan feathers and trimmed with baby panda fur. In London lobster was a premium item. It was a pure luxury. I was 22 and I wasn't entirely sure I'd ever eaten one; here it was so ordinary as to be advertised on television, as an offering at a chain of restaurants.

I never did go to Red Lobster, but I went to many other places instead on repeated trips across America and became enthralled by its largesse. Forget bigness. We know America's big. But big doesn't necessarily mean extravagant, and everything I found was extravagant, even the stories I was covering. I pursued a sex pest Congressman from Oregon who'd been caught with his hand in his staff, and doorstepped the indicted leader of the Navajo Nation at his mobile home in the middle of the New Mexico desert. In Riverside, California, I met a man who was convinced he knew how to live for ever and, just in case he was wrong, was preparing to have just his head cryogenically frozen at his death so he could be revived in the future when medicine had found a cure for what had killed him. (He couldn't afford to have his whole body frozen.) I reported the aftermath of the race riots in Brooklyn's Crown Heights, hung out with an overweight porn mogul in Manhattan who bought his clothes in three sizes – the size he wanted to be, the size he was, and the one he suspected he was going to be – and talked to NASA scientists in Pasadena about the search for extraterrestrial life.

And, of course, I ate. In restaurants I was served steaks the size of my pet cat, with a glorious char, and the luscious texture that only comes from being grain fed; I was presented with bowls of pasta that could feed a family of five and introduced to the lobster roll, the most shameless use of that luxury ingredient I had fretted over in my hotel room, the entire contents of the shell slathered in mayo and then laid on a soft white bun like it was a two-dime hot dog. For the first time I met real hamburgers, served rare in the way that too many health and safety nuts in my country would not allow, and I wallowed in breakfasts of fluffy pancakes and butter and maple syrup and crisp streaky bacon which would leave me fed until dinner time, of the next day.

From all of this I quickly learned that America's relationship with its food is also partly a result of physical geography. There's just so much of the country: it is grassland and desert, forest and mountain, and all the things in between. Tiny Rwanda has a fragile fecundity to it, as if, at any point, it could slip from growth to rot and decay and ruin. Its red earth may seem fertile, but those endless 'thousand hills' are the enemy of cultivation. Rwanda has fed itself in spite of geography (or, to be more exact, geology), not because of it. America is the other way round. It's a place engineered for large-scale production. The numbers stand this up. Unlike Britain, the US is hugely self-sufficient in food. It has the rolling prairies of the Midwest, the country's bread basket, where wheat and corn and soya beans grow on fields the size of English counties, and cattle graze in their millions. To the west in California is the Central Valley, which, on just 1 per cent of US land, produces 8 per cent of American agricultural output, and where the five counties in the US with the top agricultural sales are all located. It is the primary source of America's grapes, tomatoes, almonds and apricots, among much else. Meanwhile over in the east are the orange groves of Florida, which produce nearly 70 per cent of all the citrus fruit consumed in the country, and quite a lot of it consumed elsewhere too.

I also got to grips with the desperately dysfunctional nature of the American relationship with its food. We know it has one of the most industrialized, sugar- and fat-sodden food production systems in the world. Films like *Food Inc* have done much to shine light into dark, musty corners. We know the

US is the fattest country in the developed world, with nearly 35 per cent of the population classified as obese. We have seen pictures of vast bottoms, restrained within tents of denim, bellies still overflowing like so much expanding bread dough. I feel small there and I am not. I feel my appetites are normal there, and they are not. Everything in America is big, including dinner.

Terrible, terrible things are done in the name of food. One summer a couple of years ago I took my family for a holiday on Cape Cod, the thick spit of land that sticks out deep into the Atlantic from the Massachusetts coast and which, therefore, should have a booming shellfish culture. Indeed it has. Not far from the house we were renting was a big slat-board café – more a canteen – advertising clams. I love clams. I love sucking the soft, sweet meat from the shell, and the hit of sea and salt you get as you run your tongue around the inside. I was looking forward to a big bucket of clams, smiling up at me, just waiting to be prised and pulled from their sticking place.

No such luck. This café didn't do shells. Taking things out of shells required effort, and who wanted that? They pulled the clam meat out for you, dredged it in batter, and then dumped the whole lot in the deep-fat fryer. Tons of the stuff. You could have anything you liked there, as long as it had first been for a swim in boiling oil. Perhaps I care a little too much about my dinner. Perhaps I'm an obsessive, but I found it all a hideous disappointment.

Many Americans think so too. It is a massively polarized food culture; one which is constantly at war with itself. Whatever the virtues or otherwise of organic food, it speaks volumes that sales are – though still relatively small – much higher in the US than they have ever been in the UK, at 4 per cent as against 1.5 per cent. It feels like a repulsed reaction to something deeply unappetizing. Food scandal after food scandal has broken across the country: E. Coli outbreaks in spinach production; aquifer contamination around giant hog plants; school boards ruling that pizza can be counted as one of a child's five fruit or vegetable portions a day on account of the tomato sauce; the growing outrage around the use of a beef-based additive commonly – and appetizingly – known as 'pink slime', made with the ground-down connective tissue and scraps that can't be sold as prime cuts, which have been used by big-name fast-food and manufacturing companies.

And those are only the headline grabbers from the past few years. The announcement in early 2011 by the superstar TV chef Paula Dean that she had been diagnosed with Type 2 diabetes, the form of the disease most intimately related to lifestyle, appeared to mark something of a watershed. Dean had made herself famous by promoting a shameless brand of fat- and sugar-smeared cookery – chocolate-covered, deep-fried cheesecake, a quiche made with a pound of bacon, a bread and butter pudding made with Krispy Kreme doughnuts – which sounded like the sort of things even late-career Elvis would shy away from on health grounds. She justified these dishes by describing them as an expression of the hospitality of the American South. If that was so, then she was literally killing herself with kindness, and others too. 'I am who I am,' she said when the news broke, fessing up that she was also now taking a serious wedge of cash to promote the diabetes treatment Victoza. 'It is,' she said, 'the American way.' Cue endless pages of soul-searching in the comment pages of the American press.

The result of all this is, on the one side, a slab of the population feasting on junk, and on the other, a huge group of people attempting to challenge what is happening by retreating to a world of farmers' markets, advocacy and protest.

And, of course, there's a special kind of emotion-drenched, sugary, feel-my-soul, know-my-pain language which for a granite-hearted and suspicious Englishman can be a little too much to take. It feels as if they think you can combat the worst excesses of the industrial food machine by emoting, by feeling, by adoring. Forget flowery menu language: this is the vocabulary of the Hallmark greetings card. Everything will be OK, it seems, if we all just have a group hug and think about our feelings.

Oh God.

'If you cook this dish with love,' I was once told by a chef from Florida, 'it will work every time.'

'I genuinely think you can taste the love in this dish,' another American chef once said to me.

Each time I was told something like this I would flinch, as if a red-hot poker had been waved near my face.

In 2009 I worked as a judge on the US food reality TV show *Top Chef Masters*, in which a group of big-name chefs competed in a set of cookery challenges to win $100,000 for charity and bragging rights to the title. At the end of each episode the judging panel would have to interview the chefs on camera about the dishes they had cooked for us in response to the challenge they had been posed. The shoots went on for hours.

One night, about halfway into the series, one of the chefs made the mistake of telling me that the dish they had prepared had been 'made with love'. I'd had enough. 'Listen,' I said. 'If I want a blowjob I'll call my wife. From you I want technique and good taste.' My fellow judges, all highly regarded American food writers, stared down the table at me, slack-jawed.

For some reason, my terribly witty line didn't make the final cut.

This, of course, is not the whole story. For lying beneath this thick, fatty layer of wobbly emotion is another story about food in America, because in any critique of the modern global food system the US always looms large. It is, as ever, portrayed as a place of hard business and hard numbers. It is home to the huge agricultural biotech combines like Monsanto and DuPont that dominate the seed business. It is home to agricultural services companies like Cargill and Archer Daniels Midland (ADM), the grain purchasers, processors and refiners who manage the food supply chain. And it's home to the commodity traders who are so often fingered as the true villains of the piece for ramping up prices of the world's food – for leading billions to the very edge of starvation – in pursuit of a quick buck.

In some quarters even just questioning the conventional wisdom on the evils of all this is considered heresy. It's buying into their PR, they say. It's allowing them to shove a foot back in the door of public opinion. Give them an inch and they'll take every damn acre they can get their hands on. Then again, the game is changing. We have an awful lot of people to feed. The political, social and economic stability of our world depends upon our ability to do so. Which means questions need to be asked. The hard questions. Like: is the American-dominated industrial food complex really all bad? Or, to put it another way, might it actually be a part of the solution?

Perched at the very top of the 184-metre-high Chicago Board of Trade Building is an aluminium sculpture of Ceres, the Roman goddess of grain, by the artist John H. Storrs. She is the crowning point of the limestone building, completed in 1930, and stands with a sheaf of wheat in her left hand and a bag of corn in her right, staring far down the shadowed canyon of LaSalle Avenue in the Windy City's downtown. Or at least she would be staring if she had any eyes. Or indeed any face at all. When it was finished it was the tallest building in the city, a title it would hold until 1965. Legend has it that, as a result, the artist concluded there was no point going to all the effort of getting the face right. Nobody would ever be able to see it, so he left her blank.

As a metaphor for the anonymous and blind brutality of the modern financial system, in which the lives of millions are blighted by the capricious decisions of a tiny number, you can't get much better. Thanks to one lazy artist who couldn't be fagged to go the extra mile, we have Ceres the faceless goddess of big business, atop a building completely disconnected from the very things it is selling. It is all just so many numbers now. It's all about electronic data whizzing in millions of megabytes along glowing fibre optics or through the charged ether. It's about tiny slivers of margin in a gargantuan market where corn is the same as wheat is the same as ten-year gilts. It's all just money.

Except when you get inside the Chicago Board of Trade it simply doesn't feel like that. My guide, a trader with twenty-five years' experience called Jim Iuorio, leads me up a succession of escalators and through a set of security checkpoints to the trading floor and it's all I can do to stop myself rocking back on my heels as we enter. I had expected something that looked like a call centre: desks, banks of computers, phones, dead-eyed keyboard jockeys strapped to their consoles, like mariners against hurricane winds, but it's nothing of the sort. It's a vast, cavernous space on the scale of a major basketball stadium. Around the sides in tiers, so that the occupants can view the action down on the floor, are indeed stacks of desks and computers, but nobody is strapped in anywhere. People are moving in all directions. Above them, running all the way around the walls, are screens six to ten feet high, firing out the latest commodity prices in digits the colour of fresh, arterial blood. And then there are the famed Chicago 'pits', large octagonal gouges in the floor with stepped sides, so the dealers can get a good view of one another as they bawl and caterwaul their orders. They are wearing distinctive striped and patterned jackets of various hues, and many are wearing headsets which link them to their colleagues up in the stands. They have tablet computers held flat in front of them via straps around their necks and they are shouting. And waving their hands. And shouting some more. It's like a premiership football game in which members of the fifty-strong heaving, swaying crowd are also the competitors.

True 'open outcry' trading like this is very rare these days. Other markets – both the London and New York Stock Exchanges, their Toronto equivalent, the Borsa Italiana in Milan and many more besides – have abandoned it. 'But it makes a kind of sense here,' Jim tells me as we make our way across to the corn futures pit. I ask him to explain a corn future.

'OK. So you're a farmer and you have 100 bushels of corn you want to harvest in three months …'

'You still talk in bushels?'

'We still talk in bushels. Currently there are 166 bushels to an acre, roughly. And a single contract is 5,000 bushels.'

A late-middle-aged woman, her peroxide blonde hair pulled back into a ponytail, jaw clenched, turns and chips in. 'And 5,000 bushels is the amount to fill a whole train container.

That's why a contract is called a train.' She fires these words out the side of her mouth like bullets. These people talk in italics, like every syllable deserves emphasis.

'So every contract is called a train,' Jim says, like it's a call and response in some Southern Baptist church. 'Here's the thing you gotta understand. Chicago is like this because of what happened here. It's not just that the city is surrounded by all the farms. It's that the railroads came here. So that's why we trade commodities.'

Chicago is the riverhead. It's the gathering place. It's the hub.

'So you're the farmer and you have 100 bushels and you set a price with a trader of ten per bushel.'

'Ten dollars?'

'Ten of whatever. It's a simple example. If when we get to harvest the price of corn goes to eleven, you the farmer didn't do so well, but the trader did OK. But he can go on. He can make a deal with someone else to sell that futures contract if the price goes to, say, 11.5. That way he's locked in his profit. You can also do it in reverse to limit losses. And then you can put together packages of puts and calls, of bets against losses and for profit, a whole bunch of options. And that's what's happening here.' I'm not sure I entirely understand, but I nod anyway. I can see that this is a loud and physical business.

'Open outcry is better for this,' Jim says, 'so you can talk to the guys and work out what sort of prices you should be offering.' Here, in the Chicago pits, information is everything.

Jim introduces me to a huge man called Scott Shellady, wearing a black and white jacket in a Friesian cow print that strains at the buttons across his vast belly.

'How come the Friesian thing?' I ask him.

Jim says, 'What's a Friesian?'

I point at the jacket. 'A breed of cow. I may know nothing about options and futures but I recognize a cow pattern when I see one.'

Scott laughs and his huge shoulders heave, one big, fleshy Mexican wave. 'My family originally came from the Netherlands, where they were dairy farmers. So I wear this. There's a benefit in here to being visible and large.'

'True, true,' says Jim, who is short and wiry. 'I used to wear these six-inch stack heels so people could see me.'

'And I wear the Friesian cow jacket.'

'That's the thing about Scott,' Jim says. 'His family still own a farm.'

I'm stunned. A food commodities trader, on the floor of the Chicago Board of Trade, who actually knows something about farming?

'Yes indeed,' he says. 'I've been in a barn freezing my nuts off at 2 a.m. helping a cow to be born. There's probably only about four of us guys like that here.'

Jim asks Scott how the corn harvest is looking. 'It was OK until three weeks ago.'

Then what happened?

'Drought happened. We've had drought for the past three weeks.'

Interesting, I say, because as I was arriving it had just started raining.

Scott points up at the screens on the wall above our heads. 'Which is why the bushel price has dropped by eighteen cents this morning. Rain could mean a bigger harvest. A bigger supply means a lower price.' Corn futures prices are marked by the letter C followed by an alphabetical letter for the month: July is represented by N, September by U, December by Z. There are many things to learn here on the floor of the

Chicago Board of Trade. We can see under CN – corn delivered in July – that the price this morning has dropped from
$6.08 to $5.914. I am surprised that what's happening here
amid all these computers is so desperately responsive to the
weather outside.

'Ninety per cent of it is about the weather,' Scott says. At
present they are expecting thirteen billion bushels of corn to
be harvested in the US in 2012, which is worth around $78
billion. 'But that $78 billion is nothing compared to the busi-
ness being done on the financial markets in general. It's tiny.
And here's the thing you have to understand. More corn is
traded right here every day than will be grown in America this
year.'

Jim nods. 'Because it keeps changing hands.' He tells me
they also trade livestock here. He shows me a graph for beef
prices which is heading inexorably upwards. Beef is more
expensive than it's ever been. I want to know why that is. Are
the commodity traders here to blame for ramping up the
price?

'No,' Scott says. 'Supply and demand. There's a shortage.
You remember the food price spike of 2008? Soya beans, corn,
all grains go through the roof?' I say I remember it well. I say
it's one of the reasons I'm here, on this journey. 'Well, cattle
farmers in 2008, because feed is so expensive they can't afford
to feed their animals any more, they cut their losses and send
the animals to slaughter, including their breeding herds.'

No more baby cows?

'No more baby cows. There weren't enough animals to
replenish the herd. Hence, four years on, we have a
shortage.'

Why, I ask, have food commodities seemingly become so
popular? Years ago you never heard of people making big

bucks out of corn or wheat or soya beans. But now it's the big thing.

'There's nowhere else to go,' Scott says. Equities – shares in quoted companies – have been tanking for years. Likewise, interest rates have been hovering around zero. Making money in both of those is very, very tricky. So everybody has been piling into the tangible assets: minerals, like gold, and food-stuffs, like wheat, soya beans and corn. And so we get to the nub of it. From what they're saying corn stops being corn – something to be eaten – and becomes merely a thing with a numerical value. Doesn't that mean the great charge against speculators like this, that they are falsely inflating prices, is bang on?

'No,' says Scott. 'Because this is the thing. By driving prices up speculators can inspire farmers to plant more crops.'

I have heard this argument before. In 2008, while making a documentary for Channel 4 about the food price spike, I met an intense, beady-eyed commodities speculator called Hugh Hendry, in the west London offices of his firm Eclectica Asset Management. He stood before a map of Africa, jabbing his finger at the European continent, barking, 'We can feed these people. We. Can. Feed. Them.' Increasing the cost of food made it easier, he said. It was a curious argument.

Clearly, to get to grips with this, I needed other sources of information. I needed to follow the commodity trail back from the trading floor to the farm gate. I needed to get away from the madness and brawl of the Chicago Board of Trade and go meet a farmer.

* * *

I am being driven alongside a field deep in corn country, seventy-five miles south-west of Chicago, where the land lies flat beneath sultry, white, summer skies. It's taking a while to get from one end of the field to the other. Even at 40 mph the journey is taking some time. I stare out across a carpet of deep green maize, already five feet tall in mid-June, and try to establish exactly where the field ends, but I can't work it out. My guide, Donna Jaeshke, who farms it with her husband Paul, admits it can be tough to see where one farmer's field ends and the next begins. 'There's precious little livestock out here, so there are no obvious fences,' she says. Not that it's an issue with this particular field. It's all theirs all the way to the treeline, way over there in the distance, shimmering in the haze of the afternoon heat.

This one field covers 230 acres or just over ninety hectares. One hectare is 100 square metres and there are 2.47 acres to the hectare. The average UK farm is around sixty hectares. So this one field alone is 150 per cent bigger than the whole of an average-sized farm in the UK. But it's only a part of the land that the Jaeshkes work. In total they farm 3,900 acres across a twenty-mile stretch of Illinois. She describes it as a 'moderately large' farming venture. She knows people who farm 50,000 acres.

Two-thirds of the Jaeshkes' land, much of which is leased, is sown with corn, the rest with soya beans. I am right in the heart of America's genetically modified farming land. Placards for seed producers like Monsanto line the country lanes, a form of advertising to other farmers who can check out how well the crop from that particular supplier is doing. Those placards have led to the legend that most of American farming is corporately owned; in truth 95 per cent is family owned. I know full well that what I am being shown is regarded by many of the food and farming campaigners I talk to as the epitome of a particular kind of corporate evil. It is everything they hate. This is grain farming on a truly industrial scale. I am supposed to hate it too. I am meant to look out at all this and think that something perverse and evil is being perpetrated here against the rich Illinois soil; that in some foul way it is being raped. Instead I'm impressed. Hiding behind those mythologized images of agriculture that consumers love to buy into is this: a vast expanse of territory turned to the imperative of growing food. I am driving through one of the places that literally feeds the world. If the twenty-first century is about the battle to make sure an emerging population of nine billion hungry people has enough to eat – a growing number of whom will, with outrageous cheek, be insisting upon joining the middle classes and consuming in the way that only the middle classes will – then here, not far from the town of Mazon, is one of the places where that fight will be won.

We drive past a soya bean field. I can see dried corn stalks protruding from the ground. 'It was a corn field last year but now we've sown it to soya,' Donna says. 'We use no-till technology so you can still see those stalks.' No-till. I know a little about that: instead of ploughing up the field and grinding the remnants of each crop back into the ground, the surface is left undisturbed and the seeds are simply drilled into the earth. It vastly reduces the amount of carbon released into the atmosphere because the surface is not broken, preventing oxygen from speeding up microbial activity. As a result the organic matter from previous crops is not broken down within the soil. Water runoff and soil erosion are much lower and, more importantly for the farmers' costs – and for the environment – it requires up to 50 per cent less use of fertilizers.

No-till has its critics. Everything in industrial agriculture has its critics, but genetically modified crops like this enrage more people than most. One of the key arguments here is that heavy industries which are spewing carbon into the atmosphere see this sort of low-carbon farming as a way to offset their own polluting. The farmers can sell a notional credit for the carbon they did not release as a result of no-till to an exchange, where those credits can be purchased by heavy industry. In short, no-till generates its own subsidy in the marketplace, and therefore stands accused of encouraging dirty practices elsewhere. It's true that most things have unintended consequences, but denigrating a more sustainable form of intensive agriculture because of the way it is used by others seems to me more than a little short-sighted.

Back at the Jaeshke farmhouse, a big, white slat-board affair surrounded by fields of corn, Donna shows me graphs of maize production in the US.

'The last three years have been so good for us,' she says, almost breathlessly. Donna is a compact and tidy woman of 60, black hair worn in a bob. She offers me a drink. She offers me cookies and apologizes for the fact that her husband is away in nearby Iowa on business. She mentions the outreach work she does with her church. But she is more eager to talk to me about the gospel of corn, not least because she is on the board of Illinois Corn, a trade body that represents farmers in the state.

I ask her why business has been so good. 'It's just been a massive leap in demand. The prices have gone up and so have the yields.' Between 1990 and 2007 corn yields rose from 120 bushels an acre to over 160. In turn I want to know why that is.

'It's the genetics. Every season the genetics seem to be better.' I had assumed GM strains of maize didn't change much once they had been developed. Instead they are more like pieces of computer software with new, improved versions being released each season. 'That's why we farm so much more corn than soya. It does so much better.' Donna pulls out her iPad and shows me the day's bid prices, the amount various grain purchasers are willing to pay per bushel of corn. She has offers from Cargill, ADM and GrainFS, the farmers' co-op of which they are a member. 'We sell probably twenty times a year, depending on the price. We have a big storage facility so we can keep the corn until the right time.'

The view from this farmhouse is pretty much as Scott Shellady had described it. If commodity traders have caused prices for corn and soya beans to rise, then that can only be a good thing because it means farmers are doing better. Donna points to a huge, bright-white shed across the gravel yard from where we're sitting. 'We built that to house our machinery because we'd had such a good few years.' She shows me what's inside: these vast planters and harvesters, polished to gleaming, right down to the last wheel nut. 'My husband is always credited with how well he looks after his machinery,' Donna says proudly. A better housing for the machinery means the kit lasts longer. That makes the business more efficient. That means higher profits so they can invest more into their farming activities. That helps them to increase yield. An increase in yield increases earnings. And so it goes on.

From here, at the heart of the US, the grain goes in multiple directions. Nearby in the town of Morris is the Illinois River where Cargill and ADM load barges with grain. From there they connect to the Mississippi and so down to the Gulf of Mexico. 'It goes to Europe and Brazil.' There's also what Donna calls the 'Inter-modal' facility at Joliet. 'The bids there have been better.' Why so? 'Because all the grain from there goes to Asia.'

Asia means China.

It is, she says, a relatively new development. Throughout the nineties and into the beginning of the last decade the Chicago area became the recipient of vast amounts of stuff from China, which entered the country at Long Beach in California: all that cheap, aspirational, eager Chinese labour meant they were making huge amounts of the clothes we wear, the electronics we use, the toys our kids play with. Container loads of product rolled into Illinois courtesy of the railroads, for distribution around America. In those boom years the containers they were carried in were considered merely a means to an end. It cost more to get them back to China than they were worth, so they were regularly scrapped.

It didn't stay that way. Eventually the price of steel increased dramatically with the price of oil and now they had to be returned. But empty steel containers are unstable on ships. They have a habit of rolling off when a swell gets up. So now they packed them with waste materials for ballast. Illinois was sending old newspapers across the Pacific.

Then the Chinese middle-class boom happened, and the one thing the aspiring Chinese middle classes really wanted was meat, lots of it. In turn what a surge in meat eating demanded was grain for the livestock to eat. No longer were the containers going back stuffed with yesterday's news. Now they were going to China full of American corn and soya beans. China does one thing really well: making stuff. America does a different thing really well: growing corn and soya beans. So they trade. This is called utilizing comparative advantage.

Let's stop for a moment and think about this.

IS THAT A PHONE IN YOUR POCKET OR ARE YOU JUST PLEASED TO SEE ME?

You care about where your food comes from. I know you do, or you wouldn't be reading my lovely book. You think about dinner an awful lot. And lunch. And all the little meals in between. Perhaps you're the kind of person who, wandering the aisles of the supermarket, stops to study the labels on pre-packed bags of fruit and vegetables. You want to see whether the strawberries have come from Morocco, or the green beans are from Peru. You understand that the best thing is for as much of your food to come from as close to you as possible. Perhaps you even shop in a farmers' market for precisely that reason. It feels like the right thing to do. It makes sense, if only intuitively. After all, nobody can expect you to be reading all the academic papers on the subject. You are smart enough to see the logic for yourself. Maybe you stop by those stalls overflowing with prime, glossy vegetables so you can phone home to find out what's already in the fridge.

Stop. Let's have a look at that phone.

It's an iPhone, isn't it? Come on. Don't be shy. Only cool people read my books. You are reading my book, ergo you are cool, and therefore you have an iPhone.

Or perhaps you're even cooler than that. Perhaps you have some Android smartphone because you want to thumb your nose at the mighty Apple. So you've got that Samsung Galaxy thing because you want to prove you're not someone who goes with the herd.

Or maybe you're a sad sack like me and you're still using a bloody Blackberry, because you're tied in to a hideous long-term contract which is too expensive to break. You like the proper keyboard with all its buttons and stuff, but hate the fact that the touch pad seizes up or, worse still, the damn thing freezes all the sodding time so you have to open up the back, take out the battery, put it back in again, and reboot it. And every now and then you throw it against the wall to see if it makes any difference. Or stand over the kitchen sink and fantasize about dropping it in there. Or dream about accidentally soaking it in meths and clumsily dropping a lit match on it. You do, don't you? You do that too.

Sorry, but I really hate my shitty little Blackberry.

Anyway, the point is you have a really complex, cutting-edge phone. And perhaps an iPod and certainly a desktop computer, and maybe an iPad. You have stuff. Do you ever think where it comes from, this pile of stuff? Sure you do. If I asked you, you'd say, oh, China somewhere, probably. If it's an iPhone you'd be right. It's probably made by Foxconn in Shenzen or at one of its other factories in China. Or by its outpost in Brazil. If it's a Samsung it will be made in Seoul and if it's an HTC it may well come from Shanghai. If you're one of those people still bothering with a Nokia – how sweet – it might have been made in Hungary, though not if you've just bought a new one. They've shifted all their production out to Asia like everyone else.

Why is this? You know why. Because labour is cheaper in China and much more flexible than in Europe and the US. The workforce in China is desperate to do these jobs, even allowing for scandals over working conditions at factories making Apple kit. The cost of living is simply lower.

This is what's called comparative advantage and it directly affects the cost of almost everything you buy.

Have you noticed that there are no local consumer electronics webs, run by earnest chaps with straggly beards called Hugo and Jake who are, 'you know, just, like, trying to make a difference by cutting down the electronics miles on people's phones in an attempt to save the planet'? Have you clocked that there is no such thing as an artisan mobile phone? This is because we understand that different parts of the world are better suited to different tasks. You don't own a local phone because they make them better and cheaper in China, which is a very long way from where you are.

Exactly the same applies to our food. Illinois, Iowa, Michigan, Indiana – the entire US corn belt – grows so much of it because it has the right climate and the right soil to do so. Bemoaning industrial-scale agriculture in America on principle is about as sensible as criticizing China for making all those mobile phones. Which you wouldn't do, because you bloody love your smartphone, don't you, you dirty little digital warrior?

And that sound is the penny suddenly dropping. Yes, you are absolutely right: this argument is going to kick ten tons of crap out of the local food movement. Have patience. We'll get there.

As the afternoon draws to a close, I ask Donna if she cares where her corn goes. She says, 'No. As a farmer I simply want to provide a safe feed and food product.' On the face of it, that's a reasonable position. Donna and her family's job is simply to grow a crop. What happens to it after it leaves the farm is not really their business.

I like Donna. I like her Midwestern openness and straight talking. I admire her commitment to the job at hand. Those 3,900 acres are farmed by fewer than half a dozen people. It's Donna and her husband and her brother and a guy who comes in during college holidays. But it's hard to simply swallow her suggestion that farmers have no responsibility for what happens to their food, especially in two areas. The first is the use of all that maize to make high-fructose corn syrup (HFCS), a cheaper substitute for sucrose, which turns up in mountains of the most processed foods in our supermarkets. It's controversial. Some researchers have claimed that it suppresses a hormone, leptin, which controls appetite. By switching off that hormone, HFCS makes us constantly hungry and encourages obesity. Other researchers say this isn't the case.

One thing is certain, however. Americans have a hugely sweet tooth. Perhaps it's a throwback to the pioneering days when work was hard and all that manual labour demanded as quick a hit of calories as possible. HFCS is big on calories. But certainly the last thing needed by any country that thinks pouring maple syrup onto salty bacon alongside their pancakes at breakfast is a really good idea is a cheaper source of sugar.

But in terms of our global food supply, even the HFCS business isn't quite as stupid as the faulty science and deformed economics behind the boom in biofuels, which are blamed for the food price spikes in 2008. Not that Donna would agree. Then again, you wouldn't expect her to. Because 36 per cent of the total US corn harvest (and rising) currently goes to making ethanol. It's big business.

A SHORT, SPITTLE-FLECKED RANT ABOUT BLOODY BIOFUELS

Edible stuff has been responsible for some really stupid ideas over the years: a major brand's kidney soup that tasted lightly of wee, fries in chocolate and cinnamon flavours, McDonald's McAfrika burgers, launched in Scandinavia at the height of an

African famine in 2002. But even more stupid than all of these put together is the notion that putting loads of food into big machines to turn it into fuel is a really good idea.

It isn't.

To be fair it's not a new one. Back in 1900 Rudolph Diesel demonstrated his new engine by running it on peanut oil. Very quickly, though, it became clear to him that if you were going to build such an engine, petrochemicals might do a rather better job of running it. It might have stayed that way were it not for the drift of history: the various clean-air acts of the seventies, the Arab–Israeli conflicts of the same decade forcing oil prices ever upwards, and, most importantly, the end of the Cold War. The collapse of the Soviet Union had many knock-on effects, not least the rise of militant Islam, which in turn encouraged the US government to think that kicking its addiction to oil from the Middle East might just be the way to go.

Biofuels seemed like the perfect solution. When plants grow they eat up carbon dioxide. By processing the sugar elements of plants into fuel you would, in theory, only be releasing back into the air the same carbon that had already been sucked up by them in the first place. It would be what everybody wanted any fuel to be: carbon neutral.

Or not quite. Because that doesn't take into consideration the petrochemical-based fertilizers required to make your plant fuel grow. Or the carbon used to build and run the tractors, or the harvesters, or the trucks to take the crop to the ethanol plant, or the stuff used to build the big plant in the first place, or to keep on running it, or to take it from the ethanol plant back to the oil refinery so it can be blended with petrol. And that's before you start factoring in all the water needed to grow the plants, which is hardly an infinite resource.

It should be said that there are endless arguments over this. One influential report, published in *Natural Resources Research* in 2005, found that it takes between 27 per cent and 118 per cent more energy to produce a gallon of biofuel than the energy it contains. That makes it rather less than the great renewable energy source everybody tried to claim it would be. Another report, by the charity Action Aid, looked at the cultivation for biofuels in Africa of jatropha, also known as the physic nut. It found that the process released a six times greater volume of greenhouse gases than petrochemical usage owing to the deforestation of the land to grow it on. Even the more positive reports – one from the National Academy of Sciences in the US, for example, which did find some positive energy production by using different criteria – accepted that biofuels were not necessarily a great idea because of how much corn, soya beans and other plant material you would need to supply US energy needs. Or, as the Academy's paper explained, even if the entirety of the US production of corn and soya beans were directed into biofuels it would still only supply 12 per cent of US gasoline needs and 6 per cent of diesel needs. As the report goes on to point out, with delicious understatement, that really wouldn't be a goer given that people would also need to have something to eat.

Ah yes, food. Directing huge amounts of grain into biofuels was always bound to have unintended consequences, and in this case it was the impact on food prices. A whole bunch of studies looked at the question and found that between 12 per cent and 75 per cent of the food price rises in 2006–8 were caused by the biofuels industry, depending on the food commodity, the country being analysed and the type of methodology adopted by the study. Why then does it continue? Because of subsidies and the vested interests of the agricultural lobby. The US government paid a large number of subsidies to make growing corn for ethanol an attractive thing to do. For a while they paid the fuel companies a subsidy of nearly fifty cents for every gallon of biofuel they blended with gasoline. Laws were passed which made using a certain proportion of biofuels mandatory. In short, the whole biofuel industry became one vast market-altering subsidy for US farming.

And bit by bit that model has spread around the world. In the past two years Britain has seen a boom in anaerobic digesters, which produce methane gas to power turbines for the production of electricity. If you have a huge volume of waste material because, say, you run a large dairy and have an excess of cow shit, that's a clever thing to do. And some anaerobic digesters have been established near dairies and food processing plants which are otherwise producing waste. But increasingly, because of 'renewable energy' subsidies, fields across the UK are being planted with corn solely to be thrown into the digester. It is a smaller version of the bizarre US bioethanol industry. We worry about there being too many people in the world with not enough food to eat. And yet, at the same time, we're growing what could be food and turning it into energy. Calling it bizarre is an insult to the merely odd.

It is a catastrophic and craven failure of global government agriculture policy on a monumental scale.

On a Sunday morning back in Chicago I have brunch with Scott Shellady at the Chicago Yacht Club. It's regatta day and the place is full of Waspy types wearing white trousers, blue blazers and deck shoes. I feel like Woody Allen in *Annie Hall* when he goes for Easter lunch with his girlfriend's Protestant family. At one point the camera cuts back to Allen and he's dressed as a Hasidic Jew, all felt hat, beard and ringlets. The hyper non-Jewish environment has made the secular, godless Jew feel like a total frummer. That's me at the table of the Chicago Yacht Club. I do not own deck shoes. I have never knowingly worn a blazer with brass buttons. Occasionally big shiny yachts float by the picture windows looking out onto the lake and everybody cheers. I frown. How do you cheer a boat? More to the point, why would you? I don't do boats. I don't *get* boats. Nor does Scott. 'They keep telling me to get a boat, but I don't want one,' he says. I tell him to hold fast.

He talks about the 800-acre farm in Iowa that his father Ron bought in 1973, how his old man insisted on working the farm, even while he had a successful career as a trader. 'I would go to work and try to buy low and sell high, but I wouldn't feel I had *made* anything. But he could put seeds in the ground and grow something.' His father is in the grip of late-stage dementia, Scott tells me, and it's a terrible thing to see a man who was once so vital brought so low. He is clearly grateful to his father for having bothered to buy the farm. 'Once he dies if my brother and sister can't afford to keep the farm then I will do everything I can to keep it because I think land is now gold. For years technology has been ahead of population demand. But I don't think technology is keeping up. Population is starting to exhaust technology. That makes land the key asset.'

We refill our plates at the buffet; two large men working the all-you-can-eat vibe carefully, trying not to draw attention to themselves. Back at the table I ask Scott what he thinks of biofuels. He looks at me. 'It's a pile of shit,' he says. 'The US government has decided to use it as a stopgap [for energy supply] while they come up with something better. But it's just not the answer.'

He says, 'What would the price of corn be if there wasn't the market for biofuels?'

I say, 'Well, it's taking a third of the corn harvest, so presumably, at least in the first year, it would drop by a third.'

'Exactly. It would be $4 a bushel instead of $6. Biofuels have caused massive price inflation.' He picks at his food. 'It is just not the answer.' Another shiny white yacht floats by. The room cheers. I flinch.

The plan was to carry on west from Chicago to Minnesota and the headquarters of what, by revenue, is the largest privately owned company in America. Cargill, which is nearly 150 years old, operates in sixty-five countries, and is all over the food supply chain like an itchy rash. It is one of the six companies which, between them, control 70 per cent of the global wheat trade. It makes loans to farmers across the world so they can buy Cargill seed to grow crops which Cargill then buys, processes, transports and sells on. The company is a major manufacturer of livestock feed and foodstuffs, like starches and corn syrup. It trades in palm oil and steel, has a commodity trading arm, runs industrial-scale slaughterhouses and has recently acquired a German chocolate company, a central American poultry purchaser and a whole bunch of other stuff besides. In its 2011 report Cargill declared revenues just shy of $120 billion, up 18 per cent on the year before. If Cargill was a country it would rank fifty-eighth in the world in terms of GDP and have a bigger economy than Kenya, Tunisia and Cyprus combined. It's huge.

I didn't have high expectations of being granted access. I was told the company could be closed off to the world; that it was a peculiarly Minnesotan trait. A friend of mine from

Minneapolis said that if I did get access I would have to dump the flowery shirts and get a haircut. They weren't the sort to take kindly to big hairy Englishman in flamboyant tailoring. I persevered. I explained I was trying to engage with the industrial food process; that I wasn't out to condemn it. I wanted to understand it. Plus in recent years senior executives from Cargill, portrayed by the movie *Food Inc* as one of the devils of the piece, had been making big public speeches about the future role of their company in tackling the great food security crisis of the twenty-first century. If they meant it, surely they would talk to me?

Indeed they would, they said, just not in Minnesota. The company PR man wanted me to meet Paul Conway, Cargill's British Vice-Chairman. But I had to meet him in Britain. To be exact I was to meet him in Cobham, Surrey, a place of finely cut lawns and carriage drives and three-car families, where every house must, by law, have a portico and many women are a peculiar shade of self-tan orange. Cargill's sprawling British HQ sits in manicured grounds at the end of a road called Fairmile Lane. It is a building of glass-walled offices, the frosted panes of which are inscribed with management babble like 'Collaboration' or 'Create', 'High Performance' and 'Customer Focus'. Conway's corner office bears the legend 'Innovation', which he tells me was not his choice. He wore a pink open-necked shirt – a tie hung on the back of the door, as if for emergencies – and neatly pressed chinos. If he had spoken with a gentle Midwestern drawl I wouldn't have been surprised. Instead he had the soft round vowels of the English barrister he was many years ago. He had a wholesome, squash-playing glow.

I say I am a little surprised to be allowed in. Conway agrees that Cargill has not always been so open; that up until 2006 the stock answer to questions from the media had been, 'No comment.'

'But we're too big to hide. In the modern media world you can't hide anything.' Before I can even broach the subject he comes over all group-therapy member and volunteers that Cargill has been associated in the recent past with controversial incidents of what has been portrayed by campaigners as malpractice. It has been fingered for accelerating deforestation in the Amazon basin because of soya-processing plants it has built there. Their name has been given in court proceedings on behalf of children trafficked into Ivory Coast to work on cocoa plantations in abusive conditions, has seen its palm oil operations accused of playing a role in damaging the dwindling habitats of orang-utans. Conway tells me that all these issues either have been or are being addressed. 'It's in the nature of the sort of company we are that these things can happen, but we have realized that we have a responsibility to protect the reputations of the companies we supply.' Big-name brands do not like it when their suppliers are accused of being bit players in child slavery, even if only by default. In the age of social media they can't just let these things float by. A small campaign can have a huge impact. In a moment of disarming honesty Conway says, 'We're a long way short of where a more marketing-focused company would be. There's a recognition that we need to go and talk.'

So now they are talking to me. In an age when individual states across the US have been debating and even passing into law acts which have been called 'Big Ag Gag' bills – legislation which prohibits the photographing or documenting of abuses on farms without the owners' consent – this really is remarkable. In Utah, for example, the Agricultural Interference Bill, passed in February 2012, in effect makes it a criminal act to distribute photos of a farm without the permission of the farmer.

I ask Conway if he thinks the business would suffer if it didn't engage with the media. After all, it is a privately owned company. There is less of a requirement for it to do so than might be the case with a publicly quoted company with a vulnerable share price. 'Not immediately, but we could see that our freedom to operate might be limited in time if we didn't discuss these things. We're in sixty-five countries. If you get an overall environment that's less conducive to trade than you might wish, then that's bad for business.'

I tell him I am intrigued by Cargill's recent statements on food security. Its 2011 annual company report runs to thirty-eight pages and most of it is a discussion between leading figures in the field about how to keep the planet fed. I said it felt like some sort of a manifesto. And yet Cargill is an agricultural supply business, not a big, huggy pressure group. In short, does Cargill regard the challenges of the food security crisis as a cracking business opportunity?

Up to this point Conway has mostly been focusing his comments out the window at the damp home counties countryside. Now he looks at me. 'Absolutely,' he says. 'All these things we've been investing in for 147 years will be in demand.'

Do you understand why people feel uncomfortable with that?

'Again, absolutely. Modern food production is an industrial activity but it is marketed to the consumer by using pastoral visions.'

We talk for a while about the recent history of food security issues: about how the years 2000 to 2007 witnessed the greatest period of global economic growth in human history, the way the Chinese came onstream as the biggest importers of soya beans, and then the systemic shocks that caused the price spikes of 2008. Why, I ask, did you start discussing the issue? 'Two reasons. Firstly we were being asked what was going on and whether we had any recommendations, and secondly because various governments were doing things that could exacerbate the problem.' Like what? 'Export bans: forty-eight countries introduced export bans on things like rice and wheat in 2008 that prevented markets from working.' Cargill, Conway says, believes firmly in free trade; that this is the way to keep the planet fed. It needs to argue the case.

OK. But if it is so keen on the free market why the hell is it in the biofuel business, which is essentially a subsidy for growing corn? 'We have always had doubts about it, especially the mandates forcing the use of certain amounts of biofuels. But our view has always been that we will participate. All of our biofuel plants are part of another facility, therefore achieving scale economies. There is a role for biofuels.'

Really? The science barely stacks up.

'Well, no, there is something to what you say. But let the market decide.'

The point, he says, is that the biofuels business has helped raise the price for corn and that, in turn, has resulted in investment. 'There's a saying: the best fertilizer is price. Farmers respond to that. If you removed the ethanol business completely you would see a massive reduction in the production of crops.'

Are commodity traders a driver of price? After all, Cargill has its own commodity trading arm, with $5 billion of funds under management. If there wasn't money to be made there it wouldn't do it. Conway shakes his head. 'We are price-takers, not price-makers. Arguing against commodity traders is a bit like saying we don't need bankers.' It strikes me he may be making a different point. We do indeed need bankers. Everyone needs somewhere to put their money. That doesn't mean we want the kind of bankers we've been given. Likewise, perhaps the issue is not commodity traders per se. It's the type of commodity traders we have.

'Look,' Conway says, as if attempting to sum up. 'Our job is to move stuff from areas of surplus to areas of deficit. We will pre-finance soya bean farmers in Brazil. We will buy their harvest and ship it to China. We will build a large processing plant in China to extract the protein and sell that to livestock farmers in China. Our job is to pay the Brazilian farmer a little more than the other guy would, and sell the product to the Chinese farmer for a little less than the other guy would.' A big company like Cargill, he says, can manage volatility.

This is what he wants me to understand.

Hating commodity traders is easy. It's fun. It makes you feel better about yourself. Look at them in their silly striped jackets and Friesian cow prints attempting to make money out of the very stuff of life. They are scumbags; ergo I am a paragon of virtue. As Conway says, however, hating them may be missing the point. If a command and control economy of the sort attempted by the Soviet Union didn't increase yields – and in the long term it didn't – then we have only the market. It's worth noting that one of the ways Ethiopia has worked to eliminate devastating grain price fluctuations is by setting up a baby version of the Chicago Board of Trade. There a 'contract' isn't the amount of grain you can get in a train carriage, as it is in Chicago. They don't have train carriages of that sort. It's the amount you can carry on the back of an Isuzu pickup truck. Food campaigners in the developed world may be waving placards at commodity traders, but in places like Ethiopia, where the market mechanism can be the difference between life and death, people are staking their very survival on their success.

Similarly we can rail against companies like Cargill, on a point of principle. As Conway put it to me at one point: 'Big is regarded as bad. Big and American is very bad. Big, American and private is seen as much, much worse.' There's a lot not to like. But in a crowded and hungry world, disdain feels like a luxury we can ill afford. Plus railing against the scale of American agriculture is like rolling your eyes at the emerging Chinese middle classes for ramping up their consumption of meat or buying up land in Africa. It's like shaking your fist at the rain in Wales. It's pointless. It's a fact of life. It's a part of the new global food paradigm.

And the success of a company like Cargill also puts a whacking question mark over one of the most basic assumptions of the belly-obsessed foodie classes. It forces us to ask a simple question:

6.

IS SMALL ALWAYS BEAUTIFUL?

Ernst Schumacher was born in Germany in August 1911, the son of a political economy professor. He studied in Bonn and Berlin before, in 1930, moving to England, where he became a protégé of the great economist John Maynard Keynes. During a long and diverse career he worked as an academic, a leader writer for *The Times*, and as chief economic adviser to the Coal Board. He travelled the world, served as an economic consultant to Burma, became intrigued by Buddhism and deeply sceptical of Western economic dogma. All of this resulted, in 1973, in the publication of *Small Is Beautiful: A Study of Economics as if People Mattered*, a book which, as Jonathan Porritt, former director of Friends of the Earth, puts it in his introduction to the 2011 edition, fixed Schumacher as 'the first of the "holistic thinkers" of the modern Green movement'. It made Ernst a bit of a star.

I was given the book to read a dozen years after its publication, as part of my politics degree. Three hours after picking it up I threw it against the wall. Even now I remember the rising surge of irritation it caused even if, after almost three decades, I can't immediately remember quite why. It may have had something to do with the tutor who gave it to us and his enthusiasm for the book. He was a little man in a leather blazer and thin tie who called everyone 'Comrade'. It was the silliest sort of affectation and, worse still, inaccurate. I was pretty sure that, as a nice Jewish boy from north-west London, I was unlikely to be in the vanguard of anybody's revolution. It was more likely that, while everyone else was manning the barricades, I'd be hanging from the third lamp-post on the left.

But a student's memory is not to be trusted, and certainly not after what I did to mine. In any case in recent years, as green politics has moved from the fringe to the mainstream, Schumacher, already a serious player in the world of economic theory, has become something of a popular guru. It's not that surprising. The word 'big' – as in big business, as in big agriculture, as in big government – has become dirty and unclean. Big is bad. Ergo small is beautiful. What's not to like?

Re-reading the book, I began to wonder. What was it that made me so book-throwingly bloody cross? In the opening chapters Schumacher proffers an idea which is now a statement of the obvious, but which back then was a remarkable insight: that the earth's resources, its minerals, its nutrients, its sources of fuel, are not infinite. They are our 'capital' much as a business has capital that it builds upon. Equally, because humans have not made all of that capital we place less value upon it and just plough through it like a convention of compulsive eaters at a sweaty pile-it-high Las Vegas buffet, thus robbing future generations of anything to work with. Schumacher's book was an argument against the burgeoning cult of economic growth at all costs, proposed that society and the world of work be organized on a 'convivial scale' that was more human, and said that 'gigantism' – his own word – was dehumanizing. All of that makes a lot of sense.

It took me a while, but I finally found what it was that had me chucking the book against the wall. It was in the chapter on agriculture. I can't pretend. Part of the problem is God. You know the chap: white robes, big beard, omniscient. Despite having started life as an atheist, Schumacher ended it as a Bible-quoting Catholic. I, however, have undergone no such conversion and don't see one popping along any day soon. As far as I'm concerned I might as well believe in fairies at the bottom of the garden as take my lead from an all-powerful deity of whose existence I have no proof.

We were, I know, raised as children to believe in tolerance and respect for the views and opinions of others. That's how you play nice. The older I get the harder I find it to muster both bits of that lesson. I can do tolerance. I'm excellent at tolerance. I tolerate lots of things that annoy me hugely: right-wing politicians, people who like their steaks served well done, homeopaths, Dick Cheney.

I find the respect bit much, much tougher. I don't understand why theists think there is some higher power. It's as simple as that. To me it seems deranged. But as long as you aren't using that belief system as an excuse for abusing kids, as a way to stop people having sex with whomsoever they want, or as grounds for mounting military interventions, then go right ahead. Worship Bart Simpson as your god, for all I care. I'll happily tolerate you. But if you start using the existence of God as a way to support your argument, well then, we're never really going to be friends. You will end up having to do a little more than tolerate me.

Schumacher uses the existence of God as a way to support his argument. He even quotes the Pope (a slightly dodgy one back then, Pope Paul VI, who went out of his way to defend his predecessor for staying silent throughout the Holocaust, during a trip to Israel). He also quotes that bit from Genesis about us having dominion over the fish in the sea and the fowl in the air and so on, before announcing that 'Man, the highest of his creatures, was given "dominion", not the right to tyrannize.' I'm with the sentiment. I make a point of never tyrannizing fish. It's bad manners.

But if you start quoting from a big book of made-up stories to make your point I am going to become deeply suspicious of your motives. Schumacher also argues that more of us need to live and work on the land to be happy; that living in cities is an unnatural thing for people to do. Or, as he puts it, we must work on the land to keep humanity 'in touch with living nature'. We must, he says, 'become reconciled with the natural world'.

Really? I'm not at all convinced by the natural world, or at least not the one he's describing. I like cities. I like the noise and the clutter, the buzz and the speed and the rush and the tumble of cities. I like the crush of humanity. I think human beings are essentially sociable animals, which is why more and more of us now live in urban areas than outside of them. I don't mind visiting the countryside now and then. My wife used to make me go hill walking in Yorkshire. When I asked her why we couldn't get a cab instead of walking over the hills, I was only joking. I didn't mind walking up and down hills. But cities do make more sense. They're the environmentally sound way to go. People in cities share resources in a way those in the countryside do not. We get around on public transport. We use less land by living in homes piled one on top of the other. We reduce the distances we have to travel to reach the resources we need. It's the country dwellers with their two-car households driving the kids ten miles to school and back every day, and living on huge plots of land, who are swallowing the resources.

But it's the notion that small is beautiful which troubles me. To be fair, Schumacher was suspicious of the book's title, and had it thrust upon him. He feared it would reduce his theories to a soundbite, and his fears were well founded. In the book he does recognize the need for certain types of large-scale organization. Nevertheless, agriculture isn't among them. Schumacher insists that small units of production are the way to go with farming, and in a modern context this seems peculiar to me. Surely we need to pool resources, just as city dwellers do? Surely, if we are worried about the way we are using and abusing our natural capital, it makes sense for us to use it in a way that gains the greatest outputs from the smallest of inputs? Or, to put it another way, a ten-acre farm could manage on one tractor. But so, for that matter, could a twenty-acre farm. Or a thirty-acre farm. Lots of small farms means lots of doubling up on equipment and labour. That can't be right.

We have an awful lot of people to feed. We can have a debate about the imperative of family planning, which makes a huge amount of sense and must be a long-term goal (though it risks over-simplifying things: families in the developing world will only start reducing their family size when health and nutrition have improved to such a degree that parents know the smaller number of kids they are having will survive into adulthood).

For now, though, we have a population of over seven billion to feed, which is projected to rise by another couple of billion by mid-century. Surely this is not the moment for us all to go running back to the land, farming it as the Rwandans do? Schumacher also has a way of making statements as though they were facts, when they are just a bit of subjective babble. Among the things agriculture must do, he says, is 'humanize and ennoble man's wider habitat', without for a moment explaining what any of this means save to say that he doesn't think modern agriculture is especially good at humanizing and ennobling anything.

What troubles me most, though, is the way Schumacher appears to believe there is this thing called 'the natural world' which humanity floats above; that modern agriculture makes it impossible to 'keep man in real touch with living nature'. It's a view shared by many, many critics of modern agriculture, the ones who bellow at us that we need to re-engineer our food production system so that it is small-scale and local to us. Huge, industrial-scale farming, they say, is just unnatural.

It's the 'n' word, you see: nature, and more particularly the idea that we and it are completely separate. I have a real problem with that.

WHATEVER COMES NATURALLY

Ideas of what constitutes natural human behaviour are a little more fluid when you've grown up with an agony aunt as a mother. Claire's postbag, which contained around a thousand letters a week, was a primer on what human beings could get up to with each other given half a chance, and none of it was a secret. She didn't believe in those. She worked from home, with my dad as her manager, a team of secretaries as support, and us kids as backstop to stuff envelopes with leaflets when the need arose. The sorting out of other people's pain, trouble and neuroses was therefore the family business. As a 10-year-old boy I knew things: what the symptoms of the menopause are, how a tub of natural yoghurt can be used to soothe thrush, how a 'loving massage' can be used to get the long-marrieds shagging again. You know; all the things a 10-year-old boy really needs to know.

The contents of that postbag could quite as easily be discussed at the breakfast table as in the office, and it often was. Much of it was mundane and obvious: the teenage girl being pressured by a boyfriend to go to bed with him; the son arguing with his parents as he fights for independence; the married man who is considering having an affair and wants to know whether it's OK. And then, inevitably, there were the enquiries about the odd, weird and wonderful but very human sexual behaviour that people seemed to indulge in. They knew they liked the way it made them feel. They just needed to know whether nice was the same as good. Some of them were heartbreaking: the gay teenagers who knew what they wanted but feared (often correctly) that they would be abandoned by their family and friends if they came out, the elderly widower who missed his wife of fifty years, craved the physical contact of sex, and wanted to know whether it could ever be OK to pay for it.

Others were just plain funny. One morning my mother opened the post at the breakfast table to reveal a life-size wooden carving of an erect cock, the glans painted a delicate shade of purple over the wood's natural grain. The sender was concerned about the shape of his erection – it leaned a little to the left, Tower of Pisa style – and had therefore 'decided' that the best way to get the issue sorted was to spend months carving a version of it out of wood, because sending a photo might have been deemed impolite. (Yeah, right.) There was the other chap who phoned Claire up at her desk one morning and asked whether she'd mind having a listen 'while I have a wank'.

'Well, if you must,' my mother replied. She placed the receiver down on the desk, got on with her work, and picked it up again a few minutes later to check he'd finished.

'Yes, thank you.'

'Jolly good. Take care.'

From decades of this sort of stuff, my mother fashioned a philosophy: that defining what was 'natural' human behaviour was akin to counting the grains of sand on a beach. It was one of the glorious things about being human. Some people liked to be spanked. Some were foot fetishists or had a thing about earlobes. Others could only do it outside, a few needed cuddly toys nearby, or for almost all clothes to be in place, or for *The Muppet Show* to be on telly at the time. I may be making some of these things up, but only because she is no longer around for me to check with, which means I'm only leaving out far weirder fetishes than the ones I have described. Her view came down to this: as long as nobody was being coerced, as long as nobody was at risk of being seriously hurt, as long as everybody involved was of sound mind, as long as it didn't involve children or animals and doing it didn't make you anxious and uptight, it was fine. (Although I do recall a letter from a quite elderly and obviously lonely lady who had somehow trained her dog – an Alsatian, I believe – to perform cunnilingus upon her and wanted to know whether this was OK. Claire concluded that as long as the dog didn't mind it seemed pretty harmless.)

Certainly, when challenged on TV and radio about the naturalness of a certain type of behaviour, she would demand a definition of natural. At best the opposition would resort to something from the Bible, because it was always the Christian right who found her most obnoxious. At which point she would know she had won. There are passages in Leviticus which say it's OK to own slaves, as long as they come from neighbouring nations, though I suspect if I tried to place my mates from Cardiff into bondage they might be a bit cross about it. Leviticus also says that it is a sin punishable by death to cut the hair around your temples. I'm obviously in the clear, but I do worry about my sons, who like to keep their hair short. Exodus insists that anybody who works on the Sabbath should be put to death, which seems a bit unfair on the lovely Kurdish family who run the convenience store at the end of our street. When it comes to defining what's natural the Bible isn't really the best of primers. If it proposes execution for a bit of Sunday trading, what in God's name – and I mean that literally for once – will it come up with for a bit of innocent foot fetishism?

One afternoon a year or two back I had a cup of tea with Vivian Moses, Visiting Professor of Biotechnology at King's College London. It turned out he and my mother had similar views, even though his didn't encompass the general fetishisms of bondage, flagellation or enemas. We were discussing the science behind genetically modified foods, and the arguments made against them by opponents. These included the fact that it wasn't 'natural'.

Professor Moses sighed, shook his head, and said, 'Are humans natural?'

I hesitated. I sensed a trick question. Plus I'd always hated philosophy seminars when I was at university. Suddenly I was back in one, and the passage of time had done nothing to make me feel more comfortable with the game of sparring that such things demand.

'Well, I ...'

'It's not a complicated question. Is humanity a natural phenomenon?'

'Well, yes, of course. Humans evolved naturally.'

'Right. So it follows that anything humans do is their natural behaviour?'

'Yes. Of course.'

'Then the idea that the use of biotechnology is unnatural is rubbish because it is an example of natural human behaviour.'

I stirred my lemon tea. It was one of those light-bulb moments, the argument so simple and so obvious, and yet it had never occurred to me in that way before. So when the great Ernst Schumacher started quoting ecologists as saying there are natural laws in relation to the environment that man cannot break, he is talking cobblers. The idea that there is a natural world and that mankind is crawling about upon it, like some grubby, disease-ridden unnatural parasite, is, to use the sort of language Professor Moses might find unseemly, also total bollocks. From the moment we cross-bred grasses on the banks of the River Nile over 5,000 years ago to produce the first arable crops we were impressing ourselves upon the life cycle of plants. Undomesticated cattle do not produce milk all year round. We made them (and continue to make them) do that. Apart from a few rare places – the Arctic, say, or bits of desert – humanity has shaped almost every bit of the landscape upon which we work, because that's what we do. That's what we are. It's only natural.

So trying to argue against certain types of agriculture because they are unnatural or because they violate rules of nature just isn't going to work. It's not just a flimsy argument. In terms of classical logic, it's not even an argument. It's just a bunch of non sequiturs. It is the logic of the placard and slogan. It's lazy. That's not to excuse everything humanity does. On this planet, as far as we know, we are uniquely blessed with a conscience. We are responsible for our actions. But if you are intent on criticizing the way we interact with that planet, and the many and various things that we have done to it, you are going to have to come up with something far better than notions of what is natural and what is unnatural. There is no such thing as unnatural. There are, however, such things as good practice and bad practice.

As a result, when we come to think about farming and whether small really is the way to go, we have to be a bit more sophisticated about it. Without some blunt, specious rule to fall back on – it's against NATURE! – we have to look at things in the round. We have to weigh up all parts of the equation. We have to understand what benefits big might bring.

To which end, anybody fancy an apple?

High on a hill to the west of Canterbury, on a plot that looks out over the Stour valley, there is a grave. Six lines of old Bramley apple trees have been grubbed out from the middle of a sloping orchard to make way for it, leaving scars of dark, tilled earth, so that it sits surrounded by an open garland of further trees which have just come into confetti-white blossom.

'It's the right place for him to be,' says Chris Lynch, general manager of Mansfield's, the biggest grower of apples in Britain. He has taken me up there in a muddied 4x4 to have a look at the grave, and we sit now studying the cleft and heave of the Kentish hills, dressed with neat rows of burgeoning fruit trees that march away from us in all directions. The company was founded in the sixties by a one-time greengrocer from London's East Ham called Buddy Mansfield. He died in September 2011 aged 88, and he lies now in the grave I'm looking at. Despite my best efforts, this is as close as I've managed to get to a Mansfield by blood all morning.

Things are not going to plan.

People had been talking to me for a while about Mansfield's, but always in hushed tones. They had told me the company was the future of food production in Britain, that it was run by an extraordinarily astute man from London's East End – Buddy's son, Paul – who was almost single-handedly revolutionizing the shape of fruit production in Britain. I was told it grew 17 per cent of all the apples produced in Britain and packed 25 per cent of them, that it was constantly expanding, adding massive acreage to the 3,500 it already owned. Paul Mansfield was eating up Kent. If I wanted to get a sense of what farming in Britain might look like in the future, Mansfield's was where I had to go.

'But he can be a little tricky,' one contact said to me. 'He's very, very careful about what he says and who he talks to.' Or, as someone else put it to me, 'He doesn't do much talking at all.'

I imagined he didn't need to. The numbers did all the talking for him.

Paul Mansfield began to sound like the Blofeld of the apple business. I imagined him in some rough-hewn lair of the sort designed by Ken Adams for the Bond movies, sitting in a black leather chair, stroking a white cat while instructing minions to take control of the global apple crop. Today the wealds of Kent. Tomorrow the world! To the left of him, Everests of Braeburn; to the right, Mont Blancs of Jazz. There would be perfect, shiny, grade-A uniform apples as far as the eye could see. Not that I really need to over-work this dusty old imagery because that's pretty much how many opponents of 'Big Agriculture' see it.

'In its short shameless history,' the highly regarded American journalist Verlyn Klinkenborg wrote on the Environment360 website in April 2012, 'big agriculture has had only one idea: uniformity.' Action Aid has talked about how agricultural behemoths 'are draining wealth from rural communities, marginalizing small-scale farming, and infringing people's rights'. Food and Water Watch, a US-based lobby group, has talked about 'a tiny cabal of agri-businesses and food manufacturers' which has 'a stranglehold on every link of the food chain'. It's all about dominating the landscape, bending nature to its will, asserting human superiority over the resources provided to us and putting the demands of big business first. If small is beautiful, then it would stand to reason that big would be ugly.

And some of it is. Trying to argue that massive global agricultural combines have only the happiness and well-being of consumers at heart and aren't focused on profit is a bit like trying to claim that the rain doesn't really want to get you wet.

Except that the more I investigate, the more I look at other examples of farming and consider the growing demands of the planet's appetite, the more I find myself concluding that it doesn't have to be this way. Or, to put it in the language that one of the tutors who taught me philosophical logic at university would applaud, just because some companies practising large-scale agriculture do not do so with either the environment's or consumer's best interests at heart, it does not immediately follow that all large-scale agriculture is bad.

The reality is that, given the challenges we face, large-scale agriculture makes an awful lot of sense. It just needs to be pursued by enlightened people. It needs to be practised by people who aren't looking to suck the landscape dry of what Schumacher called the planet's 'capital', who don't just mouth the words 'sustainable intensification' but know what it means.

And that's the language people use when they talk about Mansfield's.

Paul Mansfield's big, they say, but he's sustainable.

'You have to go and have a look,' says Adrian Barlow, who heads up the growers' organization English Apples and Pears. 'He's doing some very interesting things.' Companies like Mansfield's are necessary because, Barlow says, the English apple business has been in serious trouble and is only now fighting its way out of that trouble. In 2003 we grew only 23.9 per cent of all the apples we ate in Britain. The rest were imported. That had risen to just over 30 per cent by 2006 and 36.8 per cent by 2011. 'And I expect to continue seeing increases.' If a country like Britain needs to continue getting more self-sufficient in food to help protect consumers from food price shocks from abroad, if we really need to get growing much more of the stuff we eat, then the apple business is providing an important example.

Plus I like apples.

I ask Adrian Barlow if he will make an introduction, which he agrees to do. There is an exchange of emails. From the Mansfield's end the responses are all from Paul's wife, who, for those with an affection for old movies, is called Jane. Apparently Paul doesn't do email. It's not part of his skill set.

But a plan is made. They are going off on holiday to the home they own in Portugal and they'll see me the day after they get back. I take the high-speed train to Canterbury. I take a taxi to Nickle Farm, out on the A28. I am dropped by huge sheds, the size of aircraft hangars, fashioned from pale-cream corrugated metal. There are manicured lawns and well-kept car parks. I ring the buzzer and announce myself. There is a brief pause before the woman on the intercom says, 'Oh, well. I suppose you'd better … you know … come in.'

I make my way upstairs to a set of huge, echoing office suites clearly too big for the desks in them, and I'm met by a woman, who is squinting at me over her glasses.

'I thought it was you,' she says. She had been looking at me through the video intercom but had somehow still recognized me from some of the television work I do. 'What are you doing here?'

I am not expected. They have completely forgotten. Paul Mansfield isn't even on site. He's gone off for lunch with a bunch of other growers. Jane Mansfield, Chris Lynch and their colleagues gabble their apologies and run off to 'make arrangements'. I take the time to look around the offices, which are located on a raised floor of the new sheds that were only built a year or so before at a cost of £8.6 million. There are wood-laminate floors and sofas in apple green leatherette (or perhaps it really is leather; after all, there must be serious cash in apples). There are trophies declaring Mansfield's to be grower of the year, and a certificate for being runner-up in the BBC's Food and Farming Awards. There is a glossy brochure printed on thick card full of photographs of grading lines and packing lines and refrigeration units.

Most impressive of all is the aerial view of both the building I am standing in and the land around it. The stuff about the thirty-three new cold stores and their capacity to hold 20,000 bins of fruit at any one time – a ton of apples fills three bins

– is interesting. It's good to know it has six loading bays with a pneumatic bag system even though I haven't a clue what one of those is. Apparently there are sixteen speed baggers that can pack eight bags of fruit a minute, and a water filtration process that uses a carbon-based system to extend the usability of the water from two days to six months, thus saving three million litres of water each year. All of that is fascinating. But there's something even better to look at.

It's the bloody great hole they've dug behind it. It's a reservoir, capable of holding 22.5 million litres of water, all of it to be collected from the one-hectare roof of the building I'm standing in. I look up at the ceiling as if expecting to see water dripping through. It seems such an obvious thing to do and yet not everybody is doing it.

Suddenly Jane is back with Chris. He'll take me on a tour of the site and then drive me the twenty miles or so across Kent to meet Paul, who will be in a pub somewhere. Briskly, I am asked to remove any jewellery – ring, bracelet, watch – and put my ludicrous hair away inside a hat. We put on insulated yellow hazard jackets and scrub up before entering the facility. While we are getting changed I ask about the reservoir.

'I think it was Paul's idea,' Chris says. 'There had been some flooding and so it seemed like a solution.'

When it's fully up and running he says they should be able to trickle-irrigate all of the trees without drawing water from elsewhere. I like the sound of trickle irrigation. It sounds careful and precise. They are also planting a nature reserve around it, and replanting hedgerows with native trees. 'Paul has a thing about native trees, silver birches and the like.'

It is May and the last of the Braeburns are being picked now, heralding the start of the great British apple gap, which will last until August or September, when some of the less popular native varieties like Worcester will come onstream. The Cox apples finished in February and won't be back until October. But there is still activity. Teams of workers are unpacking boxes of Jazz apples imported from New Zealand and rebagging them for the supermarkets.

'Until three or four years ago we only packed and graded our own fruit but now in the downtime we handle fruit from abroad,' Chris tells me. Doesn't it irritate you to be doing that? Aren't you encouraging imports? 'It's not like that. It's complementary to what we do. It maintains consumer interest.' There may be a British apple gap but there's no Jazz apple gap, because they come in from abroad. All that said, he admits the company's strategy is to keep increasing yield. Four years ago it was around 40,000 bins. By 2012 it had risen to 60,000 bins. By 2015 it should be around 100,000 bins, or well over 30,000 tons of apples.

Is that by using more land?

He shakes his head. 'Not entirely. It's by increasing yield per acre.' There are new ways of planting trees. If the branches can't spread outwards because they're packed too close together, they can at least go upwards. There is unlimited space going upwards, so they train the trees to use it. They are farming into the sky.

The air in the brightly lit shed is cold. It catches at the back of my throat and makes my knuckles pink. 'We believe in a chill chain throughout the business,' Chris says. 'Apples come in and are rapidly chilled before being put into storage.'

Doesn't that hoover up energy? No, he says, they are using the new generation of saline-based coolants, which are 60 per cent more energy efficient than those that went before. And what went before was a long way beyond the infamous and now banned CFCs, which were punching holes in the ozone layer. All that is ancient history. 'It is massively in our interests to reduce energy costs. We have regular energy audits.'

Chris takes me to see the lines of apple storage rooms. We have been storing apples in Britain since Roman times, the fruit piled into a space that's as airtight as possible so that the ripening fruit uses up the available oxygen until it's all gone, ripening stops, and the fruit falls into a form of suspended animation. The methods used now are a little more sophisticated, though the principle is the same. The apples are placed inside, the doors locked and the oxygen drawn out. Chris pushes open one of the heavy doors and we are immediately hit by a smell of apples of an intensity you would normally find in a sweet shop.

'Each of these stores holds 200 tons and can do that for between six and eight months,' he announces, looking up at the boxes stacked tidily on top of each other. That, he says, is the point. When weighing up energy usage it's worth considering the alternatives. If these apples weren't able to come out of store across the year, then even more would have to be imported from as far away as New Zealand, China or South Africa. The carbon footprint of importation would be far greater than that of low-energy storage.

THE CAMPAIGN FOR REAL ARGUMENTS

There is, of course, an alternative. It's the one the self-appointed food Taliban are shouting at this page right now: we stop eating apples altogether when the season ends. Just do it. Seasonality rules. When the last apples are picked and eaten in May, that's it. Fini. We could stew a few of them and package the result for long storage. We could make pies out of a load of them and chuck those in the freezer (though obviously that would leave its own huge carbon footprint). But essentially for five months of the year we'd go without fresh apples.

It's an idea. It's a really stupid idea.

Arguing for a food policy based on the kind of principles that would make the Amish look like a bunch of happy-go-lucky, profligate sybarites may make a certain sort of gimlet-eyed, self-regarding food warrior feel smug and self-righteous. It may make them glow with an inner purity.

Feel my deep well of virtue.

Stroke my inner goodness.

And so on.

But it will not provide a solution. We've been eating apples out of season in Britain for millennia. We have a reasonable expectation of being able to do so, because there are ways of making it happen. There is also a market designed to supply that need. Short of introducing laws banning the sale of something as basic as apples outside of specific, officially designated periods – shades of a Soviet-style command-and-control system there, and wasn't that a success – it would be impossible to stop a demand.

Back comes the argument: so, Rayner, all this seasonality stuff is rubbish, is it? We can just eat out-of-season strawberries from Morocco and out-of-season asparagus from Peru as much as we like because we can't frame laws against it? Is that your point?

I really must stop talking to myself.

But no, that's not my point. Food politics in the developed world has long been hidebound by clumsy, polarized arguments; by polemical warriors arguing that if you don't entirely buy into all of the demands of the organics movement, then you clearly support the massive, unfettered use of chemicals and won't eat anything unless it's been for a long bath in a swimming pool full of chlorine; that if you suggest for a moment that there is a place for large-scale farming you are clearly an enemy of Planet Earth who wants to see all badgers culled, all human life chased off the land into city-centre NCP car parks, and the very soil violated by the sort of big machinery that gets Jeremy Clarkson horny, until even Kent is a dustbowl; that if you make the slightest case for any form of biotechnology you obviously want to see your own children gene-spliced with a mackerel so they cry tears of pure fish oil when you beat them.

Well, no. And no. And no. The demands and challenges of food security in the twenty-first century are so big and chewy and complex that childish ya-boo politics is futile and, frankly, dangerous. Not only will the debate polarize but so will the participants, so that it becomes a shouting match between the hardcore knit-your-own-yoghurt foodinistas on the one side and the worst kind of grubby-handed climate-change-denying big business on the other. In the middle will be a whole bunch of people, the overwhelming majority, who will refuse to engage in a debate staged on those terms or, even more worryingly, simply feel excluded from it. It's too important for that to happen. We need joined-up thinking, a more sophisticated, inclusive approach to deal with the issues, sometimes on a case-by-case basis. And now I sound like a New Labour special adviser.

So no, getting asparagus flown in from Peru so we can eat Jamie Oliver's char-grilled pork leg with asparagus recipe out of season is not necessarily OK. It's a stupid waste of fuel for something that frankly we may like but we do not need. But eating apples out of season is entirely fine. What matters is that we do as much as we possibly can to reduce the shipping of apples halfway across the world from New Zealand and China. The new, shiny low-energy apple stores at Mansfield's are one of those things.

I watch Jazz apples trundling down conveyors on the way to being bagged for one of the supermarkets. Mansfield's supplies all of the major retailers here. Do the buyers demand the chucking out of lots of fruit because it isn't perfect?

'Very little these days. It's rarely more than 5 per cent and the vast majority of that can go to the juice industry,' Chris says. 'The supermarkets have recognized that there is an appetite among consumers for budget packs of apples that aren't all perfect.' He takes me for a tour of the huge orchards, where they grow Bramley, Jazz and Braeburn. We stop off at Buddy's grave and then head off to meet Paul. Along the way we take a wrong turning off the motorway and end up covering the same ten-mile stretch of road three times instead of just once.

My mission to meet the biggest apple supplier in Britain is beginning to feel doomed.

When I do finally get to meet the Mr Big of British apples it is not in a James Bond baddie's lair. He is not stooped over a map of the world, shifting model apples about from one bit of territory to the next, as he plans juicy world domination. He does not have a white cat. He's in the depths of a gloomy village pub not far from Sittingbourne and he has a plate of roast pork belly. He's with a couple of other fruit farmers, Robert Hinge and Lance Morrish, who are members with Mansfield of a growers' group called Fruition. They are also involved in a marketing organization called World Wide Fruit, which, with their sister organization in New Zealand, Enza, has the sole licence to grow Jazz apples in the UK. It is clear, however, that Mansfield's is the senior partner here. Paul is the biggest grower by a very long way.

He's also imposing: stocky, with a barrel chest and skin the colour of a conker from the Portuguese holiday just gone. He has big, solid hands, with fingers like bunches of baby bananas, and on one little finger he wears a signet ring heavy with diamonds, the one outward sign of his success. But he's disarmingly self-effacing. He tells the story of how his old dad got started in the fruit-growing business; that he was just a greengrocer from a line of them, that his grandmother Emma used to sell fruit and veg from what would have been the front room of a two-up-two-down in the East End back in the twenties.

'My dad slept upstairs in a bed with his five brothers. Six to a bed. Emma, my grandmother, she went off to Covent Garden every day, though these were the days when it was horse and cart.'

Buddy eventually struck out alone, and went from running a single shop to one of the biggest in the area, alongside stalls in local markets. He needed so much fruit that he started going direct to the growers down in Kent.

'Then he needed somewhere to store all his boxes, and this farm was available, so he bought it. This was in 1967.'

And that's how Mansfield's began?

'Yeah, but we were terrible apple growers. We had poor root stock. We had poor soil. We didn't know what we were doing. But the thing is, Buddy liked it. He liked growing apples.'

Bit by bit they learned what they were doing. And bit by bit they bought new farms. They expanded and grew. In the late eighties Paul took over from Buddy, though with his dad constantly at his side for advice and support. I ask him whether buying up farms was part of a plan.

'Scale struck me as the way to go. You know what, we are being paid today the same as we were being paid twenty years ago for apples. But our costs have gone up massively. The cardboard boxes, the tractors. Our actual costs have doubled. And the only way we can keep moving and investing and be sustainable is by being more efficient.' Efficiency means scale.

Robert Hinge agrees. 'You need a greater area of orchards to make a living now,' he says. 'Pretty farming doesn't pay.' He admits, however, that his family, which has been farming for five generations, hasn't expanded in the way Mansfield's has.

Why is that?

'I think it's because Paul's an outsider. He could see things in the way we couldn't. And he wasn't held back by all these family traditions and competing family opinions. He could just get on with it.'

Has anything been lost because of apple farming moving into scale?

Robert shrugs. 'The Weald of Kent isn't as pretty as it used to be.'

What about the emphasis on sustainability: the imperative to manage the soil, to keep the hedgerows in check, to find new means of supplying water? Where did that come from? 'At first I think that came from the supermarkets,' Robert says.

'Yeah,' says Paul. 'But we picked it up and made it work.'

Is that why he put in the reservoir?

'It made business sense to do that.'

I ask the three apple farmers if they think the British consumer understands how farming works. They all laugh.

'The good thing is that they want British now,' Lance Morrish says. 'British is a brand. It's a selling point.'

'But they don't actually know how the food is produced,' says Robert. 'A while back I dropped off a box of apples at my local village shop and one of the customers grabbed some and said you can't get fresher than that.'

I could immediately see what his point was. I said, 'So how long had these apples of yours been in store?'

'Eight months. This bloke didn't have a clue. He thought they were straight off the tree when they couldn't have been because the Braeburn crop had been over for months. And he lives in a village in the middle of apple-growing country. What hope is there for people living in the cities?'

Then there are issues around how consumers buy. 'If the supermarkets put a couple of pennies on the price of a kilo of apples,' Lance says, 'it would make a big difference to us. Many consumers don't even notice price.'

'Up to a point,' says Paul. 'A lot of shoppers are only shopping on the offer.' They are obsessed with 'bogoffs' – buy one get one free – and that damages the whole market. 'When our Braeburns are on offer in the supermarkets it doesn't expand sales. What happens is that sales of Cox and Gala drop through the floor. There's too much promotion.'

Is he seeing the impact of British supermarket pricing on the willingness of growers from abroad to do business with them? 'Absolutely. Growers come to see us from all over the world. They want to look at the way we work. Increasingly they're saying to me they have no interest in the UK market. They say it's too much hassle. Not enough money in it. They're looking to the Middle East and China.'

That, he says, is an opportunity. He's working hard to continue growing and expanding. 'Within two or three years we'll be self-sufficient in Braeburn, at least within the seven-month growing period.'

We finish our drinks and say our goodbyes to Lance and Robert. Paul offers to take me on a short tour. He wants me to see what he's been doing. Contrary to what I'd been told he's eager to explain his business, and quickly the reason becomes obvious. He may have a sharp business mind – 'We're big enough to supply one of the multiples with all their apples by ourselves,' he says at one point – but it's not the business side that drives him. He's not merely obsessed with turning fruit into money. He just adores growing apples.

Paul turns off a lane onto a rutted track and then steers his Range Rover out across a muddy field, and through a gap in the hedge. Beyond is an enormous hillside planted with new trees. Every few trees there is a concrete pole secured deep into the earth. A high-tensile cable runs along the top, linking them, with further wires dropping down to keep the bamboo posts supporting the young trees upright. What's most startling is the precision. The poles line up in each and every direction. It's mesmerizing, this endless grid of tree and post and line. The tiny saplings are just coming into blossom.

We sit in the car and stare out over them.

'That's what I like to see,' Paul says. 'Trees, planted properly, in bloom. My dad would have been so pleased with this. He really loved it when it looked like this. We used to do this together.'

I ask him how many trees are planted on the field in front of us.

'There's only about 50,000 here. We're planting 200,000 trees a year at the moment,' he says.

It sounds like a massive investment.

'We put 90 per cent of our money back into the business every year,' he says, and then, 'To be a fruit farmer these days you have to have money to burn or be a little bit crazy.'

Which are you?

'I'm a little bit crazy.'

It was what I expected him to say. I knew it wasn't true.

Learning to cook almost scarred me for life. I don't mean that I was humiliated by a hag-faced cookery teacher who ridiculed my sauce béarnaise and mocked my dauphinoise. I make a bloody nice dauphinoise, thank you very much. I mean that when I was seven I poured boiling pig fat all over my left hand while preparing breakfast for my old brother, and that this could have caused permanent scarring.

I was naked when it happened.

I want to say it's a long story because sibling relationships generally are. Our relationships with our brothers and sisters tend to outlast those with our parents and lovers. They build scar tissue and bonds in equal measure. They can be as old as us. But this story is pretty simple. Adam is four years older than me and when I was a kid I did what he told me to do. So when one Saturday morning he said I should go downstairs and cook him bacon and eggs for breakfast I went to the kitchen, found a frying pan, cranked up the gas and got cooking. Without the aid of clothing. It was all to do with the duvets bought on the proceeds of my mother's big American book rights sale. She said duvets were what people slept under in Scandinavia – we called them continental quilts – and that nobody there wore clothes in bed, so we should all be

Scandinavian and not wear anything either. To be honest I think she was just bored of washing pyjamas.

Either way, for a few Saturday mornings I went downstairs and made a cooked breakfast and all went swimmingly. I never quite understood why my parents didn't notice the smell of frying bacon in the house, but they always seemed to sleep through it. The morning everything went wrong, though, they knew about it. I'd fried the bacon to a nice shade of bronze. I'd managed to do the eggs without breaking the yolk, and had put it all on plates. (I also cooked myself a portion: it wasn't entirely selfless.) I took the pan to the sink, still full of fizzing, bubbling fat, and then, with a distracted curiosity, felt the greasy handle turn in my palm as I reached into the sink to make a bit of space. I remember the way the still bubbling bacon grease poured out onto the side of my index finger and across my thumb, how the skin fizzed and bucked as it started to fry and, in a moment of clarity, thinking about how justified screaming very loudly right now would be. Which is what I did. Gripping my still-smouldering left hand in my right I stood at the bottom of the stairs and howled.

It was all a blur after that: the rush of the cold water tap, the bowl with the ice, the trip to Accident and Emergency, the heavy bandaging. Before the crepe was wrapped around I got to see the massive blister, a great ivory bubble of smooth, denatured skin that ran the length of my index finger, expanding out to fill the space between it and the thumb. Later that Saturday, woozy with pain and shock, I watched intrigued as my mother heated a needle over a flame to sterilize it and used that to prick the blister so that it deflated like a Lilo. Then she re-dressed it. Only later did Claire tell me that she feared the damage I had done that day would be with me for life.

It wasn't. My mother also refused to let the accident become a stumbling block to learning. There is always risk in life and it has to be faced head on: you cannot learn how to use fire and knives without burning yourself with one and cutting yourself with the other. It happens. And so as a kid I was given free rein in the kitchen, though my brother would kill me if I did not now acknowledge that he was actually the family's cook during our adolescence. He specialized in what was, for the early eighties, a convincing form of home Chinese cookery; introduced me to the virtuous pairing of oyster sauce and sesame oil; and learned how to turn finely sliced Savoy cabbage into a reasonable facsimile of the crispy 'seaweed' served at our local Chinese. The secret is to bombard it with equal volumes of salt and sugar. I, meanwhile, baked banana bread, and did things with mince.

For all those efforts, however, I arrived at university a lousy cook. I did something awful with limp cuts of chicken from the Kirkgate Market in Leeds and a tin of Campbell's condensed cream of mushroom soup. (Pour one over the other. Bake. Lie to yourself about how nice it is while eating.) I massacred the cheapest bits of stewing beef, from an animal that died of old age in Kazakhstan some time in the seventies, by trying to fry them up in a fake Chinese sauce that was so much sugar it caramelized to black on the bottom of the pan. In my third year I cooked lunch for my parents in my student flat, ambitiously attempting to braise beef in red wine. I can still recall the stench of raw alcohol in the 'sauce'. My mum and dad were very polite and ate it all. Bless them.

But my greed was insistent, my endless hunger stubborn. Looking back I see now that I only really started learning to cook in my early twenties, when my then girlfriend and I moved into a flat together. It was, I suppose, a part of nesting;

a way of making sense of adulthood. For one birthday I bought my beloved a stack of cookbooks. It wasn't a subtle hint; it was what she'd asked for. But quickly I became the one who was using them, though not for recipes. Other people's dish ideas felt – and still feel – like an invitation to fail. I wanted to know about method: the way to roast and bake, how to build up and reduce a sauce, the science of the emulsion. Then I could make my own dishes and, having used no one else's blueprint, I could always claim that the outcome was what I intended. Even if whatever it was seemed to be a little eccentric.

All these years later, this should have led to me being a fully rounded cook, and in many ways I am. I can and often do get the kids' tea on. I can do the quotidian (a curiously exotic word for something that means 'everyday'). I can cook for reasons of need. But that's not how my cooking skills manifest themselves. The fact is that, despite all the endless talk of gender equality, the way many men approach cooking is entirely different to the way many women do. We treat it like it's a contact sport. We choose the team of ingredients. We consider our tactics. Then we enter the arena of the kitchen, lift the knives high above our heads, so that the blades shimmer beneath the halogens, and scream, 'Victory or death.' Take the very first thing I ever Cooked, with a capital c, way back when I was a callow youth in my twenties: that roast saddle of lamb stuffed with sun-dried tomatoes, torn basil, ciabatta crumbs and black olives which I needed to buy the balsamic vinegar for on the outskirts of Blackpool.

This was completely male cooking. First, it required me to go to the butcher's, buy a piece of meat bigger than my own head, and then ask the bloke behind the counter to 'chine' it, which was a word I'd just read in a volume called something like *Cooking with Testosterone*. (Any dish which entails talking to butchers and using jargon is bound to have been cooked by a man, particularly if the jargon refers to slicing around bones, as 'chine' does.) Then I had to take it home and do savage things to it with one of those fancy Japanese blades fashioned out of a single piece of stainless steel. Next I had to brutalize a whole bunch of things for the stuffing, before trussing the saddle together with twine like I'd just got a distinction in advanced bondage and domination.

Finally I got to crack the oven up to the 'hotter than hell' setting and throw the whole thing in there. I shoved the knife blade into the waistband of my apron like it was a pirate's cutlass, pulled the cork on a bottle of Rioja, and stood swigging in the kitchen as if it were my lair. Later I did all the stuff you are meant to do. I rested the meat. I deglazed the pan and made a jus. I carved. I took the applause. This is what we are like. Men do not cook because they – or even anybody else – is hungry, like women do. We cook because we are greedy, not just for the end result but for the congratulations the finished article brings. We cook because we want to prove supremacy over ingredients and equipment. We make things that require the endurance of multiple stages to reach completion. Ideally we make things that require knife work and the threat of amputation. Mostly we indulge in what my beloved calls 'show cooking'.

This can take many forms. A man can make a salad, as long as it requires a lot – and I mean an afternoon full – of chopping and slicing. (You should try my pepper salad. You will marvel at the knife work.) A man's salad will usually also involve a certain amount of heat, if only to make the croutons or the completely unnecessary shards of crispy bacon. Men will cook with vegetables, if they have to, but only if they get to char-grill them on a skillet. Men don't do steaming. Advanced pasta dishes are a favourite, though mostly because, in the closing stages, they demand a lot of serious tossing and throwing about of wet stuff which makes us think we're professionals. Naturally we love anything involving booze from which the alcohol then has to be burnt off, in a roaring sheet of flame that will terrify the cat.

So what don't men do? We don't make soups. I mean, why would we? Shove ingredients in stock. Boil them to buggery, then shove them in the Moulinex. Where's the skill – not to mention the artery-severing risk – in that? We also rarely make bread. You know how people say cooking is an inexact science? Well, they are right, apart from when it comes to making bread. That is an exact science. Get the measurements wrong and you won't have food. You'll have house bricks. Men are not good at the exactness business in the kitchen. Why do you think almost all the pastry chefs in top restaurants are women? It's because they can be fagged to do all that spooning stuff and staring at scales. Men can't. Which is why in our house She does the puddings and She bakes the bread. Me? I just wage total war on ingredients.

And now we are teaching our sons to cook. The younger one, Daniel, helps with baking. He's a whizz on the shortbread and the bread kneading. Perhaps he'll break the mould on the 'men and baking' thing. Eddie, who is 13, has developed an obsession with maki rolls. He has a kit. He knows how to do the rice. The things he can do with a sharp blade and a cucumber are really quite thrilling. I look forward to watching him bleed some time in the near future. What matters here is the transference of skills, and we are trying to do our bit.

Which gently brings us back to the question of whether large-scale farming really is the big evil. A lot of the self-appointed guardians of our food culture bang on endlessly about provenance. They want you to know how good the ingredients they cook with are, and how clever they are for locating them. They want you to know all about the narrative of their lunch. Every meal, and every part of it, must come with a story. I too like a story. I adore good stories, as a man who has written novels should. It's also obvious that the story of big agriculture is far less compelling and far less sexy than the story of small agriculture. It is less about the personal and it is people who make good stories sing out.

But when it comes to the nitty-gritty of how people really live, all that guff about provenance and human narrative misses the point. We agonize, rightly, about obesity levels, especially among those on low incomes. We worry about people losing the skills essential to cook food from raw ingredients, rather than just shove fat- and carb-heavy ready meals into the oven. But we don't agonize enough about it. For if we really do care about our food culture what really matters is *how* we eat, not how soft and cuddly the narrative of the ingredients is.

The great chef and food writer Simon Hopkinson once said to me that he would prefer to have the cheapest chicken roasted for him by someone who knew what they were doing, rather than the most expensive, artisan-raised, frottaged and fondled chicken cooked for him by somebody who didn't. I am completely with him. In the end what really matters most is not how the chicken – or the onion or the potato or the apple – was produced. It's not about whether it comes from a small or big farm. It's about whether it ends its life in the deep-fat fryer.

* * *

Only an idiot would argue that all farms now need to be big, and I really do try my best not to be an idiot. Idiocy is a terrible waste of time. What's more, that would be indulging in the sort of polarized arguments I so hate. There will always be a space for small farms, even if it is only to offer examples of good animal husbandry and agricultural practice to those working on a much larger scale. Plus what will eventually be large-scale farming often has, by necessity, to start small. If farming on a small scale makes the people doing it happy, if it produces enough to be self-sustaining, especially if its product has a certain uniqueness, then only an idiot would object to it. And as we know I do try not to be one of those.

And yet, even as I say that, I know people will still be curling their lip. Because what's striking is just how emotional some people get about large-scale farming. God but they hate it.

Back in 2010, during a slightly ropey TV series I made for Channel 4 about the state of our food supply chain, I looked in detail at the dairy industry, and the ways in which it could face up to the challenge of the consumer's addiction to paying under the odds for milk. (Let's accept that a major part of the solution lies in encouraging supermarkets and therefore shoppers to pay a little more now, so we don't end up paying much more in the future should we be required to rely on imports.) One of the new ideas, imported from other parts of the world, was the super dairy. At Nocton in Lincolnshire plans had been submitted for a dairy farm that would house over 8,000 cows and produce over 100,000 litres of milk a day. They wouldn't be out in fields. They wouldn't be chewing the cud, noses down in the cool, damp earth. They'd live in open-sided sheds, on sand, and be fed silage from elsewhere.

The critical response to this proposition was immediate. It was wrong. It was the battery farming of cows, just like the battery farming of chickens, which, during the same period, was in the process of being banned across Europe. It was, some critics said, evil and distasteful and grotesque and lots of other things besides. Anybody who even wondered casually out loud whether it had anything going for it deserved to be tied up to two tractors and pulled limb from limb as a warning to others.

I got one point they were making. The super dairy idea wasn't especially pretty.

I visited a small version of what was planned – a mere 1,000 cows – and it did have an industrial aspect to it: the large sheds stretching off into the distance; the clank of metal grilles and fences and gates banging against each other; the tractors rumbling up and down to refresh food and sand and clean away the crap that cows have a remarkable talent for producing. The smell and the squirt and the call and response of the lowing.

But not everything is always as it looks. I'd also spent time on a traditional dairy farm down in the West Country the day before, which had a herd of about 180 cows, the average for this sort of business. The third-generation farmer, Roger Jenkins, had modern kit. It was no ramshackle affair. But he found it very hard to make the economies of scale work. A lot of his income was derived from renting out holiday homes. Roger did it because it was what he'd always done. He did it because it was what he knew, and what his father had known and what *his* father had known before him, even though it was a very tough life.

I asked Roger what he thought of the conditions in which the animals would be kept at the super dairy.

He surprised me. There was, he said, nothing especially wrong with it. 'People like to see cows in fields, but they don't need to be there,' he told me. 'Ours aren't out in the fields all year round. For up to six months of the winter they'll be inside too.' The charity Compassion in World Farming, perhaps unsurprisingly, disagreed. CIWF gets rather soppy over cows. I should say that I find the name 'Compassion in World Farming' exceptionally irritating. It suggests that they think they have a monopoly on compassion; that they are the only people in the world of farming who actually give a damn. For the record, in all the time I have met livestock farmers, be they dairy or meat – and I have met an awful lot – I have not encountered one who did not care very deeply about their animals. They may not have been sentimental. They may not have talked in greetings-card slogans. But they really did give a damn. Anyone who argues otherwise simply hasn't spent enough time with them.

CIWF set up a website to challenge the Nocton super dairy plans entitled 'Cows belong in fields' – or, more precisely, 'COWS BELONG IN FIELDS' – even though there was no particular evidence that it was the case.

Cows are, Roger my traditional farmer told me, sociable animals, who would be quite happy bedding down on sand, as long as they were together. And, he added, 'unhappy cows don't produce good-quality milk, not in the long term'. Keeping the cows in conditions which would make them unhappy was not in any farmer's interests. It went further. He told me that the cows at the back of his herd could take ninety minutes to two hours to get through the whole milking process, a lot of which time would be spent standing on the concrete milking parlour floors awaiting their turn, a stressful experience. At the proposed super dairy the whole process would take around forty minutes, meaning far less stress for the animals. What's more, the super dairy would have a veterinary unit on site, able to deal with any problems as they arose, and a dedicated maternity unit; traditional farmers had no such luxuries. Their vets had to get to them when they could. And there was one more intriguing thing about the super dairy plan: it was proposed eventually to build massive anaerobic digesters which would use the huge volumes of cow crap – 400,000 litres a day – to generate electricity. The plan, I was told, was for a dairy that was as close to carbon neutral as possible.

All that said, I was not surprised the Nocton plans were eventually withdrawn. During a question and answer session at the NFU's 2011 conference, before the developers threw in the towel, I said that there were local issues around the site which could well make it very difficult to approve the plan. It had become clear that there were problems to do with ground-water systems at the proposed site. But that didn't mean the notion of the super dairy was a bad one in principle. If we want milk at an affordable price, radical solutions like that may well be the way forward. It was clear to me, though, that the opposition really was to do with what it looked like, and what it sounded like, rather than what it was.

It was the same with Thanet Earth, a massive greenhouse complex in Kent the size of eighty football pitches, using hydroponics which, when fully up and running, could supply 15 per cent of all of Britain's salad vegetable needs. The growing methods were not new. They've been around for decades. As far as Britain was concerned, though, the scale was. Yes, it was an odd place: an enormous amount of it was automated. Driverless trolleys moved almost soundlessly up and down the aisles collecting crates of picked vegetables. Nutrients were fed into the plants according to computerized schedules. The vegetables grew in packages of stuff that looked nothing like good old-fashioned mud. It felt like something out of the classic seventies sci-fi movie *Silent Running*.

But this unit was taking vast numbers of trucks off the roads from the Netherlands to the UK. It too was almost carbon neutral. There was a gas-burning power plant on site, used to produce electricity, most of which Thanet Earth didn't want. It took the heat and the CO_2; the power went back into the national grid. 'The closer we get to a carbon-neutral model,' one of the executives of the company behind it told me, 'the better our bottom line is. Being carbon neutral makes sound business sense.'

As unfashionable as it may be to admit it, I found the whole environment rather thrilling. It had something of the modernist secular cathedral about it: the acres of glass, the vaulting, brightly lit spaces, the thick green fronds reaching graspingly for the sky. I understand, of course, that lots of people won't feel this way. They think of growing stuff to eat as an expression of the natural world and regard the way it is being managed at Thanet Earth in such an apparently hard-nosed way, using so many hard-edged, man-made materials, as somehow wrong. These are, incidentally, exactly the same people who are taken in by all the clever marketing on food packaging, the stuff with the ears of corn and ruddy-faced farmers leaning over five-bar gates, and images of deliriously happy pigs flogging themselves unto slaughter, like the talking cow in Douglas Adams's book *The Restaurant at the End of the Universe* which had been genetically bred to sell itself to diners at the table. They're the deluded consumers who are more than gagging to be fed a total fiction about our food supply chain, courtesy of the ad men.

They are also the ones who will react with the most outrage when food prices go bashing through the roof because we failed to invest in enough large-scale domestic agriculture to increase our self-sufficiency, and are instead being held to ransom by the international markets.

Of course, they will tell you, there is another way. It is exactly the opposite of large scale. It is small scale. It is ultra-small scale. It is teeny-weeny, touchy-feely scale. It is grow-your-own. If we all just grew exactly what we need, surely we'd all be fine.

It's a thought. It's an interesting thought, albeit one that dredges up terrifying memories. Come with me, then, back to the long, hot summer of 1976 and meet my culinary nemesis: the spaghetti marrow.

7.

THE CURSE OF THE SPAGHETTI MARROW

I don't think my mother ever meant to be cruel. Then again, life is full of unintended consequences, even if they are not all necessarily unforeseeable. In 1974, when Claire agreed to become a TV chef, I imagine she saw it as an opportunity. Everything in her career to date had been an accident and it all seemed to have worked out nicely enough. Good work had been done. Money had been earned. Nobody had died. Why shouldn't she be paid to put on an apron and teach the nation how to cook produce from a kitchen garden?

Perhaps because the nation included her own family?

Perhaps because, if she hadn't said yes, we wouldn't have been tortured by the produce of our own vegetable plot?

In the early seventies food television was still in its relative infancy. Fanny Craddock was still hectoring the nation, assisted by her husband Jonny. (Did he really once finish a show by saying, 'And I hope your doughnuts end up looking like Fanny's'? I do hope so.) Graham Kerr's achingly camp series *The Galloping Gourmet*, in which he dragged women up from the audience to dine with him, intimately, just the two of them and the millions watching, continued to be shown on a loop, even after he'd left TV to find God. Otherwise, it was mostly cooking slots on general-interest magazine programmes of the sort fronted by a young woman with a charisma bypass called Delia Smith, part of the BBC's local show *Look East*. It was about experts leading the viewers by the hand.

ITV's *Kitchen Garden* would be different, mostly because it involved non-experts or, at the very least, people who were known for other things. In the first half a DJ called Keith Fordyce would show people how to grow vegetables; in the second half an agony aunt called Claire Rayner would show people how to cook them. And only them. Because *Kitchen Garden* had another ace up its sleeve. If Keith couldn't grow it, Claire couldn't cook it. As a result the show would be entirely vegetarian, and for a while so would we. Not that it was ever explained to us in this way. On the level of the family it was simply a matter of expediency. Today TV cooking shows are overrun with home economists and nutritional advisers and food stylists. In 1974 there was none of that. Instead there was just my mother and a box of vegetables delivered to the doorstep with a note from the producer which said something along the lines of 'see what you can do with this', the 'this' being sticks of salsify, or curly greens with the texture of canvas but none of the nutritional value, which she had never cooked before.

That is how I came to meet the spaghetti marrow, a tough-skinned, oval vegetable the colour of an anaemic lemon and the size of a fat baby's head. It simply turned up at the house one day, uninvited. Its Latin name is *Curcubita pepo*; in Japanese it's kinshi uri. As an 8-year-old boy I would have called it cruel and unusual punishment, had I been well enough versed in the law. To prepare the marrow it has to be boiled for a good half hour. Very little good can come from any food that must first be boiled for half an hour. It then had to be split open and the flesh scraped out, whereupon it would form into long strands of empty, vapid, cucumber-like ... stuff. That's the only word I can use for it. Stuff. Even from a distance of nearly forty years, the only word that seems to do it justice is 'stuff'. Claire would smother this stuff with a tomato sauce and tell us that it was just like pasta. Eat up.

And it was just like pasta. In the same way that nuclear war is just like peace, and Wales is just like somewhere dry. Which is to say, not at all. As a fat, greedy 8-year-old, dinner mattered to me. My mum was a good cook, and did great things with whole chickens and oven bricks, which was about as cutting-edge as it got in north-west London in the seventies. I liked curry night. I liked the little bowls she put out with the over-sweetened chicken curry containing chutneys and chopped-up bits of banana and that crumbly material called Bombay Duck which smelt of old men's armpits and wasn't duck at all but salted, dehydrated fish. I loved it when she cooked chops, or when she made shepherd's pie or roasted sheets of lamb ribs.

But this?

This was a betrayal. It was claiming to be one thing when really it was another. Sure, it was filling. And, of course, it was good for me. Perhaps if I'd eaten a lot more of that as a kid and a lot less of the lamb ribs and the McDonald's burgers and the Dayville ice cream I might not have been the last one chosen for football by team captains. Except I didn't (and don't) care about football. I just didn't give a damn. But dinner: that mattered. It was a serious business, and spaghetti marrow with tomato sauce was a mealtime wasted. Still, I thought to myself, it won't haunt me for long. She's just testing the dish out. Once she gets it right, once she's certain she knows how to cook it, she'll turn instead to torturing the British public with it and leave those she loves in peace.

How wrong I was. Some time in the mid-seventies an area at the back of our garden next to the garage was dug up. It was almost precisely as a comedy series called *The Good Life* was launching on the BBC, in which suburbanites Tom and Barbara Good attempted to live off their own Surbiton garden. To be fair, my mother was not at all interested in self-sufficiency. She had shown absolutely no interest in hippie chic; she was far too radical for that sort of posturing. I think she just thought that it would be a good idea, what with *Kitchen Garden* getting a second (and then a third) series on ITV. There were now vegetarian cookbooks to write. What had started as a simple job of work had spread like melting ice cream across a warm plate, to fill up significant parts of our lives.

Of course, one of the first things to go in to the ground were *Curcubita pepo* seeds. And the bastards grew. The spaghetti marrow bloomed like an outbreak of chlamydia in a student house. Nothing would stop them. They were like Audrey, the plant in *The Little Shop of Horrors*, their thick tendrils ending in yellow blooms which would soon wither and die to reveal the marrows. Some things are hard to grow on private vegetable patches. Spaghetti marrows are not one of them. I would watch with undisguised horror as the damn things flourished. Alongside them were rickety frames of green beans which always seemed to be woodier and harder than the green beans we bought from the greengrocer, and tomatoes which always seemed to be less sweet. This, it has to be said, was one of the oddities of our vegetable patch. We now had a garden which was filling the kitchen with a limited range of edible things on a daily basis and yet the size of our weekly vegetable order from Robert the Greengrocers did not diminish. I think my mother felt responsible to him, and didn't want to do him out of income just because of her hobby. That, or she didn't much like what she was growing either.

And so this verdant plot, this endless suburban fecundity, this wretched, festering scab of green, came to mock me, not least when the violently hot summer of 1976 arrived and I was tasked with keeping it all watered. I couldn't refuse or do it badly. She checked up on me. Plus I had standards. So now I was utterly complicit in the too, too dismal nature of certain mealtimes. Most afternoons after school I would float around the kitchen while my mother was there, as fat boys are wont to do, trying to work out what was for dinner. Catching sight of the heavy, yellow curve of yet another bloody spaghetti marrow, I would retreat wounded and bitter. When we went on holiday, at the height of the drought, I secretly hoped that the arid conditions and hosepipe bans would finally do for our vegetable plot, but narratives rarely work out the way you imagine them. The rest of Britain's vegetation may have been dying in the heat; London's parks may have become patchworks of rust and russet and beige rather than anything approaching green. But in our garden everything lived on and, more than that, burgeoned. We came back to a huge and healthy crop of spaghetti marrows.

In the spring of 1977 we finally departed the cherry-blossomed and privet-fringed avenues of that part of North Wembley for a much larger, grander house in Harrow. The vegetable patch did not come with us. Many years before, amateur gardeners who once owned our new home had planted it with a bounty of fruit. There were half a dozen different types of pear and apple. There were plum trees and red and white and black currants; raspberries, strawberries, loganberries, and, scampering up a wall as if it were heading for the roof, a quince tree that each year risked falling to the ground, so heavy was the fruit. Perhaps this was why Claire decided not to bring the spaghetti marrow plants with her. A professional job had already been done on the garden. It did not need an intervention from her. In any case the third and last series of *Kitchen Garden* had come to an end, and she had moved on to other things. She was banning butter from the house in favour of polyunsaturated fats. She was designing a high-fibre diet (long before the success of the F-Plan) which involved putting a horse pill of bran into her orange juice every morning whereupon it dissolved to look like something a baby with a digestive problem might expel. She tried to get us all to try it, but we were wise to her by then. We knew where politeness could lead us. We said no.

I have told this story before and had it thrown back at me as the explanation for why I sigh deeply whenever I am told that growing your own is a vital part of a re-engineering of our food system. And people do tell me this. Whenever a piece of mine about the pros and cons of the industrial food process turns up online, the comments extolling the virtues of home growing pile up underneath it like so much leaf fall in autumn. I just sigh, roll my eyes, and carry on. Apparently I do this because I was traumatized as a child; I had an unfortunate experience with home-grown vegetables.

Ergo.

I admit I am not very outdoorsy. I know where the outdoors is, much as I know where Droitwich is; that doesn't mean I necessarily want to go there. I would call myself very much an 'indoorsie-prop-me-up-at-the-cocktail-bar-and-mix-me-an-old-fashioned' sort of chap. I could make gags here about it being something buried deep in the Jewish DNA; that my people spent so many tedious centuries tilling the dank soil of that part of Poland, Ukraine and Russia known as the Pale of Settlement that we have won the right to do desk jobs, wear loafers and laugh at Jackie Mason gags about how Jews don't do gardens. And even if it's not genetic it's certainly cultural. I am a little suspicious of plants. I suspect plants are plotting to get me. That's why I married a shiksa. I needed a non-Jew around the place to look after the garden.

But jokes like that would be cheap. Let's bury them with a trowel (assuming someone can be bothered to show me which end of the trowel to hold). Only an idiot would be anti the idea of growing your own fruit and vegetables, and, as we've already ascertained, I try desperately hard not to be one of those. It is a brilliant thing, for lots of reasons. It's a superb way to get exercise. It is an excellent way to bring communities together: there are few shared endeavours better than the turning of a piece of forgotten hard-scrabble inner-city land into a garden producing good things to eat. And, of course, it's a marvellous way to educate people. The playground of my son's primary school, like so many other primary schools across the land, is fringed with planters, heavy with cucumber and marrow, green bean and tomato. It's so obvious why this is a good thing – helping the children to understand the link between the things they eat and the way it is made, enthusiasm for fresh rather than processed food, the value of a non-screen-based activity – that I barely believe I just wasted the energy typing out those sub-clauses. It is blindingly, staggeringly, hit-me-over-the-head-with-a-mallet obvious that growing your own fruit and veg is a good thing.

But that's not the same as it making any hard economic sense (beyond the economic value of people being more contented). And in no way can it be the route to breaking the so-called stranglehold of the industrial food process (if such a thing exists) and supplying the masses with cheap food. Indeed, it's exactly the opposite. Even if we assume that you have the spare land – and many people do not, being forced instead to rent an allotment, if they can get one – you are then faced with a series of costs, be they plants or seeds, tools and fertilizers. Even Jane Perrone, author of *The Allotment Keeper's Handbook* and therefore rather a big fan of people growing stuff themselves, says, 'You should see it as a hobby that might occasionally get you something nice, not as a money-saving exercise.' Hillary Osborne, who edits the money pages of the guardian.co.uk website and who is pretty keen on a bargain, gave it a go. 'Several months of toil produced a handful of carrots, strawberries that were around twice as expensive as those on the menu at Wimbledon and a pile of shrivelled apples that weren't even good for cooking,' she wrote rather forlornly. 'The only successes were the cherry tomatoes and rosemary, but taking the cost of seeds, equipment and compost into account these were more delicious than cost-effective.' The UK government's website promoting growing your own hardly goes out of its way to big up the economic advantages. Among the seven reasons given for doing it – educational value, sense of achievement, exercise, increased smugness quotient (I made the last one up) – only one mentions hard cash, and even then rather limply. 'It could save you money on expensive items like salad leaves.'

Aha! It's brilliant for self-absorbed foodies. In 2011 Steve Mercer, resident vegetable expert for the magazine *Which? Gardening*, published by the Consumers' Association, ran a year-long trial on a one-metre by two-metre plot. His harvests only supplemented one or two family meals a week and then, obviously, only in the growing season. Another trial of 'Gourmet Veg' in 2010 'showed that you could save pounds by growing Jerusalem artichokes, kale, Florence fennel, tenderstem broccoli, pattypan squash, banana shallots, watercress and spinach,' the magazine wrote, 'but arguably these veg, while tasty, are probably best considered "treats" – they're not family staples'. Quite.

Let's try to put some hard numbers on this by looking at something that's increasingly popular: keeping chickens for eggs. It's a lovely image, isn't it? Sweet, plump, feathery things, strutting about the place, pecking at the earth, filling the air with the soft hum and chuckle of their calls. I do not doubt that it's a hugely rewarding thing to do, and that you can become attached to them as pets. If you can afford it. Obviously you will have to buy a hutch. The Eglu Classic, one of the most popular modern-style hutches, will cost you £425. There are cheaper options, but not much cheaper. At best you'll be paying around £300 and it can go up to as much as £600. There will be the fencing for the run to think about (which, if you live in an urban area, will have to be completely fox-proofed). There's the cost of the chickens themselves, say two at anywhere from £20 to £40 each. You've got the running costs of feed – the general consensus is that, if you care about the bird's welfare, formulated feeds really are the way to go – and, of course, various running medical treatments to keep them healthy, not to mention the terrifying prospect of vets' fees if things go wrong. It is hard to see how you could keep the basic set-up costs of a couple of chickens and the facilities to house them in below £500. Of course, they should produce around a dozen eggs a week for you. At the supermarket twelve free-range eggs will cost you around £2.50, or £130 a year.

You do the maths. Go on. I've got time.

Oh all right. I'll do it for you. It's a minimum of four years to almost break even on those start-up costs, though, as I say, that doesn't include the long-term running costs. Nor does it include the fact that by the time those four years are up you'll probably need to have replaced the fencing or the chickens or both. Or, more likely, got completely bored with the damn chickens and the mess they are making of your garden, and taken up macramé or the tango or dogging. Leo Hickman tried raising hens for the *Guardian* (they're very keen on these kinds of larks at the *Guardian*). He fell in love with his birds. Well, of course he did. For it's obviously a delightful thing to do. 'I sometimes pull up a garden chair and just watch them scratching around,' he wrote. 'And the fresh produce it provides. There's just no going back once you've tasted those sunset-coloured yolks.' But cost-effective? No. 'It is,' he declared, 'a complete fallacy that keeping hens saves you money.' Even Jane Howorth, founder of the British Hen Welfare Trust, which rehouses battery chickens, agreed with him.

Am I being horribly cynical? I don't think so. It's simple economics. Not long ago I visited a bunch of nuns who live in the Monastery of the Visitation in East Sussex. A nice group of women. Difficult to tell them apart, but nice all the same. They were getting on a bit, but still they were up and at it every day, working their fingers to the bone in their kitchen garden. That was why I went to see them. As a community they were attempting to be self-sufficient, at least in vegetables and fruit. They owned an enormous plot of walled land, at the back of their glowering red-brick home, which had been ploughed up to make beds. Being nuns, they weren't exactly short on time. Apart from regular outbreaks of praying they could dedicate themselves to the business of growing food. Even they admitted they had to go to Tesco for top-ups. And they were supposed to have God on their side.

The issue here is the one thing nobody considers when calculating the cost of home-grown food: your labour. When farms work out how much they need to charge for their produce to make a profit they include the wages they are paying their staff. Not to do so with the things we grow at home is to give it a false value. Of course, we have to be realistic. You may be a highly paid lawyer or accountant, earning £175 an hour (you bastard), but that's for skilled work. So let's agree that when you are heaving away at the dark earth in your back garden you are essentially an unskilled labourer likely to receive little more than the minimum wage, which stands, at the time of writing, at £6.19 an hour. It's both not very much and, in terms of the vegetables you are growing, an awful lot. If you add all the hours worked together and then divide it by, say, the number of carrots grown in that time, the results can be startling. The food you have spent all that time growing is suddenly going to be costing you an awful lot more than its equivalent in the supermarkets. (And while we're at it, if you are renting an allotment a mile or two from your house, which you have to drive to, so as to carry tools there and produce back, you will quickly bestow upon your food a carbon footprint of the size that would embarrass a multinational oil company.)

Ah, but what if you are unemployed? What of it? That doesn't make growing your own the systemic solution to the problem of food supply. It makes it at best a stopgap for you, which will become redundant the moment you find a job.

Because this is how it works. Over the centuries we have continually delegated responsibility for certain industries to smaller and smaller numbers of people, as a result of growing efficiencies. In 1900, 40 per cent of the US workforce was involved in agriculture, which was almost half the proportion of the country's workforce so employed thirty years before. By 2008 it was just 1.7 per cent. We are happy for other people to grow our food for us, so that we can get on with doing more economically viable things, like pursuing careers in management consultancy or posting those pictures of kittens sleeping in hats on the internet. The romantics, like Ernst Schumacher, who have bought into every sweet mythology about rural life, would regard this as a disaster; they would say that it has broken mankind's link with the natural world. But that notion is loose and fanciful. Allowing for the fact that the planet is grossly over-populated, it makes sense for more of us to live in cities and let other people grow our food for us outside of them, while we do things that are more fulfilling.

I fully recognize that there are a lot of people who will still disagree with me; who will still say that growing our own food makes economic sense. I also understand why this is. Facts are great and sturdy things. So are statistics, and properly mustered arguments. But they are as nothing in the face of emotion. Food is very, very emotional. It's about how we feel about ourselves. What we eat and how we eat is a reflection of our world view, the sort of person that we like to think we are. Which is why it's so hard to challenge so many of our assumptions about food. Which, in turn, is why my views on farmers' markets have also brought me so much abuse. People feel very emotional about them too. They bloody love farmers' markets, just as they love their hens and their vegetable patches. And I love them too. The difference is that many people believe they are the way forward for food retailing, and I don't. Let me explain why. And let me do so by taking you back to preparations for my wedding over twenty years ago. I promise not to get slushy.

A cool spring morning in 1992 and I am striding down the same street in London's Soho where my dad was called a black-bearded, bollock-faced bastard almost thirty years before. I am on Berwick Street, looking for a tailor. Obviously Savile Row is only a ten-minute walk away on the other side of Regent Street but, while the suit I want is for a special occasion, the prices there are too rich for my blood. And anyway, I wouldn't feel comfortable over there. These are much more my people, the grafting Jewish tailors who get much of their trade from the film, television and theatre businesses that operate around here. The wedding isn't going to be that traditional. The ceremony will be at the high-columned registry office on Marylebone Road; the party will be at the Eagle on Farringdon Road, which will eventually become regarded as Britain's first gastropub. For the moment it just happens to be a rather nice pub that's opened near the offices of the newspaper where I work. It has an open kitchen and serves big-flavoured Mediterranean food. Certainly it's not the place for a man in a monkey suit, though in a way that's what I'll end up with: a suit made by a man who makes suits for monkeys.

I want something simple and classic in a hard-wearing material. I am a big man, and we do strange things to suits. We stress and strain cloth in the way skinny men do not. We are an engineering challenge. So far none of the tailors I have talked to seems up to it. They offer me inappropriate bolts of woollens and silks or shrug their shoulders when I ask them if they regularly make suits for people of my shape, as if to say, 'Does anybody?' So I have pushed on and found myself standing in the deserted workshop of Paul the Tailor. I look around. There are, as there often are on the walls of these places, a number of those cheesy showbiz pics with a white space beneath the image for a signature, sellotaped up because this was the studio responsible for making their stage suits. Here on Berwick Street the walls are a collage of Bernie Clifton, Bobby Davro, Mike and Bernie Winters, and Alan de Courcy. And if those names mean nothing to you, what a golden age of light entertainment you have missed. Those were the good years, my friends, when a working-class lad from St Helens could go all the way to *The Royal Variety Show* by putting his legs into an ostrich suit.

Here in Paul's I notice a set of pictures I have not seen before. They are of chimpanzees. In suits. Big, bright, wide-shouldered suits in blisteringly saturated colours. Each of the chimps is grinning towards the camera and holding up a mug of tea. I look around this simple, unprepossessing room. It may not look like much but I am clearly somewhere very special. I have come to the tailor who made suits for the PG Tips chimps, which featured in the adverts for the tea company from 1956 (and would go on doing so until 2002). Suddenly the tailor is at my side. He is a slender man, with a row of bright-white teeth, an eighties mop of greying, curly hair and something of the game show host about him. I point at the photographs.

'Did you make suits for the PG Tips chimps?'

He gives me a twinkly game show host wink. 'I did indeed.'

'Right then,' I say. 'You're the man to make my wedding suit.'

He was, and he did. It was a simple and elegant affair in surprisingly hard-wearing black linen. It was perfect and it cost me around £500. (Come inside these parentheses for a moment. A year or two later I bumped into a friend who was wearing a fantastic suit. I asked him where he got it from. It's a funny story, he said. It's made by the man who makes suits for the PG Tips Chimps. Really, I say. Paul the Taylor? He looks baffled. It's another tailor on Berwick Street. Clearly there were a whole bunch of them dressing chimpanzees.)

Two decades later and I am getting another suit made, again on Berwick Street. There is no special occasion. It is just something I want and which I am lucky enough finally to be able to afford. I think I have reached the sort of age when a chap should have a bespoke suit for everyday wear rather than just to get married in. This time a friend who is a very highly regarded wardrobe consultant for British film and television has directed me to a man called Chris Kerr.

'He makes the suits for Phill Jupitus,' she says, referencing the not-small comedian. I like Phill Jupitus and I recognize him as a kindred spirit. His suits will also be an engineering challenge. He is my modern version of the PG Tips chimp. If Kerr can make a suit for Jupitus he can make one for me. It will not cost me £500. It will cost me a lot more than that, but I can afford it.

Of course, I don't need to spend this money. I could go to M&S and buy something adequate off the peg for £160, or perhaps £250 if I really wanted to push the boat out. It would be eminently wearable and would doubtless look fine. Nobody would ever comment on the detail: the golden lining or the matching rust-coloured button holes or the half-velvet collar, because it would have none of that. It might not last for ever but it would do the job. However, I am not doing that. I want something much more exclusive, and much more special. Let me be shameless and admit I like the fact that it will be something nobody else has. Plus there is the rosy glow that comes from knowing I will be supporting true craftsmanship. Chris Kerr is an expert. He is an artisan. That has to be worth supporting.

It's not for everybody, but it is for me.

Which is where farmers' markets come in. I adore good produce, always have done. More than that, I love produce with a story. When Borough Market, down by London Bridge, first began to emerge around the turn of the millennium as a Mecca for obsessive greedy people like me, I would try to go every Saturday. I was convinced that by shopping there and talking to the people who raised the food I was buying I would make myself a better cook. I think it probably did work like that, and unsurprisingly so. When you think about nothing else except your dinner for the whole morning, it's bound to make a difference. I knew it was expensive. I used to joke that I'd only go there with cash rather than plastic, to stop me spending the mortgage money on a leg of Herdwick mutton, some artichokes and a bag of salted Marcona almonds. The point is, I always knew why I went there. It was the same reason I commissioned a tailor to make me a suit: it was purely to do with the aesthetics I was lucky enough to be able to afford.

When I reference Borough Market today, advocates for farmers' markets get cross. It is not representative of the movement, they say. And I see their point. Today there are still a few very good retailers there, but there are also too many stands flogging ready-to-eat food and pointless fripperies. The fact is, however, that Borough Market isn't an aberration: it's merely an exaggerated example of the problem with the movement in general, or at least the problem as defined by its own supporters. Farmers' markets, we are told, are a clean form of vertical retailing in which the filthy middleman, the supermarkets, is cut out, thus bringing food consumer and food maker closer together. And that does go on. Small-scale farmers have found a new and lucrative route to market which helps them to bypass the leviathans of the industry. There's nothing wrong with that. It's a good thing.

But this can only be promoted as a true social good if the consumers benefiting are the ones who can't afford the prices being offered by the supermarkets. And yes, occasionally you will find a fruit stall selling its premium produce at a lower price than you would find the equivalent in the chilled fresh produce section of your local supermarket.

However, when you look at farmers' markets generally, you find expensive, bespoke produce aimed at the affluent who have the wherewithal to afford to indulge themselves in this way. They convince themselves that by shopping there they are doing something to revolutionize the food supply chain. They aren't. It is a lifestyle statement, just as buying a Chanel handbag is a lifestyle statement or buying a pair of Manolo Blahniks is a lifestyle statement or getting the bloke who dresses Phill Jupitus to make me a suit is a lifestyle statement. Only this lifestyle statement now comes with a greasy veneer of false self-righteousness. Paying £12 for a chicken from your lovely poultry producer is no more a challenge to the meat counters of Tesco, Sainsbury's, Asda or Morrison's than buying that bespoke suit is a challenge to M&S.

It goes further. It is in the nature of farmers' markets that the produce they sell is biased towards the premium end of the market. Even on the very rare occasions when the prices charged for that organic chicken or those free-range eggs are slightly lower than those available in supermarkets, the exercise is still exclusive because there is little or no budget choice for shoppers with less money. The market traders, not unreasonably, guard their competitive advantage fiercely; generally they get guarantees from those running the market that theirs will be the only stall selling their kind of produce. Unlike in a standard street market, nobody is ever allowed to undercut anyone else on price. They are merely allowed to offer points of gastronomic difference. And again, that is all about aesthetics. It's nice if you can afford aesthetics. It's bloody lovely. But not everybody can.

Still, let's look at the idea that farmers' markets are a genuine alternative to the supermarkets; that, in an ideal world, they could come to offer a different model if only we shopped at them more and they became more widespread.

Oh dear. That is to completely underestimate the scale of the food retail sector in a developed and industrialized nation like Britain. Think about pork for a moment (as I often do). There are currently about 750 farmers' markets trading in Britain today, most of them on just one or two days a week. Let's be generous and say that each one of those sells the meat of a whole pig every day. Actually let's be more generous than that. How about we quadruple it? How about we imagine that the volume of pig being sold by farmers' markets in Britain has increased by 400 per cent. Not optimistic enough? Fine. Let's say there's a tenfold increase in the number of farmers' markets trading in Britain. That's 7,500 pigs sold a week.

It's nothing, not compared with the size of pork sales in Britain. The British supermarket Morrison's, one of the big four, slaughters 22,000 pigs a week itself. That's only for its fresh pork business. It has to import most of its cured products, like bacon and hams (Britain's pig farmers have had such a bad deal from the supermarkets over the years that enormous numbers have left the industry; there is simply not enough capacity to supply British needs.) Of course, Morrison's is only one of the big four. There are the other supermarkets and food operations all needing pork. So just how many pigs do you think we slaughter in Britain every week? Are you ready for it? Here it is:

Somewhere between 150,000 and 160,000 animals.

Every seven days. And that does not account for the vast volume of pork products imported from Denmark and the Netherlands.

Imagine we do as has been proposed by a number of campaigners and academics and cut our meat consumption by half (we'll get to meat in the next chapter). We will still be slaughtering more than 75,000 pigs a week. Against which even a farmers' market sector ten times its current size is still just a piglet's lame squeak. No wonder the offering is a premium one. It doesn't make sense to do anything else.

Ah, but it's not just about that, say the defenders of farmers' markets. It's about the supply chain. It's about sustainability. It's about localism, for we are all locavores now. Away with food miles. Bring food closer to us all.

Well, yes, it's time we got to all that, isn't it. And as we do so you might just like to get out your smartphone and place it next to you as a kind of visual reminder.

In November 2009 I lost my temper in front of a television camera in a way I have never done before or since. Or, to be exact, I lost my temper in front of eight television cameras. I was in Los Angeles working as a judge on the second season of that American television series *Top Chef Masters*. For the final, the three remaining competitors had been asked to cook a series of dishes that told their story: their first food experiences, where they are now, where they are going, and the like. For the dish that defined where he was going the Las Vegas-based chef Rick Moonen had cooked a venison dish, using meat imported from New Zealand.

This was baffling. Throughout the competition Moonen had described himself as 'the fish guy'. He was also 'the sustainability guy'. He cared about the planet, he told us day after day of the competition. He cared about his impact upon it. I can't pretend. I had not warmed to the man. The sustainability guy? His flagship restaurant was in Las Vegas, one of the least sustainable cities on the face of the planet. I had no doubt that he sourced his ingredients sustainably, but just being in Las Vegas, a city that gulped water and petrochemicals like they were going out of fashion (they are), was in itself an unsustainable act. Plus he had a grating, humble, man-of-the-people line in patter which got my back up. Oh, and in an earlier challenge he had cooked the worst Thai green curry (using a shop-bought paste) that it had ever been my misfortune to taste. He had only survived that round because someone else had done an even worse job.

And now here was the fish guy, the sustainability guy, announcing that he had used meat imported from halfway across the world. When he was in front of us I asked him some pointed questions. Once the competitors were gone, and we were deliberating, I let rip. Admittedly, after a month in LA I was knackered, desperate to get home to see my family, and pissed off with a city and a population which, compared with Europe, appeared incapable of spelling the words 'carbon footprint', let alone doing anything about it. In LA the lights were always on and nobody cared.

I shouted. I raged. Veins bulged.

HAD THE MAN NEVER HEARD OF THE BLOODY CONCEPT OF FOOD MILES?

I was furious.

The producers saved me from myself. They included none of my rant in the final edit. I made up for it, once that episode had aired, by writing a piece for my newspaper explaining my fury. Moonen responded online by calling me out; the venison had arrived in LA by sea, he said. It was fully sustainable. His supporters in Vegas alleged that I had robbed their man of the prize. I can say firmly that the Kiwi venison was not why Moonen lost. The cooking by Marcus Samuelsson, an intriguing Ethiopian-born chef who had been adopted and raised by a Swedish couple before making his name in the US, was so much better. Samuelsson deserved to win. But Moonen and his well-travelled Bambi did himself no favours.

Cut to three years later and I am reading an academic paper with a very snappy title: 'Food Miles – Comparative Energy/Emissions Performance of New Zealand's Agriculture Industry', by Caroline Saunders, Andrew Barber and Greg Taylor. I'm citing the full title so you can look it up. It's not a breezy read but it is an important one. At the very least it requires me to apologize to Rick Moonen. Having read it, I can now say that while it's in no way certain it's possible venison raised in New Zealand and shipped to California could well be more sustainable than the alternatives in California. At least he deserves the benefit of the doubt.

Sorry, Mr Moonen.

I'm still not a fan, and it really doesn't change the result of the contest. There were three other judges. But on this point it looks like he may have been right and I may have been wrong.

Because, according to this exceptionally detailed study from 2006, lamb, apples and dairy produced in New Zealand and shipped to Britain have a smaller carbon footprint than the equivalent products produced in Britain. To be exact, Britain uses twice as much energy per tonne of milk solids produced as New Zealand, and four times more than New Zealand for lamb. I was so baffled by the report I wanted to know whether I had read it correctly. I emailed Tim Benton, Professor of Population Ecology at Leeds University, who is also the government-designated 'UK Champion for Global Food Security', charged with coordinating work on the subject between research councils and government departments. He truly understands both the global food challenges that we face and what sustainable intensification means. He had been an invaluable source of academic papers and scholarly advice for this book from the very start. I wanted to know whether the report was simply a function of the New Zealand agriculture sector attempting to protect its commercial interests by ferociously massaging some numbers.

He threw in some caveats (which we'll get to later) but, he said, 'the overall picture is probably true'.

For me it was the final nail in the coffin of localism. Then again, I'd been listening to the hammering for months.

In the late nineties, when the term 'food miles' was first coined by Tim Lang, Professor of Food Policy at City University, it was a vital and important part of the debate on how our food system worked. It was a simple and easily understandable notion: the further your food travelled from point of production to point of retail the worse for the environment it was, by dint of the amount of fuel that journey took. It was that simplicity which made it a rallying cry for food campaigners across the developed world. Here, finally, was a tangible way in which to describe what was wrong with our food system. It is hardly a coincidence that both the concept of food miles and the farmers' market movement emerged at exactly the same time. It also gave environmentally minded consumers a simple way to judge whether they should buy a product. Had it come from as close by as possible? If yes, then into the basket it went.

The problem is it's far *too* simple. Looking only at transport costs for your food is not just to miss the bigger picture: it's to miss the picture entirely. The only way you can get some sense of the footprint of your food is by using what's called a Life Cycle Analysis, or LCA, which brings everything about the production of that item into play: the petrochemicals used in farming and in fertilizers, the energy to build tractors as well as to run them, to erect farm buildings and fences, and all of that (and so much more) has to be measured against yield. It's about emissions per tonne of apples or lamb. The New Zealand report used nearly thirty different measures in its LCA. And it's when you start drilling down into those that the point is quickly made.

Using a wide sample of apple farms in both Britain and New Zealand, the researchers found that the actual weight of nitrogen fertilizer used was roughly similar in both countries (eighty kilos per hectare in New Zealand to seventy-eight in the UK). However, in New Zealand they were getting a yield of fifty tonnes per hectare, as against fourteen tonnes in Britain. Where lamb was concerned yield was higher in Britain than in New Zealand, but so was nitrogen fertilizer use, by a factor of more than thirteen. New Zealand simply has a better landscape and climate for rearing lamb and apples. China has long had a comparative advantage in its cheap workforce, which has made it the go-to country for consumer electronics; New Zealand has a comparative advantage in its agricultural landscape. Of course, as Tim Benton pointed out to me, some of these figures may be out of date, but not by much. There are also endless arguments about what things ought to be measured and what ought not to be measured. But even if it is the most extreme example, it makes its point.

Jan Kees Vis, global director of sustainable sourcing development at Unilever in the Netherlands, has overseen research which puts the proportion of the global carbon footprint of your food as a result of its transportation at 2–3 per cent. Not convinced? After all, Unilever would have rather more than a small vested interest in this. Fair enough. Look instead at the detailed and independent 2008 study by Christopher Weber and H. Scott Matthews of Carnegie Mellon University. They put it at 4 per cent. Or as Professor Benton explained it to me, 'If you want to wipe out all the food miles in what you eat, all you need do is swap from one day's red meat eating a week to white meat. Not even to a vegetarian diet. Just to white meat.'

There's an awful lot of research to back this up. I am up to my nipples in research papers and pointy-headed bits of analysis and strident hunks of arithmetic which show just how much extra land you would need if food production moved from where it is now to be conveniently close to you so you could feel good about your food miles. But even I would find that tedious.

So instead come with me briefly to the fens of Lincolnshire, Norfolk and Cambridgeshire. Generally I hate flat places. They sap the will, drain away ambition. If there are no hills you have no need to find out what's on the other side. Huge, flat plains and big, dreary skies make me brood. But I'll put up with it to make a killer point about comparative advantage in agriculture. If you look at a map of potato growing in Britain you'll quickly see that it's concentrated here on the flat expanses around King's Lynn and in the Scottish borders. It's no accident, as potato farmer Bill Legge explains to me while he gives me a tour of his fields, hemmed in on each side by the grassy banks that keep the waters at bay. Legge has been farming potatoes around here all his life, on land which was under water until the seventeenth century. 'It's peat soil here, so we need to use less in the way of nitrogen fertilizers,' he says. Not only that. This dark, loose soil is good for the harvesting of potatoes. It's not as good as a sandy soil, but that needs more carbon inputs to make the potatoes grow. 'Here we get about twenty tonnes of potatoes an acre,' Bill tells me.

So how about if potato production was moved closer to the capital? After all, there's more people living in London than, say, here around King's Lynn. 'Well, it's a clay soil there and it's not as productive. Plus it's bloody hard to harvest them from the solid clod.'

How much less productive is it?

'You'd get sixteen tonnes an acre there.'

So the yield would be 20 per cent less. In other words, to get the same amount of potatoes to grow local to London you would need 20 per cent more land. Or you'd have to bombard that land with military-strength doses of fertilizers. Either way the footprint of your potatoes would be bigger. And that's why potatoes are grown in Norfolk and Lincolnshire and not in Essex.

It's exactly the same reason why that smartphone of yours is made in China. You can put it away now.

Of course, if you live in Norfolk or Lincolnshire that's where you should get your potatoes from. They're local to you. They are the most sustainable option. Look, I never said this was simple. It's anything but. Just as food miles made everything *too* simple, the end of food miles as a single measure makes everything very complicated. It should also be said that, just because meat and fruit from New Zealand may be more sustainable than those produced in Europe or the US, that doesn't mean we should rely on being able to get them from there. In fact, that may well not be a choice. Remember, the hungry Chinese and Indians, the Brazilians and the Indonesians are out there with the fast-growing economic strength to suck up all the surplus food that New Zealand can produce.

And let me make it a little more complicated: there *are* other good reasons for buying local food which have nothing to do with sustainability. It can be great for rural economies, and viable rural economies can be good for communities. As with growing your own, anything that reconnects us with where our food comes from has to be a good idea. But if you get caught in the corner of the supermarket by some goggle-eyed food warrior examining the contents of your basket for signs of food-mile transgression you can tell them that I said they should sod off. Go on. Have a practice. Shout at the mirror. It feels good, doesn't it?

It should be obvious by now that all of this also applies to issues around seasonality. The argument has long worked like this: if an ingredient is available out of season it must have been grown somewhere far away. Therefore, by dint of the miles it has travelled, it is unsustainable. But as we now know this may well not be the case. A strawberry ripened beneath the winter sun of Morocco can easily have a smaller carbon footprint than one raised in a polytunnel at the height of a so-called British summer. You can make lots of arguments about seasonal British strawberries tasting nicer. Once again that's purely about aesthetics. You can, I suppose, also argue that it's healthier for our food culture if we only eat with the seasons, though in an increasingly globalized world, where we happily consume film, music, television and books from all corners of the globe, the argument does not exactly have legs of steel. What you can't immediately assume is that it's the less sustainable option. Explaining this to people who have built entire patterns of behaviour around the idea of seasonality is tough. Nevertheless, they do need to be told.

And while you're at it you might want to have a word with them about the whole organics thing.

In the early autumn of 2003 I was locked in a kitchen in south London with the Australian chef John Torode, still then a few years off becoming a fixture on British television as a judge on *Masterchef*. Surrounding us were about eighty products, mostly available in the British supermarkets, some own-brand, some not. All of them carried the legend 'organic'. The value of organic sales in Britain had just slipped past £1 billion a year. It was still (and would remain) a tiny proportion of Britain's retail food market, which is worth about £155 billion – never more than 1.5 per cent. But with percentage growths into double digits year on year it wasn't unreasonable to think that the future would be more to do with organic food than less so. The supermarkets had piled into the sector. What, we wanted to know, was all this stuff like? After all, it was sold at a premium. It cost more, often a lot more. What did that money get you?

It got you depression and misery; it got you angst and indigestion; it got you anger, fury, and aching eyeballs from all the rolling.

It was, in short, a dismal afternoon; sometimes, for men who cared a little too much about what they ate, shockingly so. Across the sixteen categories that we tried – organic apples and cheddars, marmalades and tomato sauces, spaghetti, muesli, sausages, butter, and onwards – there were some great products, to which we enthusiastically gave the maximum five stars. There was Swaddles' Green Back Bacon. 'Gosh,' we said in our summing up, 'a yummy bit of bacon with great fat.' Or, as John puts it, 'That's no bullshit bacon. Give it six out of five.' We raved about Yeo Valley Organic Butter ('That almost cheesy edge you look for in a great butter'), eulogized Riverford Farm Foods' Pork Sausages with Herbs and Black Pepper ('You need all your own teeth to eat one of these'), and were suitably impressed by the yoghurt from Neal's Yard Creamery ('We expected a good product from Neal's Yard and got one').

But those were the exceptions. The majority of what we tasted that afternoon was awful. Tooth-grindingly, mind-numbingly, shoot-me-now-I've-suffered-enough dreadful. Our notes were littered with products that received one out of five or even zero. 'We only ate it because we had to,' we said of one yoghurt. 'It's only just coffee,' we said dismissively of some brown dishwater produced by something that had made a wasted journey all the way from Papua New Guinea. 'Absolutely pants,' we said of a Tesco's ham. And then there were the cheeses. Our verdict on the whole lot appeared as a single sentence separated only by ellipses. The first couple received two stars, but it was downhill to zero from there. 'Has a crumbly texture and a certain creaminess …,' we said of the first, before continuing under the second, '… as does this one … [two stars] … but what's the point of an organic label if all you produce are a bunch of dull … [no stars] flaccid and insipid cheeses that are not a patch on … [no stars] … the non-organics? It shouldn't be a marketing tag. It should offer a better product and these aren't [no stars].'

Almost ten years have passed since that miserable day. In all that time I have seen nothing to convince me that the organic tag is proof of anything other than what you are buying is likely to be more expensive than if it were not organic. That doesn't mean there aren't great organic products. There are. But from my experience of meeting with and talking to organic farmers I have come to the conclusion that this has far more to do with the care and attention involved in the whole approach to food production that comes with obtaining organic status. In other words, if you are the sort of obsessive person who is willing to go to the effort and quite considerable expense of getting your produce certified organic, you are also likely to be the sort of person who will generally make a greater effort to come up with something very good; to lavish more care on your plants or your animals. You will be deep in the premium market and will know there is someone out there willing to pay more for something that's obviously better. Or not, as the case may be. It is hardly surprising that organic sales started falling across the developed world in 2008 for the first time in fifteen years when the first credit crunch started to bite.

The quality of the food is, of course, only one of three reasons why you might choose to buy food designated organic. There is also its impact on both human health and the environment. The evidence for the first is what might, politely, be called scant and, impolitely, cobblers. Time and again there have been studies and, more importantly, meta-studies – reviews of many different studies, looking for trends – and each time they come up with the same result. Nutrient levels might be slightly higher in some organic produce than in conventional. There may, for example, be more polyphenols in organic tomatoes than non-organic, more minerals in organic milk than non-organic. But the scientific evidence that any of this has any impact on human health, especially on people already eating a generally balanced diet, isn't there. In the developed world we may be over-nourished occasion-ally, but we're not malnourished. As a major study by the UK's Food Standards Agency put it in 2009, there were 'no important differences in the nutrition content or any addi-tional health benefits of organic food when compared with conventionally produced food'.

Ah, but what about the pesticides used in conventional farming? Haven't there been studies which have shown that they have been linked to higher incidences of Alzheimer's and Parkinson's? By eating non-organic food don't I risk ending my life not recognizing my own kids and wearing an adult nappy? No, you don't. There have been such studies. But in each case those studies were of farm labourers in direct contact with the filthiest of chemicals, not of consumers who had eaten the produce they had been used on. Calling flimsy the evidence that eating organic food is better for you would be a terrible insult to the sturdiness of tissue paper. The chef Antony Worrall Thompson may say things like, 'Instead of popping pills we should eat more organic food,' but that just tells you more about him than it does the food.

The biggest problem with the organic movement is that it is based on a false premise which says: man-made really bad, non-man-made really good. Oh yes? Antibiotics are man-made and they are a very good thing. They have saved hundreds of millions of lives, perhaps billions. The next time you or a loved one develops a raging bacillus infection, or a suppurating abscess eating away at your innards, trust me, you will be grateful for every single man-made antibiotic in the medicine cabinet. (The fact that some of them have been overused, resulting in resistance in certain cases, does not make the antibiotics themselves bad, only the protocols around their prescription.) Likewise, E. Coli O157 is entirely non-man-made. People have had nothing to do with it. It's found in the guts of cattle. It can cause haemorrhagic diarrhoea, kidney failure and, funnily enough, death. Being dead is absolutely no fun. There are lots of things not made by us which can do that to you. There are berries and mushrooms, spider bites and radioactive minerals. Not being made by people does not prove anything. Copper sulphate is also naturally occurring, which probably explains why the Soil Association, which accredits organic farms in the UK, allows its use to tackle potato blight. It's horrible stuff, toxic to wildlife and not great for people either, causing major damage to the liver.

'If somebody attempted to introduce copper sulphate as a pesticide now,' says my Fenland potato farmer Bill Legge, 'there's no way it would ever get approval. It's just too nasty. It's only still around now because it's been in use for so long.'

That mother nature: she really can be a bitch sometimes.

Copper sulphate aside, the most persuasive argument in support of the organic movement is its impact on the environment and, more importantly, the debate we have around our stewardship of it. On issues like biodiversity, soil replenishment and water management, organic farmers have clearly been leaders. Indeed it's arguable that they have been too successful, at least if their aim really is to see all food move into a certified system of organic production. Notions of sustainability in agriculture have shifted from the fringes over the past two decades to become so completely mainstream that the organic movement has been left looking redundant. Even Patrick Holden, who was director of the Soil Association for sixteen years from 1995, admitted as much to me during a question and answer session at the NFU's annual conference in 2011. 'We have been too exclusive,' he said. 'We have separated ourselves from the rest of agriculture; and we have said we are right and you are wrong. That has to end.'

On top of that comes the 'intensification' bit of sustainable intensification. If we need to produce more food to feed more people, is organic really the way to go? In 2012 the highly respected journal *Nature* published a paper by Professor John P. Ragnold of Washington State University which said that 'organic farming systems in developed countries produce yields that are 20 per cent lower than their conventional counterparts'. (The paper was a meta-analysis of multiple studies into the yields of organic farming systems.) Ragnold could hardly be dismissed as a critic of organic farming: he ran the only undergraduate course in organic agricultural systems in the US. In an interview with Julian Baggini, working on his own book about the philosophy of food, Patrick Holden's successor as director of the Soil Association, Helen Browning, acknowledged there was a problem. 'On biodiversity, organic clearly has a lot to offer,' she said. 'On climate change, on the greenhouse gas side of things, it does in some areas and not others.'

Except even on biodiversity it's not that great, because the benefit is entirely local. We have to think globally when it comes to food production. If organic yields are 20 per cent lower than those of conventional farming, that shortfall will have to be made up somewhere. And that somewhere will almost certainly mean a conventional farm abroad. The biodiversity issue is simply being shunted to another country. Plus there is the issue of 'virtual hectares'. All the food we eat requires land for its production. Any food we can't produce domestically requires the economic annexing of land – those 'virtual hectares' – in a another country. It is as if we are pretending the land mass of the country in which we live is millions of hectares bigger than it actually is. And if that land is growing food for us, then it's not growing food for the people who live on it. This is a Very Big Problem.

Left out of all this is the issue of raising livestock under organic standards. While there's little doubt that the intentions of organic livestock farming are good – to give the animals as good and healthy a life as possible – there are long arguments over the virtues of the way it is meant to be achieved. For example, is it really in the interests of animals to not vaccinate them, unless there is a specific threat of disease nearby? We don't treat our own children like this. We vaccinate because of what we know about the way diseases might spread in the future, not because of what's already happening. Indeed, were cannibalism to be less of a tiresome old taboo – I can think of a whole bunch of people who would make good eating – it's hard to imagine that any of us humans, even the most head-banging, locavore, grow-your-own, farmers'-market food warrior, could ever be certified organic. Most of us would be fit only to be ground down and turned into the lowest-quality value-range sausages, the protein levels bulked up through high levels of our own ground-down skin.

Then again, the amount of meat we consume and the way it is raised under all farming systems leads to such messy arguments that the pros and cons of the organic system are frankly little more than a sideshow. Be in no doubt: killing animals for your dinner is a filthy business. That was something I got to grips with a very, very long time ago; indeed, well before I got that lovely wedding suit made.

It was three decades ago, to be exact.

Let me explain.

8.

SOMETHING TO CHEW ON

When I was 16 I took a Saturday job as a butcher's boy. My greatest advantage in the position was my size. I was bigger than the butcher, and in a shop full of large bits of dead animal this was a good thing. I was built for carrying carcasses. This also meant it was very difficult for me to damage the stock. My one other Saturday job had been in a delicatessen in Stanmore, where so many of my Jewish brethren lived, and it had ended badly. There I filled up on sweet, crumbly fish balls nicked from the walk-in fridge out back, and disgraced myself with a huge tray of cream-heavy cakes. Going to restock the front window, I carried the tray high over my head, trying to prove my dexterity, balance and poise, none of which were words anybody would ever have associated with me then or now. Naturally I lost control of the tray, but only once I'd reached the display. I destroyed both the cakes in the window and the new ones I was bringing up from the back. At the end of the day I did the decent thing and resigned. They didn't try to stop me. They may actually have held the door open for me.

So now I had a new job, in a butcher's shop, and that seemed a much safer place for a boy like me to be, even allowing for the knives and the graters and the mincers and the bleach. Plus I liked meat. When I was little I was the one who was always given the bone to gnaw on: the narrow end of the roast leg of lamb – the ankle, if you like – which was more tough, crisped skin than meat; the chicken's wing and drumstick; the curving rib from a proper joint of beef. We made jokes about cavemen and how really I was still one of those. I was the short, squat boy with the bone clasped between his teeth. Mine was a childhood marred by softness and roundness. From the age of 10 to about 12 I was constantly mistaken for a girl. Once a man came up to me outside a train station where I was waiting to meet friends and said, 'Are you a boy or a girl?' I sighed wearily, 'I'm a boy.' The man turned to a colleague on the other side of the pavement and said, 'You're right. I owe you a fiver.' My gender was so unobvious, people were taking bets over it.

So the bone thing mattered. It suggested a certain hardness. I defined my boyness by eating animals with my hands.

It would be helpful now if I could say that I understood then that the meat I was eating came from animals, and I suppose, in the abstract, I did. Curiously, given that we lived in the London suburbs, there was a farm not far from where I lived, a real one in the shadow of Harrow on the Hill, where black and white cows grazed. Given they were Friesians, it was probably a dairy farm. I quite liked looking at them. As a very small child I did the endless pointing and gasping thing. But that enjoyment in no way interfered with my ability to eat their sisters. There were no flirtations with vegetarianism, fuelled by youthful outrage and disgust. As far as I was concerned, meat came from my mother's bountiful nature.

She was a deeply unsentimental woman. I think the privations of childhood had led her to regard sentiment as at best an affectation and at worst a luxury she could ill afford. She rolled her eyes at slush and dewy-eyed posturing. The meat we ate was just part of dinner, for which the animals had always been destined. I liked it very much. Certainly the job in the butcher's where my parents did their weekly shopping made a kind of sense.

On my first morning I was introduced to George, the owner. I had expected someone big and heavy with tree-trunk arms, a machete tucked into the waistband of his apron, blood on his hands. He was nothing like that. He was short and thin and his nose was sharp and pointed and had a little groove at the end so he looked not unlike a weasel. And he smoked far too much. His cough rumbled upwards from the soles of his boots, a lank forelock bouncing on his forehead each time his lungs twitched. He balanced his burning fags on the edge of the butcher's block, red smoking tip over the edge, ash tumbling to mingle with the sawdust on the floor, where I would later sweep it up. Distracted perhaps by a customer, or stock coming in, he would often forget that he had placed it on the block and light another. The neglected cigarette would burn all the way down and leave a blackened groove where it had taken the wood away with it. All of the butcher's blocks had these charcoaled grooves. Eventually George's smoking would kill him.

His hands bore the mark of a hundred missed chops and slices. I expected by the end of my time to have become like him, to have hard, grooved hands to show to my friends, trophies of some courageous struggle with real, working life. That such scars would have been gained in combat with dead things, not exactly known for fighting back, and therefore would be proof only of my incompetence with blades, never occurred to me. I was a butcher's boy. On Saturday's my A levels could go to hell. It was meat that mattered.

The only real cut I ever got was on my little finger. I was washing up a sink full of mucky knives and watched with surprise as the bubbles turned pink. That was the only time I got to play with them, thankfully. On my first day George took one look at me and recognized where my talents lay. 'Here,' he said. 'Get that leg of beef and take it to the fridge. And mind, pick it up from the bottom or you'll do your back.' I quickly discovered that in a butcher's shop a lump of dead animal becomes just another weight to be moved. I heaved it up and stumbled the ten feet to the large walk-in fridge. I weighed it: 115 pounds. George was pleased. 'You'll do all right.' Cough. 'It's a bit of a mucky business, this one.' Cough. 'But you'll soon get used to it.' He returned to disembowelling chickens.

The fridge was my domain on Saturdays. I was the one who fetched and carried from it and the one who cleaned it out. Being a butcher's boy was an unending battle with congealed blood. It wasn't so much the floor that was the problem. These were still the days of sawdust, and it soaked up the blood brilliantly. At the end of the day a hard broom would get that off. It was the white porcelain tiles. They loved the blood, couldn't bear to let it go. I spent my days with my hand in a bucket of hot water and bleach, scrubbing and running from one end of the shop to the other mopping round the fridge and then starting all over again. At the end of the day I would collect my money, capital for whatever night out I had planned, and head home to stand under the shower for hours on end in the hope that I might be able to wash away the smell of raw dead animal and bleach. I lived in fear that it might limit my chances of copping off, that some girl I fancied would get close to me only to recoil from the whiff of something akin to the cleaning fluids used in public toilets.

I stayed for the best part of a year until the revision time-table for my A levels called. George gave me double my £9 salary that day and wished me well. I'd been all right as a butcher's boy, he said. Not the soft-handed nancy boy he thought I was going to be. I was proud of that. People may have stopped mistaking me for a girl a few years before. But I hadn't exactly turned into some big hunk of man; softness and roundness were still my calling cards. So to be told I had measured up in a task that required physical strength mattered to me. In later years, as a journalist writing about food, I would find myself in a butcher's and would tell them that I had worked in a shop just like this one as a Saturday job. They would nod at me slowly, approvingly. Against all the odds, this made me one of them.

Then again, butchers have always seemed pleased to see me, perhaps because I have always looked like a good customer. A man cannot hide his true nature, and in my restaurant reviews I have never tried to. I eat meat. I like the taste of crisped fat and well-aged muscle seared outside, and the way the Maillard reaction – the browning process which gives a steak its big burst of flavour – delivers a huge hit of that something savoury the Japanese call umami. (It's also found in big-flavoured foods like fresh Parmesan cheese and salted anchovies.) I like cutting into a steak and finding it still to be the colour of a baby's hot cheek. I like birds roasted in butter, and the crunchy skin on hunks of lamb and pig and their cured brethren, the sausages and the bacon that ensure very little of the animal is ever wasted. I like cooking these things and I like eating them. I could dress this up with flowery self-justifications, and there are a few of those to come, but I don't have the feet for dancing on a pinhead. Better for now, I think, to face straight on those who object to my meat-eating and say I do it because I like it.

A lot of my writing about meat cookery has been taken as a shameless attempt to goad vegetarians. Some of it is. There is such clumsy, muddled thinking among so many vegetarians that they deserve to be goaded. They deserve to be made angry. And anyway, they need the exercise. The dairy- and egg-eating vegetarians – the majority – fail to recognize that they are as complicit in animal slaughter as I am. Only females produce milk and lay eggs. What do these cheese soufflé eaters think happens to all the males at birth? Do they think they are freed to gambol across field and brook, over stream and through forest, to end their lives of natural causes? Of course not. The overwhelming majority are killed at birth, superfluous to requirements. Bull calves are shot in the head with a bolt, because too many of us won't eat veal. (The farmers hate it; many have told me they leave the farm on the day it happens.) Chicks are asphyxiated or have their necks broken or worse: look up 'maceration of chicks' online. Animal husbandry is an ugly business, even when it's pretending to be neither ugly nor too corporate. Dairy- and egg-eating vegetarians are as deep steeped in the blood of it all as the rest of us.

Vegans occupy the moral high ground here, of course. Their arguments are philosophically robust. They have an internal logic, which is to say they believe eating animals is wrong and by swearing off dairy and eggs – and, God help us, honey – they are consistent. That doesn't mean they are right. It is possible to survive on a vegan diet. Millions do so. But there's an awful lot of evidence that it needs to be supplemented with other things to make it complete. There are issues around protein deficiency. It is labour intensive.

Oh, and it's not very nice.

I know. I used to be a vegan. Not for long, mind, though it was for longer than I experienced poverty. It was just five days, to be precise. Oh God, how I suffered. Sometimes I still wake at night, the sweat-stained bed sheets clenched in my fists as I live and relive the memories. Forget the silence of the lambs; I am haunted by the silence of the Puy lentils.

Here's what happened. One of my editors, who must have hated me, called me up and asked me to go vegan for two weeks. I haggled her down to one week, and then almost halfway through, drained and crotchety and tired of barking at my kids owing to the low levels of protein in my diet, I decided a week meant a working week. Five days. It was enough. I couldn't go on. They could send me to report wars, make me the badminton correspondent, force me to report council meetings in Nuneaton. I was prepared to do absolutely anything for my newspaper. But I couldn't take another day of veganism.

It was, to be fair, an intriguing experience (though I imagine having a limb amputated isn't short on drama and distraction, but that doesn't mean I'd recommend it). I was fascinated by the way a vegan agenda sent me rushing into the arms of non-Western food. I used up a lot of white miso paste and a lot of soy and chilli. And enormous volumes of noodles. It was a hugely carbohydrate-heavy diet. I felt bloated and uneasy on it, or at least more bloated and uneasy than I usually feel. I shared the pain of vegans, tripped up by unexpected outbreaks of milk powder in products that had no good reason to contain it. Why, in God's name, is there milk powder in bags of flavoured nuts? Why? Nuts are meant to be the vegan's friend, a reliable if relentless source of protein. The milk powder thing contaminated them.

For all the insights that my short flirtation with veganism gave me, it did nothing to dissuade me from the imperative of eating meat. After all, we have been doing it for a very, very long time. When anthropologists begin looking for evidence of human civilization at a dig one of the first give-away clues has always been animal bones, gnawed bare by heavy-browed early humans, probably by the fat little boys in the tribe who didn't want to be mistaken any more for girls. In 2010 the celebrated anthropologist Richard Wrangham published a book, *Catching Fire*, which argued that it was cookery which made us human. Heating food makes it possible to extract the maximum amount of energy from ingredients. That meant our ancestors could waste less time foraging for stuff to keep them going and could instead concentrate on really cool things like inventing machinery, developing language, and becoming artists so they had something to talk about. Without the appliance of fire to food we really would still be hanging about in trees grooming each other for the protein in flies and lice. Wrangham's argument is rigorous and compelling. You would have to be an A-grade, gold medal-winning, premier-league arse of mammoth proportions to dismiss it as bunk. The same argument applies to eating meat. It is a quick and efficient way to get the sort of nutrition and energy humans need to do the things we do, including all the stupid stuff like tweeting each other pictures of kittens. Without it a greater proportion of us would be dedicating vast amount of our lives to arable farming, to growing the things we need to substitute for the animals which are such a tight and clever nutritional package.

This was all brought home to me in the middle of the last decade when I was sent to interview Hugh Pennington, now Emeritus Professor of Bacteriology at the University of Aberdeen, who came to public prominence as a result of his investigation into the outbreak of E. Coli O157 in Lanarkshire in 1996 which killed seventeen people. He was the man who identified the causes of the BSE outbreak, and over the years he has become the oracle on all things food-poisoning related. In 2005 the *Observer Food Monthly* decided to give him their lifetime achievement award in recognition of the work he had done to make our food safer, and I had been sent along to profile him.

During the afternoon, by a crackling log fire in a central London hotel, we fell to talking about factory farming of fish but more particularly of chicken, which had been slated by many in the food world as a terrible evil, not least because it was a reservoir for infection. As many big-name chefs and food campaigners liked to tell us, factory-farmed flocks of chickens were often infected with salmonella and campylobacter, which could both have fatal consequences.

Professor Pennington acknowledged that this was so. Though, of course, he said, both of those could be dealt with by cooking the meat properly. So it's not really an issue? He nodded and said he wanted to go further than that.

'If you look over the twentieth century,' he explained, 'at the beginning lots of kids got diseases that we don't see any more. There was lots of symptomatic tuberculosis, for example, because they were not eating an optimal diet. Things like cheap chicken have solved that problem.' Of course, there is a downside, he said, including the spread of those bugs like campylobacter and mass-produced salmonella. 'Though if you look at it brutally and over the long term it's not a bad trade-off.' In short, the benefits for public health of factory farming far outweigh the downside. In the short term we have come to blame the industrial food process for making so many of us in the developed world obese. We talk about over-supply of calories. We bemoan the over-use of sugars. All of these things are true. But sometimes the longer view is necessary. The fact is that the wide availability of cheap, factory-farmed animal protein has helped us to live longer. A lot of people may not like this fact. That doesn't make it any less true.

This argument is, however, entirely from the human side of the equation. It's about what is good for people, and I make no apologies for the fact that if you ask me which species I am going to side with in any argument, it's more likely to be the people. Most of my best friends are people. But, as many have pointed out, that is not good enough because the eating of meat involves animals – sentient beings which have no one to speak for them other than those of us who eat them. So before we even get to questions of the sustainability of eating animals, and the whopping carbon footprint their rearing leaves behind, we do need to give them a place in the moral arguments, beyond that of object. We have to engage with them as things that live and then die.

Certainly I felt I had to. I know I can be horribly flippant about my meat eating, use it as a vehicle for crappy, mallet-heavy jokes. I don't apologize for any of that. Lord save us from the self-regarding, self-appointed moral arbiter who claims they are thinking about the implications of every decision they take all the time. That's not how we live our lives. That's not how I live mine. Sometimes a chicken is just dinner and nothing else. Then again, that isn't always good enough. Certainly it wasn't for me. If I was going to think seriously about the role animals play in my diet I had to engage with the process that got them onto my plate. I had to go to work in an abattoir.

I had to get involved in the killing.

It is early on a Monday morning. I have been put to work on the pig tank and I'm trying hard to regulate my breathing to deal with the sensory overload. Danny and Alan, the two blokes I'm working with – and they are blokes; lean and hard-bodied and sinewy, with a clench-jawed sense of purpose – are getting on with it. They are doing the thing. They do this thing every day, sometimes for six or seven hours, and I can't quite imagine how. For all the extra weight I carry I am fit, as a result of all those trips to the gym. I am probably fitter than I have ever been in my life, but I am genuinely afraid that this job on the pig tank will defeat me; that I will crumple at the knees and disgrace myself, overcome by the noise and the smell and the heat and the sheer relentless heft of it all.

I am intimidated.

The morning started for me not long after 6 a.m. and I had already thought it had been full on. I am in the abattoir of John Penny and Sons in Rawdon, that part of Leeds where it bows its head to the smudge of Bradford just over the hill. J. Penny is a rare business, an integrated beef farm, slaughter-house and butcher's, famed not just for sending some of the highest-quality meat to market, but for its complete openness. The slaughterhouse industry in Britain – the world over – is notoriously secretive, and unsurprisingly so. Animal welfare campaigners can and have made the lives of those who work in it very difficult, and with good reason; the worst abuses of animals at the moment of death have generally been identi-fied by exceptionally brave campaigners, who have made it their job to record the suffering – let's call it torture, which is what it is – perpetrated by people to whom we have delegated power.

For that is the reality. We want to eat meat but we want to have no part in what obtaining that meat requires. We turn away from it. We ask others to perform that role for us, and we do not look. While the BSE crisis of the nineties vastly overhauled the regulation and oversight of abattoirs in Britain, they still remain very wary of any outside examination by the media. I have attempted to investigate various stories involving slaughterhouses over the years, but have been repeatedly warned by people with knowledge of the sector not to get involved.

'There are a lot of dangerous people involved in that industry,' one contact told me. 'You're a married man. You have kids. Don't take the risks.'

The current Penny in charge of the business, John, believes in letting people in. He's a big, solid Yorkshireman who keeps his hair buzz-cut short, as if to save time. 'We have nothing to hide,' he tells me. 'Look at everything.' The beef animals they raise travel only a matter of metres from the farm down the hill to slaughter, which reduces the levels of stress. They also slaughter for other farmers, but their livestock travel from pretty close by in Yorkshire. It's also relatively small. In a month J. Penny will slaughter around 2,000 sheep, 6,000 pigs and 1,000 cattle. There are industrial-scale abattoirs in the US which kill 5,000 cattle *in a day*. There are records showing the Penny family have been farming around these parts since the end of the eighteenth century. Certainly they've been on this site since 1891, opening the first abattoir here in 1938.

But it is, as they like to joke, a dying trade. Once there were sixteen slaughterhouses in the area. Now only J. Penny's remains, sustained because it diversified into wholesale butchery, turning the animals it kills not just into carcasses but into beautifully shaped, well-aged cuts of meat.

I have been here once before, for an article in which I followed a bullock from hoof to plate. I had gone to a farm in North Yorkshire with a butcher, to be taught what to look for in a live beef animal: the well-developed arse, the lump of fat where the tail meets the body, a lack of definition at the ribcage. I had been schooled in objectifying something with a pulse; to look at it as both a butcher and later a cook. We chose number 365, a thirteen-month-old Limousin chestnut cow, dark of eye, furry of coat. From there I had followed the animal to J. Penny, and had been standing above the 'crush', the metal cabinet designed to hold it in place, while it took the bolt to the forehead which rendered it unconscious. I had very briefly glimpsed the point when it was bled out. It was an educative day. It was dramatic and full on and left me thinking very seriously about the way we let others perform this task for us. It might have been easy for me to imagine I was playing God but I knew the reality was far more prosaic. The animals had been reared by farmers for the purpose of being killed and eaten. If I hadn't chosen cow 365, it would still eventually be slaughtered. And if the likes of me hadn't been here to eat it, this animal would never have existed in the first place.

But it occurred to me that, in bearing witness, I had failed to engage with the experience in an authentic manner. For the fact is that I was present for just minutes, rather than day after day as the slaughtermen are. To really understand what was going on, to understand the relationship between ourselves and our once-sentient dinner, I had to go for long-term exposure. I had to be there for long enough to be inured to what was happening around me. John Penny agreed that I could come back for a couple of days, that they would put me to work on whatever unskilled tasks there were.

And so early one morning in high summer I turn up at the site and am invited to follow a herd of sheep through what are called the 'layers', the shed of holding zones, separated out by clanking metal gates. As the gate in front opens to let through the flock, the one behind closes, in a continuous corridor that snakes back on itself as it rises up the gentle concrete incline, bringing the animals ever closer to the point of slaughter. Clive, a former butcher who now runs the slaughterhouse, leads me to a spot just above the chamber at the start of the 'kill line'. There a young man by the name of Josh – 'They call me the special one,' he says with a grin, when we are introduced – would be using a pair of huge electrified paddles shaped like tongs to stun the sheep.

'It's only Josh's mum who calls him the special one,' Clive says, with a shake of the head.

The sheep are let into the room in tight batches of eight or so, a hatch clattering shut behind them as they come in. Josh positions himself with his legs either side of a sheep's hind quarters. He presses the paddles to the side of the head and down they go, unconscious. Running over Josh's head is a long continuous rail from which hangs a set of chains. He hooks one of these to the animal's front leg and it's immediately lifted up so that it is dangling, head to the ceiling.

It moves down the line to where an older man in a plastic apron is waiting, the sticking knife in his hand. Allan is coming up for 65 and retirement, after being here most of his working life. He is grey and solid and a little round at the belly, where the apron bows. He grabs hold of the sheep as it passes and shoves the blade in below the ear to sever the artery. There is a quick but contained spray of blood. The animal twitches. It is done.

'The pigs twitch even more than the sheep,' Clive tells me, as we stand there watching.

Josh stuns another sheep. 'That's a perfect stun, that is,' Clive says. 'Front legs out, back legs in.'

I ask Josh, who is in his twenties, 'How long have you done this?'

'It's the only job I've ever done,' he says.

'Why?'

He shrugs. 'They offered me the job.'

Clive says, 'How many GCSEs have you got, Josh?'

'None.' Josh grins, then stuns another sheep and it passes onwards to Allan.

It occurs to me that this is an entirely male environment. There are a couple of women in the front office, but none here, where the killing is done.

I ask Josh if he would like to have some women in the workplace.

'I wouldn't mind,' he says.

'But they don't apply for the jobs,' says Clive. It is a place of men. This is how it has always been.

As we talk, the sheep keep coming through. Josh keeps stunning. Allan keeps sticking. I am staring down a white-painted corridor, its walls sprayed with some of the sheep's blood. At the end, the rail turns, taking the dead sheep to a long line of men each with a different task: the sheep will be beheaded, skinned, disembowelled, the bodies sawn in half. All of those men are waiting. We can chat but the work must not be stopped. There are 700 sheep to come through here.

I ask Clive if they ever have to look carefully at the type of people they employ.

'Of course,' he says. 'You get some. You see if they're getting something out of the experience they shouldn't.' They are taken off the job. That said, he refuses to deny how the kill line can make you feel. 'No mistake. It gives you a sense of power doing this. You see a big animal and realize how easy it is to put them down.' He does not say this boastfully or with enthusiasm. He says it with the thoughtfulness of a man who has been in the trade all his life, who knows there are certain facts of life that must not be avoided. We stand and watch the sheep dying for around half an hour. It stops being quite as dramatic as it was at first. There is a rhythm. But it does not stop being compelling.

This is life, halted.

The sheep are through and it is time for the pigs. Clive invites me to work on the tank and I know I can't decline. This is what I am here for. It is a tank of hot water – 62°C – around twenty feet long, four feet deep and ten feet across. Behind the wall at our backs, in the kill-line corridor, the pigs are being stuck by Allan. I can hear the noise of them squealing and grunting in the holding area before they receive the stun from the electric paddles. I can hear the chains clanking. At one point I look around the wall and see the slaughterman. Our eyes meet. He is weary. With the sheep, Allan was merely a little splattered. Now he is drenched. He is covered in blood, from his ankles right up to the transparent visor of his face mask, though it is across his face too. It is everywhere, and the pigs continue to bleed out as they come round the corner, a huge, swirling scarlet tide. As they get to us, one of my colleagues lifts a handle which in turn lifts an articulated section of the overhead line. He can now lift the pigs up and over the lip of the tank so he can deposit them into the water with a huge splash. There is the smell of fresh blood and the tang of urine and shit and above the top of it all something familiar which I eventually identify as pork stock. Which is what happens when you dunk just-dead pigs in hot water.

When the pigs hit the water our job is to grab hold of the chains around their legs, three or four at a time, and hook the end over the side of the tank so the bodies aren't lost to the depths. Then we must drag the animals down the length of the tank, heaving them against the fluid tension, straining to get them moving. Danny, who is working alongside me, is short and wiry and prefers to push the chains down; I prefer to use my weight to pull, but sometimes find my feet slipping on the wet concrete floor. Then again, I am trying to move around 300 kilos of pig at a time. Waiting at the end is the bristling machine. We push them through the water onto the platform – a little like the scoop at the front of a forklift – which raises them out of the water into an open-sided chamber. There they are flailed by furiously rotating rubber paddles with metal teeth at the end, which strip off any hair and, while they're at it, toenails too. Every minute or so there is a searing burst of violent flame designed to finish the job. Finally they are spat out the other end, re-chained, and sent off down the line.

It is ninety minutes of pig drama, as scripted by Hieronymus Bosch. There's the stench and the splash of the hot water and the drag of the pigs. There's the roar of the machine and the heat of the belching flame. And over the top is the noise of the animals and the splatter and spray of the blood that cannot help but get you. Occasionally an animal comes round that is twitching and bucking more than the others and Danny takes a knife to them just to check they are properly gone, hunkering down under the gush of something hot and arterial to finish the job as quickly as possible.

And, of course, it is continuous.

I do what I can to keep up, to not be a hindrance. Occasionally I lose a pig to the water and somebody has to come to my aid to retrieve it from beneath the surface. I feel ashamed and literally unmanned. I am a writer. I sit at my desk. I type. I have never done anything that feels remotely male. That soft-cheeked 11-year-old, who looked like he had budding boobs, who was mistaken so often for a girl, is still in there trying to measure up. I feel I am failing. And then I feel ashamed, not for trying to measure myself in this way but for thinking like this when really what's going on around me, the deaths of pigs to feed my own intense pork habit, is so much more important. Then there is the strain. I feel the effort in the core of my abdomen and in my arms and in my neck. I feel it everywhere. And when, after ninety minutes or so, Clive invites me to try my hand at something else, I grab the chance, reasoning that I have to do as much as possible while I am here. I leave Danny and Allan to it. I am happy to say goodbye.

The next day I go to work on the sheep kill line. My job is to help skin them. The line runs in a kind of U shape. They are stuck on the down stroke, come round the bend, and are beheaded and the skin loosened around the legs. When they get to me I am invited to punch my fists down between the skin and the still-warm, greasy body to loosen the skin further. Then I am shown how to grip the skin around the neck and yank hard. Get it right and it comes away in one long piece that ends up dangling around their arse end. The job will be finished by the next station in the line, after which they are disembowelled and the carcasses bisected, as with the pigs.

At first I am not bad at the skinning, even though I find the heat given out by the newly slaughtered sheep's body disconcerting. But it's all about tensile grip, and I simply don't have it. My hands are not strong enough. I have other skills. I can type fast. I am a reasonably accomplished pianist. I have precision and dexterity, more of it than average, but I have no power, not like these men around me. I am soon taken off the job.

The sheep are finished. The kill line is cleaned down to make way for the seventy-five cattle which must now come through. Clive asks me if I would like a job, but very quickly I decline. When I first changed jobs on the kill lines I quickly realized that not all animals are the same. A sheep is not the same as a pig. Size changes things. Species changes things. This is brought home to me on the cattle kill line. The cattle are completely different. It is all just too big, too immense, too damn huge for me to identify any manner in which I could possibly participate. I watch the animals receiving the bolt to the head from the gun. The side of the crush goes up and they roll out senseless onto the abattoir floor, legs stiff. A chain is attached to a back ankle and close to a ton of animal is lifted high to the ceiling. It is sent round to the slaughterman, the only Muslim in the company, who is killing them in the halal style, by cutting their throats from ear to ear. He turns them towards the wall as he does this, so that the blood sprays out against it. There is an awful lot of blood in a beef animal. A huge amount of blood. The slaughterman does not flinch. This is what he does.

And that is what I am left with most of all: the sense of serious men doing a serious job. There is the little bloke whose task is to get under the beef animal as it is still bleeding out, stick his hand into the throat gash, find the oesophagus, and attach a clip which cuts it off so the contents of the bowel and stomach can't be drawn back down by gravity. There are the men who take out the liver and lights, impaling them on a candelabra of spikes so they look like Christmas trees of viscera. There are the meat inspectors, men in their sixties whose word is law here; who, at the slightest sign of disease, can condemn a whole carcass and will not hesitate to do so. There are computerized traceability systems, operated with an extraordinary degree of precision by men who know that the entire functioning of the process depends upon them making sure that a link can be maintained between the beast that came in through the layers first thing and the carcass that hangs, cooling, in the vast walk-in fridges out the back. What happens here is important. It's really important. And yet we treat its product with a shameful degree of casualness.

It's a good word, 'shameful', especially where meat consumption is concerned. So many of us feel so many different kinds of shame about it. There are those who find all and any kinds of factory farming repugnant, regardless of what Professor Pennington might say about the value of cheaply available meat to human health. The chef and food writer Hugh Fearnley-Whittingstall made a series of films about the way the cheapest chickens are raised, crammed together in sheds, their feet burning from the ammonia in their accumulated shit, their legs barely able to hold up the huge, Pamela Andersonesque tits they have been bred to grow. Understandably, he wept on camera. If he was looking for the truly ugly face of animal husbandry he certainly found it.

The highly regarded American novelist Jonathan Safran Foer wrote a book called *Eating Animals*, full of shock at the way so much meat in America is farmed (again understandably: in the US things like the tethering of sows in stalls – banned since 1997 in the UK and across Europe from 2013 – is still legal). Ever the philosophy major, he started from first principles, which is to say the regard in which we hold animals. The issue here, of course, is one of what some would call sentiment and others would call realism. Either you fully identify with animals as equals, who are therefore deserving of our complete protection, or you regard them as not equal, in which case – accepting their absolute right to be spared cruelty – it's OK to eat them. It will come as no shock that I fall into the latter camp, and there was nothing in Safran Foer's text to shift me over to the other side of the argument. He lurched from unsupported statement to unsupported statement, refusing to accept, for example, that certain animal behaviour is just instinct and therefore ascribing to it a higher intelligence.

In the way of the polarized arguments that infect the food world the opponents of intensive livestock farming always run in the other direction when asked for an alternative. The only solution, they say, is that everything should be free-range. Every chicken should be able to strut daintily across the pastures; all pigs should be outdoor-reared. They should be massaged with essential oils every day, bedded down on duck-feather duvets and slaughtered to the soothing tones of Vivaldi's *Four Seasons*. Or something like that. I would be hard pushed to disagree. All animals *should* be reared like this. In a perfect world. The problem is that our world is horribly imperfect. It's a dreadful place with many competing pressures, especially if you're somebody's dinner. According to Compassion in World Farming, Britain slaughtered 850 million chickens in 2011. Can you imagine how much space would be needed to allow all those chickens the ability to range free and far and wide? There simply isn't enough land, unless you're willing to move out of your lovely house and let a bunch of fat hens move in. The landscape would be nothing but chickens as far as the eye could see.

And by God would they be expensive. The £31 I paid for that chicken from Lidgate's in Holland Park was obviously stupid. Insane. Barking. But what about the £15 chicken? Or the £18 chicken? Or the £22 chicken? Meat prices are already rising in response to feed costs, without us even attempting to set up animals with slabs of land to call their own. And as meat prices rise the willingness of people to grant them greater welfare falls away. In 2010 I interrogated shoppers in Croydon on just this point for a TV show. Almost all of them said at the start that they cared about animal welfare. They loved animals. Adored them. Wished them only the best things in life and death. But when presented with the cost of meat reared to high standards they said they were not prepared to pay that much and would buy cheaper meat. What? Even if it meant lower welfare standards? Yes, they said. Even if it meant lower welfare standards.

Given a choice between their own well-being and that of the animals, they chose their own. It isn't an unreasonable response. This is not to condone the very worst excesses of the industrial livestock rearing process; genuine cruelty should never be acceptable. But perfect practice should never get in the way of acceptable practice, if it means meat costs too much.

Certainly the joint of beef I presented those shoppers with was just too expensive. Indeed beef is a case in point. As I write it is the early autumn of 2012, and beef prices are going through the roof.

In fact they are rising so fast it's worthy of a sweaty, panicky 'stop press' moment.

STOP! PLEASE! I CAN'T KEEP UP.

Newspaper articles of the sort I write week in week out are generally a snapshot in time. The comment piece of mine published in the *Observer* newspaper, ahead of the G8 meeting of the world's wealthiest nations at Camp David in May 2012, was just such a snapshot. The intelligence coming from within international aid and charity circles was that US President Barack Obama was poised to announce a global food programme initiative to help deal with exactly the kind of chronic malnutrition in childhood that I had witnessed in Rwanda. Seize the moment, I bellowed, self-importantly. The world's leaders needed to understand that we were teetering on the edge of another food price spike like the one that caused so much chaos and hardship in 2008. Quietly, almost unnoticed, the commodity prices for both soya beans and corn, the main livestock feeds, had spiked at close to the highs of the crisis four years before. At its peak in 2008 maize had cost $287 a tonne, or about $6 a bushel; in the spring of 2012 it was back around $280. Soya beans were trading at around $545 a tonne in Chicago, just shy of the historic high in July 2008 of $552. And that's pretty much where the prices stood when I visited the Chicago pits a little over a month later, interviewing Scott Shellady and the other commodity traders.

Within days of my departure from America, farmers across the US began to report severe drought conditions. (I'm pretty sure these events weren't related.) Crops were dying in the fields. Yields were drastically down. Words like 'catastrophe' and 'disaster' were being pressed into play, and for once it didn't feel like hyperbole. By September 2012 corn was at $330 a tonne, or $8 a bushel. It had increased in price by over 30 per cent in just six weeks. Soya beans were at $672 a tonne. That, in turn, was having a massive impact on the price of beef, because soya beans and corn are what beef cattle are fed on. The beef shortage caused by the 2008 price spike, when cattle farmers decided feed was so expensive it made more sense to send their breeding herds to slaughter, was being compounded. So now, not only was there a shortage of beef animals. Those animals which remained were again hideously expensive to feed. The wholesale price for beef in Chicago had gone from just over $1 a pound to, at its peak, just shy of $2. Once again US beef farmers were liquidating their herds; they were now the smallest they had been since 1973. Cargill, which had told me that food security issues were 'absolutely' a business opportunity, was suddenly proving it by announcing that profits for the quarter of 2012 to the end of August were up 300 per cent from $236 million to $975 million. The last time it had revenues anything like that was during the food price crisis of 2007–8. Meanwhile the risk analysis company Maplecroft issued a Food Security Risk Index, which showed vast swaths of the world at risk of societal unrest owing to people not being able to access enough to eat. Countries like Ethiopia, Somalia and Chad were shown as at extreme risk, but even countries such as India, Libya, Iraq and Pakistan were in the high-risk category.

Here I was trying to write an incisive, thoughtful book about the coming food crisis, the tsunami of food price rises and shortages that was heading our way some time in the future, and the damn wave was already breaking over me as

I typed. The crisis wasn't some time in the future. It was here. Things like this can make life very tricky for a man with a book to write.

When you ask the 'free-range or die' lobby what people on low incomes are to do about the cost of non-intensively reared meat, they always come up with the same response: there are lots of cheaper cuts. And indeed there are. I'm a huge fan of cheap cuts. Give me skirt steak over fillet any time; it's where the flavour is. It may require a bit more cooking but it's worth it in the end. And I love offal; I adore those inner organs with their ripe, big-fisted tang of real animal that is so often missing from the more dainty and prime pieces. I love andouillette, that French sausage made from the business end of a pig's intestine, which smells like a farmyard before it's been cleaned of the shit. I love liver and kidneys and sweetbreads. Calves' brains in browned butter are a thing of beauty. I firmly believe that if we are going to bang an animal on the head we have a moral responsibility to eat as much of it as possible, to suck the marrow from its bones and the cerebellum from its skull and work our way out from there.

But the notion that those on lower incomes should be banished to eating this and only this while the fat wallets get the sirloin and the ribeye makes me deeply uncomfortable. Too much of our modern food culture has already become a cocktail party for the chattering middle classes, in their Boden wrap dresses and mustard-coloured cords, from which a whole stratum of society is excluded; making that division real through brutal economics is surely not the way to go. We have to balance the demands of welfare against the economic imperatives.

But there's another issue around our consumption of animals which makes all of these issues even more complicated: the fact that my meat habit is killing the planet and leaving people hungry. Obviously not just my meat habit. I mean, I like my dead pig and dead cow, but even I can't be blamed for everything. It's your meat habit too. And yours. And, while we're at it, yours. The problem is multi-faceted. First, there is the volume of grain that could be fed to people which instead is fed to livestock. To produce a pound of chicken (live weight) it takes a little under two pounds of feed. It takes three pounds of feed to produce a pound of pork and a whole seven pounds to produce a pound of beef. If we are going to keep the coming nine billion fed we will have to give more of that grain to people and less of it to animals.

And then there is the impact all that livestock has on the planet. Globally the sector is accused, in a report by Cranfield University, of producing 37 per cent of all the world's methane (which has twenty-three times the global warming potential of CO_2). Sixty-five per cent of the nitrous oxide (N_2O) released into the atmosphere (which has 296 times the global warming potential of CO_2) comes from farm animal manure. More than 55 per cent of all agricultural emissions come from the meat and dairy sector. They use 70 per cent of all agricultural land and 30 per cent of the land surface of the planet. The UN's Food and Agriculture Organization says it is the largest source of water pollution. The impact on biodiversity is also vast. Farmed animals account for 20 per cent of the total terrestrial animal biomass.

And you thought you were just having roast chicken for tea.

You aren't. You're serving up a weapon of mass destruction.

Naturally there are many who have argued that vegetarianism is the only way forward. It's a nice idea. Even if you love pork belly and ribeye as much as I do, it makes a certain kind of sense. Get rid of all those farting, shitting cows and pigs so we stop poisoning the planet. Dig deeper, however, and it becomes clear that it's neither completely desirable nor absolutely necessary. Swapping the entire planet's agricultural production to arable farming will have impacts of its own, especially on water usage. It would also be bound to lead to an uplift in the sales of meat substitutes – awful things like Quorn, fashioned from dismal fungal growths – the production of which leave their own massive footprint. And there is another point. There are huge regions of the planet which are not suited to arable farming. Vast areas of upland Britain are really only good for the raising of ruminants; it's impossible to plant crops on them. Likewise, you can't feed people from the green hillsides of the Lake District, Wales or Scotland, but sheep bloody love the grass. The same applies to many other parts of the globe.

Farmer and former co-editor of *The Ecologist* magazine Simon Fairlie made exactly this point in his 2010 book *Meat: A Benign Extravagance*. Fairlie is no apologist for the livestock industry. He'd spent years living on a commune surrounded by vegans, and now lives at a centre 'for sustainable living' in Dorset. As a result of these experiences he had concluded that so many of the ingredients vegans used – chickpeas, lentils, rice, soya milk and olive oil – came with their own huge footprint. Furthermore, he said, the issue with livestock was the way it was being raised now, on grain, not the keeping of animals for meat per se. He calculated that by feeding cattle on the kind of straw and grasses that human beings could not eat, and pigs on residues and waste, we would need only

reduce our consumption by half. He also pointed out that raising livestock is good for the environment. 'Livestock provide
the biodiversity that trees on their own cannot provide,' he
wrote in *Permaculture* magazine. 'They are the best means we
have of keeping wide areas clear and open to solar energy and
wind energy. They harness biomass that would otherwise be
inaccessible, and recycle waste that would otherwise be a
disposal problem. And they are the main means we have of
ensuring that the phosphate which leaks out from our arable
land into the wider environment, and that is crucial for agricultural yields, is brought back into the food chain.' He also
challenged authoritatively all the figures for both water
consumption and greenhouse gas emissions.

But we really do have to eat less meat (I say, with tears in
my eyes and a knot in my tummy). The idea of a Meat Free
Monday, as proposed by Paul McCartney among many others,
doesn't just sound like a good idea. It sounds like a vital one.
Meat-free Tuesday and Wednesday may well be up for grabs
too. Indeed, as far back as 2008 Dr Rajendra K. Pachauri, chair
of the UN's Intergovernmental Panel on Climate Change, was
arguing for a massive cut in meat consumption globally, to
save the planet. In many countries in the developed world the
notion is gaining purchase. People are getting it. The problem
is selling that to the emerging economies, especially China
and India. Telling the newly affluent there that they can't
gorge on the meat their new-found economic heft is allowing
them to buy, because the rich bastards in the West have
already buggered up the planet by doing so, is going to be a
very hard sell.

It is also a potential point of conflict, as reports seeping out
of Tehran on 23 July 2012 proved. According to Saeed Kamali
Dehghan, writing on the *Guardian*'s website, a sudden rise in

chicken prices in the city of Nishapur in the country's north-east had led to angry demonstrations on the streets. 'Shame on the rise,' the crowds chanted, as what the Iranian media called 'the chicken crisis' deepened. The government responded quickly by distributing discounted chicken, which resulted in long queues. We are used to the idea of bread riots and rice riots and, as they were nicknamed in Mexico during 2008, tortilla riots. As the Arab Spring proved, the rising price of staple foodstuffs, inciting the mob to rise up, has been a challenge to governments down the centuries. But suddenly there was the prospect of a meat riot, and that was something entirely new.

A solution is required, a new source of animal protein to go alongside a vastly reduced supply of the conventional kind. There is one out there. But it's one many self-proclaimed food lovers in the developed world will find very hard to stomach. It goes against everything they believe in or have ever championed. Nevertheless, as food prices rise and supplies become scarce, objections will start to crumble. Indeed, if we really are going to make sure everyone is fed, if we are going to embrace a future of sustainable intensification, we will find ourselves with no choice. We will have to dump hackneyed and fuzzy ideas of what is natural in our food supply chain and head to the lab.

We will finally have to embrace biotechnology. Which in turn means we will finally have to engage with science.

9.
N IS FOR NARCOTICS

Arranged along the top shelf in my mother's office at home when I was growing up was a series of box files. They were in alphabetical order. 'A' was for allergies, 'I' was for impotence, 'M' was for the menopause, and so on. Inside each of these box files were academic papers and research studies culled from the numerous publications that came into the house every week. We received *The Lancet*, one of the oldest and most respected general medical journals in the world. There was the *British Medical Journal*, the *BMJ*, published by the British Medical Association. There were countless nursing quarterlies and scholarly works on everything from psychiatry to midwifery. She would read each one of these, tag them, and pass them over to her team of secretaries and assistants so they could cut them up and get the relevant papers into the right boxes. This was a part of the serious and formidable body of work which underpinned her non-fiction books and the answers she gave in her newspaper problem pages.

Claire had a secular rationalist's commitment to, and respect for, rigorous science. She was fascinated by it; by the beauty that lay at the very heart of biology. One of her pleasures was collecting antique medical equipment and textbooks. She had a tray of early Victorian glass eyes, in a velvet-lined box, each pair with a slightly different-coloured iris, which I loved to stroke with the soft pad of my middle finger. There were the exquisitely detailed and delicate nineteenth-century anatomy guides – one for each gender – made of countless cut-out pieces of paper which turned back to take you deeper and deeper into the body: first the skin, then the muscles, followed by the skeleton and nestling within it the vital organs. There were terrifying metal implements which made you grateful for the wonders of the modern age. She had a huge disdain for anything that smacked of hucksterism and had no time for fraudulent theories passed off as 'New Age' enlightenment. For example, she always said there was no such thing as 'alternative medicine'. You double-blind tested whatever the substance was. If it worked it just became medicine.

As an inquisitive, questing, restless adolescent I found this bedrock of scientific knowledge that had become part of the fabric of the house extremely useful, although not necessarily in a way my parents would have either anticipated or approved of. For sitting on the shelves in that office was a series of box files marked 'N'.

'N' was for narcotics. I got an awful lot of use out of those.

I smoked my first joint when I was 13. It was rolled for me by one of the managers on a Jewish youth group away weekend, somewhere deep in the Gloucestershire countryside. I was not at all religious, but as a result of moving house and changing schools to one far from where I lived, I'd ended up short of friends. To be honest I was so short of friends I didn't have any. From the age of 10 to 12, weekends were bleak and empty. Seeking a solution, my parents had eventually swallowed hard and packed me off on a summer camp run by Reform Synagogues Youth, held in a very English public school in the Dorset countryside. It worked. I returned home with a tight, intimate circle of just 150 friends, all Jewish, scattered all over the country. I knew an awful lot of girls called Danielle. There was a bit of the religious stuff, but mostly, this being the Reform movement, it was ritual-lite. Though *my* parents didn't give a damn – they just didn't like the fact that I was lonely – most other parents sent their kids off on these holidays in the hope that they would meet a nice Jewish boy or girl rather than end up with someone who wasn't of the tribe. Snogging and fumbling was positively encouraged; if we weren't all copping off with each other the youth workers would worry that the venture had been a failure.

At the summer camp, and both the winter camp and various away weekends held at Outward Bound centres in the English countryside which happened to have kosher licences, it really was more about the social side. There were organized games. There were – oh God – sports. Jews should never be made to do sports. No good can come of it. Occasionally, for a bit of light and shade, they'd show us the gruelling films made by the legendary television journalist Richard Dimbleby of the liberation of the Bergen-Belsen concentration camp at the end of the Second World War. Holocaust education was regarded as a key part of the project and as teenagers we became very used to watching films of atrocity. It wasn't all bleak and awful. Sitting in the dark, it was often a good excuse to try holding some girl's hand, just for, y'know, a little moral support.

Inevitably, at some point during these trips away, somebody would play 'The Sound of Silence' on the guitar and we'd all sit around looking very intense and profoundly moved. We'd then try to grope each other in the sweetest way possible in an attempt to prove how intense and moved we were.

Getting stoned with the youth workers wasn't an official part of the programme but it did happen quite a lot. Now, as a parent myself, I can't just shrug my shoulders and say it was fine. I know it wasn't fine. It was outrageous; my own parents would have been appalled. Their trust had been betrayed. I would feel the same way if it involved my kids now. But I can't pretend, just for the sake of appearances. At the time – we're talking the very late seventies – it felt like a safe and comfortable environment in which to find out what being out of your head on hash was really like. I enjoyed the high. I loved the accessories involved, the way words like 'red Leb' and 'sensimillia' rolled off the tongue. Then there was the camaraderie; I welcomed the sense of being a part of a culture. I had a privileged, safe and very comfortable upbringing. This made me feel just a little bit mad, bad and dangerous to know. It made me feel less safe. I quickly committed myself to the notion that, whatever other sort of teenager I might be, I was definitely a stoner; one who recognized the infinite variety of drugs that might be available to a resourceful kid, if only he could get the cash together.

And yet, for all that, I did regard myself as smart and responsible. If I was going to consume lots of drugs I really ought to know what the hell I was doing. Which was when I remembered the box files. Ferreting around in there on nights when my parents had gone out, I found endless academic papers on the general impact and addictive qualities of everything from grass and hash, through its opiated cousins, to barbiturates, psychotropics, and speed, coke and heroin. I was determined to be a discerning and educated drug user. I wanted to be learned. For example, the evidence of the effects of ingredients with which clumsily produced amphetamine sulphate might be cut soon helped me decide it was not for me. Domestic cleaning materials really didn't sound like fun. Heroin was clearly too serious a drug; I hated the thought of both dirty needles and cheap cutlery.

But when I heard there was a little opium floating around the neighbourhood I determined to read up on it in detail. I quickly deduced, from the academic studies collected in N for Narcotics, that it was not an experience I should repeat too often. It's addictive qualities were obvious. Still the romantic, slightly literary part of me wanted to give it a go. All of the papers I read warned of temporary impotence in men. However, as I was only 16 years old, grossly overweight and terribly clumsy, the opportunities for getting laid were extremely limited. I didn't see a touch of impotence as a major issue.

An opium high (or, to be more precise, low) was, as it happens, soft, gentle and a little dull.

Of course, I eventually got into trouble for all this. How could I not? After the last night of a school production of *The Taming of the Shrew* in which I played a cleric, my Semitic curls held in place by a finger full of KY Jelly (it's a brilliant hair gel, and sets hard when it dries), there was a party held at the house of the boy who had played the lead. The school laid on a coach to get us all there. Knowing what form an all-nighter like this might take, a group of us had talked long and hard about how to approach it. We reckoned alcohol was not the way to go. We'd all drink too much, too quickly, and end the night throwing up. Alcohol poisoning was no fun. Better to get gently stoned. A dozen kids gave their money to one of the group who scored the hash for them; I had my own dealer, a whippet of a man who lived in a squat that smelt of damp dog, with a foot-long iguana in a hot glass tank. It's often the way with dealers.

It was a great night. We all got quietly stoned to *The Dark Side of the Moon* and pushed on until the first smudge of an early summer morning.

It was never going to be that easy. Nothing ever is. One of the other party-goers split on us. An inquest was started at the school. A dozen or so of the accused coughed immediately and were suspended for a week. I tried to hold out. I denied it all, aware that there would be deeper, darker consequences for me, until they related in exact and fetishistic detail what I'd been seen doing ('You were seen heating a piece of cannabis hashish on a safety pin over a flame; you were seen crumbling said …'). I should have held out. I should have demanded they bring the witness in front of me, but my fight had gone. I crumpled, admitted everything, and my father was summoned to take me home. We drove in silence. It was May. I was told I was not welcome back that term; that they would decide in due course whether I would ever be returning at all.

They did let me back to complete my A levels, although not before the deeper, darker consequences I had feared had come to pass: the story had been splattered across the national press, courtesy of my mates Charlie and Ted, who flogged it to the *Daily Mail* for £150 (thanks, boys; if you were going to sell me out, you could at least have haggled). I was the problem son of agony aunt Claire. I was Claire's Agony. I was delinquency in smudgy, black 72-point. (A few years later, after university and a period as a student journalist, I obtained work experience in almost all the national newspaper groups in London. These were the days when yellowing cuttings were kept in named files. I found all of the files with my name on them, in each of the cuttings libraries, sneaked them out, and destroyed them. The only person who would be reminding the press of my early brush with fame was me.)

Though I did continue smoking dope for about eighteen months after that, I returned to N for Narcotics just once more, to look up the peer-reviewed studies on psilocybin, as found in 'magic' mushrooms. They grew in volume in a field not far from my house and I'd heard interesting things. That said, I really didn't want to read about the upside. The positive impact could reveal itself to me at the time. It was the negatives I cared about. On this, those academic studies were in general agreement: a bad trip could engender paranoia, anxiety, depression and uncomfortable hallucinations.

Science is a clever thing; they were bang on. The first couple of experiences were fine. Indeed, they were more than that. They were joyous and funny and relaxing. By now I was in my first year at Leeds University, and I was happy to sit in my student flat in Headingley, staring for hours at the weave of the cheap dog-poo-brown carpet and all the patterns that danced and shimmered there.

The third trip was different. I took them in a mushroom cup-a-soup with a friend, in his battered flat, high in the eaves of a tall Victorian house as the wind and the rain of an early winter Leeds night battered at the windows. The previous trips had been so much fun that I had doubled the dose. I believed I could take it. I was hardened. After all, drugs had been a part of my life since I was 13. After all, I knew what I was doing. After all, I had read the academic papers. It took about an hour for the panic to slowly fall across me, like high grey clouds filling a once sunny, blue sky. Within ninety minutes my heart was at double speed. I was sweating and fearful and I just needed to get away. I ran from the flat, and all the way home, and spent the night clinging to the bed and praying that morning would come soon and doubting that it ever could again.

Morning did come again and with it a general, disconnected sadness that did not lift for days. When at last it had passed I decided to celebrate by rolling myself a joint. The papers that I had read had said flashbacks were a possibility, and once again they weren't wrong. Within minutes I was right back where I had been a few days before. I was panicking. I was sweating. I was terrified.

That was that: the complete end of my drug career. I was only a couple of months past 18 years old. Again, I won't pretend. I had enjoyed it immensely. It had been a part of me. When Ecstasy and the second summer of love came around a couple of years later I was merely a spectator, and a mournful one at that. I knew that I was missing out on something. Still I wasn't tempted. The person who had done all of that had been subtly different. Magic mushrooms had changed me, just as the papers I had read had told me they might.

Later, a lot later, when I had left university and married and had children of my own I would often find myself standing in my mother's office at the house where I had grown up chatting to her, while she sat behind her heavy wooden desk. As we talked my gaze would slowly drift upwards to the shelf of box files and N for Narcotics. Sure, it was just a pile of peer-reviewed scientific studies. It was just so much paper and ink. But it was also an important fragment of my childhood. It was a piece of me. It made me feel terribly wistful.

* * *

In later years, as I found myself covering more and more stories involving scientific studies, I realized that my approach to those box files had been a robust one. True, I had been a little too quick to think that I would dodge the negative effects of magic mushrooms that all the studies had told me were possible. But at least I had looked for multiple sources of information, and read multiple studies rather than relying on just one before making choices, which is exactly what you should do. Not that you would know this from reading about science in the mass media. Most popular newspapers and television news broadcasters leap upon each and every passing scientific study as if it were gospel truth, because men in white coats were involved. A single study apparently reveals an increase in cancers among people drinking red wine and suddenly it's proof that ALL WINE WILL KILL YOU. A small study finds lower blood pressure among people who regularly eat dark chocolate, and it's time for a banner headline about chocolate being THE ELIXIR OF YOUTH. Cheese mustn't be eaten in pregnancy. Hot baths make you impotent. Facebook gives you cancer.

IT'S THE TRUTH.

I may have invented one of these. Or maybe not.

Knowledge doesn't work like this. Scientists may wear crisp white coats and have benches full of neat stuff to play with but even they – or at least the good ones – know that they are not in the truth business. They are in the 'studying things, observing outcomes and reporting them in a way which will help us move towards a generally agreed version of the world in which we live' business. Each new study adds to the growing pile of evidence. We inch towards conclusions. It is why scientists often carry out studies which involve no direct experimentation at all, but instead simply do literature reviews: meta-studies looking at all the studies that have already been done on a particular subject to see what patterns emerge. (Interestingly, a new meta-study published in the *American Journal of Clinical Nutrition* in December 2012 looked at all the papers claiming that various foodstuffs were linked to cancer risks: coffee, sugar, salt, butter, and so on. Their close examination of the results found that many had 'borderline or no statistical significance'.)

Just basing conclusions on one study is a little like flying into Britain on the one sunny, blue-skied day of the year, announcing that it's always sunny here, and flying out again. To come up with a reliable assessment of the climate in a country like Britain you would have to spend years there recording the weather every day. And even then the climate would still manage to bowl curve balls at you – periods of unseasonable cold or heat or rain – which would force you to accept that your summary of the British climate is not universally reliable.

Which brings us to the hideously complex and viciously fought over question of genetically modified food (from here on in, to be called GM) and whether it is safe or not. Many, many books have been written on this subject, from both extremes of the argument. Rarely do people sit in the middle, attempting to weigh up the pros and cons. In 2008 I did try to do just that. In an early exercise in crowd-sourced journalism, I used the Word of Mouth food blog published by the *Observer* to solicit contributions from all sides of the debate before writing an article about the subject. I asked people to send me links to reputable academic papers and they took me at my word. Working with an assistant I printed out everything about GM that had been sent my way; it produced a pile of paper the height of which could be measured in feet. It was striking that both sides of the argument were represented equally, as they were in my final report. To my immense pride, readers on both sides accused me of being part of both the staunch pro- and staunch anti-GM lobby.

The negative aspects to modern GM are clearly pronounced. The most obvious of these is that, across America, strains of corn genetically modified to be herbicide resistant have led to an increase in the use of some herbicides, even though they were meant to do the opposite. That, in turn, has led to super-weeds that are resistant to the very chemicals the corn was modified to allow free use of in the first place. More generally some of the huge corporations responsible for developing these strains of seed, like Monsanto, have behaved at times in a staggeringly clumsy and bullying manner. It's certainly the case that Monsanto's practices have engendered a deep mistrust. The company has vigorously pursued through the courts farmers suspected of illegally planting their seeds without paying royalties. It and many other companies have created seed 'technology packages' that force farms into a dependence on the company. Equally many people do not like the notion of a multinational corporation owning plant life through patents, a move that only became possible as a result of a change in US patent law in 1980.

However, many of the other criticisms of GM foods don't stack up. There is the allegation that their use has resulted in environmentally damaging monocultures in various parts of the world, for example Argentina. Monocultures – the over-planting of and reliance upon a single crop, in this case soya beans, across vast tracts of land – are a terrible thing. Poor water management, overuse of nitrogen-based fertilizers and the failure to rotate crops adequately are equally terrible, a dismal failure by farmers to take their role as custodians of the landscape seriously. But all of these things can and do happen in conventional farming too, as the dust bowls of the Midwest in the thirties proved. It is not a problem which has anything specifically to do with GM.

On another matter anti-GM campaigners argue that these crops have not delivered the increases in yield they promised. There is a good reason for that. Regardless of what Donna Jaeshke may say about the increased yield on her farm in Illinois, none of the GM strains developed so far has ever promised increased yields. They were designed to reduce costs by being resistant to certain pests, or by being adaptable to no-till technology. Increased yield may be possible in the future as a result of GM but no one has made any such claims for it yet.

Of course, the biggest charge against GM is that it's dangerous to human health, and this is where it gets very complicated indeed. On the one side its supporters argue, very convincingly indeed, that with 90 per cent of soya beans grown in the US now being GM, people have been eating it for decades with no ill effects whatsoever. Europe has been exceptionally resistant to growing GM. For example, no GM crops are currently grown in the UK. However, GM animal feeds are constantly coming into the country, and again there is no evidence of any damage to human health as a result of people eating GM-fed meat. The response of the anti-campaigners is that lack of evidence is not proof of safety. In 2008, for that article on the ideological battles over the subject, I interviewed Dr Michael Antoniou of the Nuclear Biology Group at Guy's Hospital. He was once a member of the British government's advisory group on GM foods and knows an awful lot about genetic modification. 'In our research into therapies for diseases such as multiple sclerosis and cystic fibrosis, we work with genetically modified organisms all the time,' he told me. It is because of that experience that he believed – and continues to believe – that GM foods are potentially very dangerous.

The problem, Dr Antoniou explained, is the unintended consequences of genetic modification. 'It's a highly mutagenic process,' he said. 'It can cause changes in the genome that are not expected.' So had this happened with the GM crops on the market? 'These crops that have come along seem to be doing what they claimed they would be doing,' he replied. 'The question is what else has been done to the structure of that plant? You might inadvertently generate toxic effects.' The answer, surely, is that the regulatory regime is there to catch these things. No, Dr Antoniou said, because it is not based on detailed genetic studies or even animal feeding tests. It is based on the doctrine of 'substantial equivalence', in which the original plant and its GM version are compared and, if found to be similar, passed as suitable for cultivation. He argued that it was like comparing a conventional and a nuclear weapon of the same yield and deciding they are substantially equivalent because of their explosive power. So what of all those Americans endlessly scoffing the stuff? Why haven't they all started showing ill effects? 'That,' he responded, 'is only because nobody is looking at what the effects might be.' Later he sent me complex academic papers on unintended consequences of GM crops. They did appear to establish mutations along the genome, but, again, the researchers could not say for sure what the consequences of those mutations might be.

Vivian Moses, the man who grilled me on the notion of 'natural' human behaviour, was sure he knew. As both Visiting Professor of Biotechnology at King's College London and a member of CropGen, a pro-GM lobby group, he was experienced in arguing about the science. Arguing with Dr Antonio was almost a part of his daily job description. 'It's simply not true that there are mutations all over the genome,' he said. 'There was a paper published recently which looked at this. They found that the changes were specifically where the researchers intended them to be.' In any case, Professor Moses told me, resistance to GM is not merely about the science, but about perceptions of the science. He pointed out that, in the late nineties, GM and non-GM tomato purées were stocked side by side in British supermarkets for two years, and sold in similar amounts. 'The consumer saw the product and they were not put off.' Then the newspapers started filling up with headlines about 'Frankenstein Foods' and the market collapsed.

Professor Moses raged against the culture of what he called 'catastrophism and protest. There is a cultural problem that some people have. If they don't understand it they bash it.' It does seem that the anti-GM side can be prone to misunderstandings or exaggerations. For example, I was sent a briefing paper by Britain's certifying body for organics, the Soil Association, an organization which is avowedly anti-GM. It referred to the same research papers on unintended consequences in the genome sent to me by Dr Antoniou. The Soil Association briefing took an unproved thesis in the research papers – that unexpected mutations might cause toxic reactions – and turned it into fact. 'This,' it declared, with impressive assurance, 'explains why [GMOs] have been associated with allergic reactions.' And this despite the fact that the research papers didn't explain anything of the sort. They simply raised questions around the possible impact of changes to the plant genome that they could not answer.

More confusion swamped the subject in the autumn of 2012 when the most recent study (at the time of writing) was published. It appeared to show that 'safe' levels of GM maize and the world's best-selling herbicide, Roundup, 'can cause tumours, multiple organ damage and premature death in laboratory rats'. The study's USP was that it followed the rats for their full lifespan of two years, rather than just for ninety days as is more usual in such research. It was a complex study, with the 200 animals – 100 of each gender – separated into a variety of groups, for a variety of different feeding regimes. The findings received major media coverage, with the *Daily Mail* – the British newspaper most responsible for 'Frankenstein Foods' headlines – running photographs of tumour-ridden rats alongside the headline 'Cancer row over GM foods as study says it did THIS to rats'.

Which is when the arguments really started. First, critics of the new study said that the type of rat used was a species especially prone to tumours, a fact not discussed in the report. Second, they took issue with the size of the 'control' group, the rats which were not on any special feeding regime so that you could compare the results of the experiment with what had happened to the animals leading normal lives over the same period. The standard procedure is for the control group to be of an equal size to the subject group so you can compare like for like. If you have 200 rats on a feeding programme, you would have 200 as a control. In this study, of the 200 rats studied only twenty were the control. Anthony Trewavas, Professor of Cell Biology at Edinburgh University, took specific issue with the size of the control group and said it was too small to enable anybody to draw meaningful conclusions. 'To be frank, it looks like a random variation to me in a rodent line likely to develop tumours anyway.' The highly regarded 'behind the headlines' section of the National Health Service website, which does a forensic job of digging behind newspaper and television reporting of each new banner-headlined 'scientific finding', described the study as 'poorly conducted'.

No matter. You can guarantee that when anti-GM campaigners want to make their point it is this study to which they will point, for years to come. It is the equivalent of that British weather report based on that one sunny day (though, to stretch the metaphor until it snaps, the study is so flawed that it's actually a little more like the one sunny day where the researchers left the country before the clouds piled in, the skies darkened, and the rain came down. But they missed it because they weren't there. Or something.)

In the past, as the response to that 2008 article of mine proves, I have genuinely sat on the fence with regard to GM, but it's cards on the table time. I have read countless studies and reports and listened to countless arguments. Whatever legal, business and social issues are raised by GM, nothing I have seen has ever convinced me it is dangerous to human health.

At the heart of the arguments against it is the claim that in some way the science is fundamentally different to other sorts of gene mutation that humanity has used on its crops since we first started cross-breeding grasses for grain on the banks of the Nile thousands of years ago. As Professor Moses explained to me, what the oppositionists fail to recognize, indeed refuse to recognize, is that the process of genetic modification in our food crops is hardly unique. He was referring to the little-discussed mutagenesis breeding programme that took place in the early part of the twentieth century, when Marie Curie's science of radioactivity was still in its relative infancy. 'Around eighty years ago researchers began to irradiate seeds and treat them with carcinogenic chemicals in the expectation they would cause mutations, some of which might be useful,' he said. Many of these experiments produced seedlings which were useless, but a significant number were successful. 'About 70 per cent of our [conventional] current crop plants have such an event in their history.'

What troubles me most, though, is the attempt by many campaigners in the developed world to close down research into GM altogether, which has had a massive impact on policy in parts of the developing world which could most benefit from it. Proposals to conduct crop trials in Britain have been met with threats to invade the land and dig up the plants, alongside the vilification of the scientists involved. For the fact is that there really is immense potential in the science. Drought-resistant strains of wheat or corn, crops modified against site-specific diseases and pests, crops designed to grow on salinated land all offer immense hope to parts of Africa and Asia which need all the help they can get. Right now, for example, there is major work being done in Uganda to find a way to genetically modify bananas to make them resistant to Xanthomonas wilt, or BXW, which both kills the plant and contaminates the soil. On average Ugandans get 30 per cent or more of their daily calories from bananas and it is a vital cash crop. If BXW disease took hold globally it would be economically disastrous for countries like Uganda which depend upon the banana harvest, and a genetic modification is the quickest and most accurate way of sorting the problem. In turn an economically unstable Uganda could have massive ramifications for the whole of East Africa.

But work like that is being challenged by an ill-informed, technophobic fear among affluent consumers in parts of the developed world. The Ugandan government has allowed the research, but has not yet said whether it will allow the new strain of bananas onto the market. Let's be honest: consumers in Europe, the US and elsewhere probably could manage fine without GM. But does that give them the right to stamp on technologies which could be a genuine life-saver in other, less blessed parts of the world? As Sir David King, the British government's former Chief Science Officer, said in a speech to the British Association for the Advancement of Science in 2008, a European resistance to GM, based purely on lifestyle choices, had 'been adopted across Africa ... with devastating consequences'. Sir David is now the director of the Smith School of Enterprise and the Environment at Oxford University. I asked him if anything had changed in his views since he had made that speech, a period during which he had been heavily involved in development work across Africa. He said, 'No. If anything my views have hardened.' As he pointed out, between 2000 and 2011 the food price index had increased by a factor of three. 'For countries in the West where food costs account for 5 per cent of GDP that's manageable. But in parts of Africa it's about 30 per cent of GDP and then it becomes very tough indeed. When food prices increase by a factor of three, people in those countries will be really struggling. In those circumstances we need whatever technologies we have available to us to improve efficiency and use of resources.'

Go stand in the aisles of your local supermarket. Or, if you still think they are too evil to be deserving of your business, go to your nearest deli or your nearest weekly farmers' market. Go look at the abundance we are lucky enough to enjoy, at least for the moment. And ask yourself: are we entitled to crush a whole discipline of extraordinarily promising science which could bring hope to millions of people who have but a fraction of the food choices we have, because some of us think it's just, y'know, a bit weird?

Sorry, but I really don't.

The reality is that, in the next few years, many of our food choices will be made less as a result of heated debate and more out of financial imperative. With a rising global population will come those rising prices. It is no coincidence that in 2011, as the cost of meat continued to soar, the European Union announced it was making grants worth €3 million available to university departments which come up with proposals for research into utilizing insects and mealworms as a source of animal protein for humans. 'While insects have not traditionally been used for food in the UK or elsewhere in the European Union,' a United Nations Food and Agriculture Organization spokesperson said at the time, 'it is estimated that about 2.5 billion people across the world have diets that routinely include insects. While many insects are regarded as pests, the UN's Food and Agriculture Organization is interested in promoting [them] as a highly sustainable source of nutrition.' From a purely nutritional point of view the announcement made a lot of sense. One study has found that small grasshoppers can be as much as 20 per cent protein and just 6 per cent fat, as against lean ground beef, which is 24 per cent protein and 18 per cent fat. Some insects can be as much as 60 per cent protein.

They are also gloriously eco-friendly. Being cold-blooded they have a very high food conversion rate. Crickets, for example, require six times less feed than cattle, and four times less than sheep, to produce the same amount of protein. They can be raised on organic waste and only a few of them produce any methane at all. Plus the meat yield is high. You get 55 per cent meat from each slaughtered head of cattle, and 35 per cent meat from each sheep. Those crickets give as much as 80 per cent.

Cue images of people deep-frying grasshoppers and muttering about how much like pork scratchings they taste, if only you season them properly. It's the territory of *I'm a Celebrity ... Get Me out of Here*. We send people once famous for being in a soap opera into the Australian rainforest and then point and laugh at them while they fill their gobs with live mealworms out of some mad, wet-knickered desperation to win the approval of the viewing public.

While they are still so much legs and wings and beady eyes, insects will never be more than a novelty food item in the developed world. But that's not how they will be offered to the consumer. The key will be the development of a proprietary product, some form of a highly flexible protein powder, which quickly takes the flavour and texture of whatever is around it. It won't be called Bug-U-Like™ or Insectelicious™. It will have some carefully manicured brand name like NaturesBounty™ or LushEarth™ and will be flogged to us with the classic advertising frottage of pastoral scenes. It will appear as an ingredient on the back of packs of burgers and sausages, which will cost a fraction of those utilizing the meat of pigs and cattle. And wanting to experience meat, but at a price we feel we can afford, we will go for it. (Although much was made of the cultural taboos in Britain around eating the meat of horses, when the horsemeat scandal broke in January of 2013, the real issue was secrecy and fraud. Because the presence of horsemeat had been hidden from consumers, there was anxiety over how the animals had been raised, which veterinary drugs they had been given during their lives, and the circumstances of their slaughter. If there had been complete transparency the debate would have been very different.)

'I really do think the consumer will be ready for this,' says the academic and food futurologist Morgaine Gaye. 'We know that meat prices are going to double or more in the future and we're going to have to look for solutions.' Gaye has done anecdotal research, interviewing a wide range of consumers from different backgrounds about what foods they thought they would be eating in the future. 'They all said insects.' This, she said, was something we could do now. 'I've already made a burger out of insects for a TV programme. It was pretty good.'

So-called in-vitro meat – animal protein grown in the lab from stem cells and nutrients – will take a little longer, but that too will eventually be a part of our diet. The pressure group PETA – People for the Ethical Treatment of Animals – has offered a $1 million reward to the first research team that can produce a convincing animal-free burger. Manufacturers of the filthy drek that is Quorn need not apply. Already two major teams are having a go. In California a vegan molecular biologist from Stanford University called Professor Patrick Brown has been at work for a few years now. 'I have zero interest in making a new food just for vegans,' Brown told the *Guardian* newspaper last year. 'I am making a food for people who are comfortable eating meat and who want to continue eating meat. I want to reduce the human footprint on this planet by 50 per cent.' Meanwhile, in the Netherlands a team at the University of Maastricht is also having a go. Both teams acknowledge the challenges. Meat is very much more than just protein. It's a complex web of protein plus fat, nerve endings, plasma, gristle and so on. It contains sugars and amino acids which, when seared, undergo the Maillard Reaction, which gives a steak its intense umami flavour when browned.

As a result a true lab-grown steak may not be achievable. But that's not the point. It's about providing a substitute for the animal protein we consume in anything other than prime cuts.

'At some point,' Morgaine Gaye says, 'we will have a device at home, a box like a microwave. We'll put our stem-cell culture in there once a week and top it up with the various nutrient-rich fluids and we'll grow our own in-vitro meat at home. There will be hiccups along the way. There will be complications along the way. But it will happen.' Meanwhile those old-fashioned prime cuts will become luxury objects. 'In the forties and fifties if we had a roast on a Sunday then we made it last through the week,' Gaye says. 'Cold cuts on Monday, pie on Tuesday, a soup from the bones on Wednesday. When it comes to the pieces of identifiable livestock, that is something to which we will return.'

Arguably, futurology is a bit of a racket. Some of it is just knowing what's going on out there before other people are aware of it. Some of it is merely about having a seriously plausible manner, the sharpest pair of glasses in the room, and a killer PowerPoint presentation. The rest is extrapolation and wanton fantasy greased with the shameless hope that by the time you get to the future you were talking about so convincingly five years ago nobody will really remember what the hell it was that you said would happen.

So take my predictions of insect animal protein and in-vitro meat with as big a pinch of salt as you think the way I have described them deserves. But be in no doubt: these alternatives to meat from animals are just an example of what's going on out there. The world of food is changing, not because media-hungry celebrity chefs say it should do so or because we're bored and we crave the next big thing. It's changing because the world itself is changing: populations are growing, financial might is shifting, new consumer tribes are emerging, every bit as greedy and avaricious as the tribes to which you and I already belong. A lot of stuff will happen whether you want it to or not. Decisions will be made for you, sometimes through changing access to foodstuffs, more often through hard, cruel economics. It is a cliché, but then clichés are only such because they are so very true: the future is already here.

Welcome to the complicated business of dinner in the twenty-first century.

10.

THE SUMMER THEY STOPPED EATING

My mother began dying in the late spring of 2010. Claire had done this before. In 2003 a botched anaesthetic during an operation on a busted tendon had landed her in intensive care for many weeks. A dormant chest infection had turned into pneumonia which in turn had led to septic shock and multi-organ failure. She should have died, and if she had been any other 71-year-old with her medical history – lung problems, a pacemaker – she may well have done so. There were switches that could be flicked, beds that could be emptied to make way for more promising cases. But she was Claire Rayner, the woman who had been agony aunt to the nation and then an ardent campaigner for, and a guardian of, the National Health Service. She had sat on various Royal Commissions looking at the best way to manage care. She had been a non-executive director of the very hospital whose ICU she now occupied. No consultant wanted to lose her on their watch, and they didn't. It was a long and slow process, but she did what none of her doctors thought she was capable of. She made a remarkable recovery and was eventually able to walk back in to the ICU and thank the staff who had saved her life. She got seven more reasonably active years that many of us had not expected.

And then in May 2010 she began dying again. This time it was a bowel obstruction – she never believed in euphemism or delicacy in matters of health and neither do I – which required emergency surgery. Once more she was back in intensive care; once more my poor father Des, her companion for over half a century, was forced to keep vigil. It had been traumatic enough the first time. The second time it was almost too much to bear. Not that we knew exactly how bad it was then. We were battle-hardened. We had seen her in intensive care before, seen this formidable woman kept alive by the pulse and glow of so many pieces of machinery, attached to her by a seemingly endless umbilicus of shiny plastic tubing. We all knew how to read the vital signs that flashed at us from screens as she lay unconscious and sedated in front of us. Only later would we learn that she came very close to checking out on us that first weekend; she would live on for another five months.

There had been many things that could have killed her over the years. There was the brush with breast cancer in 2001, which she had dealt with via a radical double mastectomy, arguing that, as fond of them as she was, she really didn't need her breasts any more at her age. She liked to say that she had gone from not having breast cancer to not having breast cancer in fourteen days, the period from before diagnosis to after mastectomy. There were the pulmonary problems, which she blamed on a childhood amid the sulphurous pea-soupers that enveloped the London of the forties and fifties, not helped, I imagine, by a few years of heavy smoking in her youth. There was the cardiomyopathy, a disease causing, in her case, a thickening of the heart walls.

(A brief diversion: cardiomyopathies can be genetically inherited, and it was decided once Claire was diagnosed that her children should be checked out too. I went to a local hospital for an exercise test, at the end of which I was told by the doctor that they would like me to wear a tape machine wired to my chest that would record my heartbeat for twenty-four hours. Only once I had left the hospital, sensors in place, cables snaking out of my shirt, did I recall that I was due that evening to review a restaurant called the Soviet Canteen, which attempted to recreate the food enjoyed by the elite during the years of the Soviet Union. To add piquancy to the review I had invited as my companion a man called Sir Gerald Warner, former deputy Director General of MI6, the foreign intelligence agency. He had recently retired and was edging out into the daylight of normal life. The moment he arrived at the restaurant I had to explain to him that I was wearing a wire, but that the only thing it was recording was my heart-beat. He said very little during dinner. After all that it turned out I had not inherited any form of heart disease.)

None of these things was going to kill Claire. She would survive endless medical procedures, including four knee replacements, which wasn't bad for a biped. (Two of them failed, on the same knee.) Instead she would die as a result of an operation on the intestine, the organ most closely associated with eating. I wouldn't call this poetic justice. There was very little poetry in a death like hers. But it did have a certain internal logic for we have always been a family that loves its food. It was my mother who had taught me how to eat. It was my mum who introduced me to my first oyster when I was 10, grinning from ear to ear as the accessories piled up around us on the restaurant table: the frame for the tray of ice, the tiny, flat, two-pronged fork, the muslin-wrapped lemon, the shallot vinegar and Tabasco. Dress it as you will, she told me. Check it's been released from its sticking place on the shell with the fork, then, whoosh, down the hatch in one. Chew if you like, but not too much. Try it with a sip of this Sancerre. Sniff it. Smells a bit like cat's wee, doesn't it? But doesn't it work well with the oyster? Yes, mother, it does.

She adored the theatre and any food which came with a bit of that was OK with her; even better if it required strict instructions. She loved steak tartare, but needed to be asked how piquant she wanted it, and would brighten further if the final mixing of the egg yolk into the chopped beef happened tableside. A few years ago I lost a bet with her; the winnings were lunch on me at the Fat Duck, the gastronomic temple of that genius of culinary modernism Heston Blumenthal. I wasn't sure she would like it. For years she had been a regular amid the red velvet plush and certainties of Rules, the oldest restaurant in London, with its brass trim and menu of game; when the Wolseley opened and proved itself reliable at the Mittel-European shtick she quickly embraced it. They did a good steak tartare there. So what she would make of Blumenthal's exuberant techno-fancies? I had no idea. But if the Fat Duck is anything it is pure theatre. The moment the waiter bathed the foamed green tea palate cleanser in liquid nitrogen, the vapours rolling out across the table, she was sold. Not that she was overly impressed by the gloss and shine of that world. True luxury didn't need spin, she said.

The night before my mother was to be admitted to hospital for her double mastectomy my wife and I met my parents for dinner. On the menu that evening my mother spotted 'lobster and chips'. She nodded slowly, in recognition. 'Now that,' she said, 'is class.' We both ordered it and sat, side by side, bibs in place, the emptied shells piling up around us as we worked.

We were happy. My mother was right. It was a special kind of luxury.

And now she lay in a drug-induced coma in an intensive care unit. My father visited every day, reading to her from the poems of John Betjeman that she so loved, uncertain as to whether she could hear; the reading as much therapy for him as for her. We kids visited regularly, trying to make sure Des had as much company as possible. We were told that there were complications, that the wound from the emergency operation was not healing as quickly as might be hoped (or in fact at all). Eventually, though, they did begin to withdraw the sedative and she did wake up. There were a couple of days of elation. There always are. But that, quite quickly, was replaced by something else. Claire was furious. She was livid. She was desperate. Damn it, she had been through this once before and it had been a particular kind of torture. Not again; this couldn't happen again. She would never really stop being angry.

Late one night, two months after Claire had landed in intensive care, my older son Eddie, then 10, awoke in the night complaining of stomach pains. By the morning he described the pain as a very clear stabbing sensation to the right of his abdomen. He said he felt bruised. I knew immediately what it was; he couldn't have described appendicitis any more accurately if he had been a medical textbook. We shipped him off to Accident and Emergency at the local hospital, where they gave him painkillers and sedatives, and ummed and aahed as to whether he would need an operation. He was admitted to hospital that morning and after a couple of days they decided they should go in. Whatever drama was unfolding in north-west London, where my mother lay in hospital, was pushed to one side. My brother and sister readily agreed they would now deal with that.

Eddie was taken down for his operation late one evening; I was at home, looking after his younger brother, Daniel. Within an hour I had a call from my wife telling me to come to the hospital. Once under anaesthetic they had used ultrasound to discover a 'closed' appendicitis. The infection had been there for so long the body had begun to close around it. They didn't like operating on those, especially when the patient was having raging fevers as Eddie was. We were told it would be better to treat it aggressively with antibiotics and then bring him back in six or seven weeks when it was more manageable. We asked if there was a chance it could flare up anyway and still require emergency surgery. They said there was that chance but that it was better to try it this way. Eddie was sent home. Five days later he was vomiting and throwing fevers. Very quickly he was back in hospital and they were operating. He came around from the operation a very ill little boy.

We knew immediately how ill he was; he couldn't even look at a bag of Haribo's Tangfastics. This was a boy who'd never met a sweet he didn't like. And as for the sugar-crusted, citric acid-boosted joy of Tangfastics, the apparatus had not yet been devised that could measure the speed with which he could neck a bag of those.

The packet sat on his hospital bedside table, untouched.

We spend an awful lot of our time worrying about the state of our food culture in the developed world. Hand-wringing over the fetishizing of food and cooking is always a good standby for a newspaper comment page short on outrage. We watch more than we cook, they say. We have pornified what we eat; as with sex we are more interested in watching other people do it rather than getting involved ourselves. Even allowing for the fact that I have a vested interest in food media – I am involved with an awful lot of food television – this fury has always struck me as a little overblown. A bunch of people on the telly cook something and nobody dies. Is it really such a scandal? The fact is that both the boom in food media and outrage over it are two sides of the same coin. We are able to indulge in both because there aren't more important things to worry about. There are obvious exceptions but, for the most part, we are affluent compared with other parts of the world and therefore able to turn a necessity into a leisure activity. Likewise, we have the luxury to be cross about it too.

That said, we do sometimes lose sight of just how elemental what we eat is; how much a part of us food becomes. And if there is anything guaranteed to bring that back to you, it is watching your son lie in a hospital bed, suffering with a post-operative infection and declining to eat. Does it need saying that he and his brother are my sons in so many ways? Just as my mother had shown me how to eat my first oyster when I was 10, so I had shown Eddie, one warm New York summer's day in the legendary oyster bar under Grand Central Station when he was around the same age. I had bathed in the admiring glances of the shuckers behind the bar, these big men with their tree-thick forearms and bald heads and chests like bank safes. One birthday Eddie had asked for a sushi-making kit so he could produce his own maki rolls. He is not afraid of chilli. He likes his steak medium rare. He *hates* football. He's that kind of boy.

And now he was languishing in bed with no appetite at all. If anybody tells you appendicitis is always a simple and routine business, tell them they are wrong. Or send them to me and I'll tell them. In all, Eddie would spend twenty-four days in hospital, going through countless fevers. Twice a week the antibiotics being used to take out the bugs in his belly had to be changed, as the search for the right weapon went on. The only thing that kept our fear at bay was that he was already in hospital, receiving the kind of treatment only the NHS at its very best can deliver. During that time either my wife or I was at his bedside and most of the time we were imploring him to eat.

It would be customary here to bemoan the quality of hospital food, and some of it was awful. Some of what was on offer was a shameful waste of calories. As one senior nutritionist at the hospital told me, they spent more on drugs to counter digestive problems than they did on the food they served which was partly responsible for causing them. But some of it was fine. Still Eddie didn't want it. And so, blessed with the money to do so, we started bringing stuff in: dumplings from the cool Chinese place across the way in Camberwell, steaming bowls of ramen, grilled chicken from the branch of Nando's up the road. It did the job. He began to eat. The fevers began to subside. Not completely. But enough. One Friday they said Eddie could go home.

The family's summer holiday to Turkey had been cancelled. There was no way we could take a boy who was still suffering fevers to a country where the temperature regularly hit 40°C. Instead we booked a chalet on a holiday park in Normandy. We went out for steak frites and for pancakes and for waffles submerged under a cumulonimbus of cream. We ate perfect shellfish and salamis and *boudin noir*, and slowly but surely

Eddie came back to health. Then, one morning during that holiday, my wife got a phone call from her sister. It was about her 88-year-old mother.

My mother-in-law, Denise de Choudens, was born in the French-speaking part of Switzerland in the early twenties, and came to Britain in the forties as an au pair. She married and had three children, the youngest of whom, Pat, became my wife. And so, as one does through marriage, I became inculcated into another culture, with its own codes and traditions. It was exemplified for me by a love for a particular brand of Swiss vinegar. Pat's family had always carted some back with them in the boot of the car from their biannual trips to the big family house on the mountain above La Chaux-de-Fonds. Kressi vinegar was light and bright and salty and not too acidic, and, as it had been with Pat's family, it quickly became a cult object for me. In Switzerland it was nothing special. It was a major supermarket brand. Indeed, it would eventually be manufactured by Unilever. No matter. It was just better than any other white-wine vinegar. A salad dressing made with Kressi needs nothing other than olive oil and the crunch of sea salt. It is civilization in a one-litre bottle.

The problem was that, until 2012, nobody imported it into Britain. I wrote once about how I had taste-tested seventeen white-wine vinegars to find something to match Kressi for when our supply ran out, as it always did. I found nothing like it. Once, for a stunt, I flew to Geneva just to buy vinegar, and found the whole city was closed. I had visited on Pentecost, the sort of religious holiday only the Swiss would ever take seriously. (I flew home with an empty bag.) I came to associate the flavour of that vinegar with Denise, with a certain good taste in everything from food to music and art. The right piece of Elgar could make her weep. She made a point of giving me fabulous Swiss chocolate for my birthday, and introduced me to the joys of classic cheese fondues to be eaten un-ironically. In Denise's life a fondue was a serious business, rather than some joke or anachronism from the seventies. It was all about the wine and the correct volume of salty powerful Gruyère to waxy, dull Emmenthal. Fondues were eaten standing up, each of us reaching in with our forks and desperate not to lose our bread to the depths.

Denise's later years were not easy. Chronic back problems became increasingly severe until she was essentially crippled, housebound, and dependent on visits by carers, though she was remarkably sanguine; she hungered more for news of her children and grandchildren rather than the chance to complain about what she was suffering. And she was suffering. We knew this. From Denise's perspective, old age was absolutely no fun at all and became increasingly less so.

The call during our holiday was to say that Denise had been admitted to hospital with pneumonia. She died there in the early hours, a couple of days later, with her eldest daughter at her bedside. We packed our bags and headed home for the funeral.

In north-west London my mother had made a stumbling sort of progress. She had escaped the ICU to a single room with a view of the trees, where she complained about the haphazard care from a changing roster of agency nurses. For a while, infected by the most virulent of bugs, she was shifted into a small isolation room at the local hospital and became angrier and angrier. She was, I think, going a little bit crazy, hemmed in from all sides, with no sight of recovery obvious, the usual punctuations of mealtimes made irrelevant by lack of appetite. Eventually, through sheer will, through sheer bloody-mindedness, she convinced everybody to let her go home; to at least be in a hospital bed in her own bedroom in the house that she loved, and with Des, her husband of fifty-three years, nearby. Here, for a little while, she found a certain peace and calm, though it seemed to all of us that she'd had enough. She no longer wished to cooperate with the physios who were trying to get her up and about. She could no longer see the point. So what if I never walk again? she said once. It just wasn't going to happen.

An infection hit. She was carted off to the private wing of the hospital whose ICU she had occupied a few years before. She agonized over this, felt it was not in keeping with her absolute commitment to the NHS, but she also knew a public ward was impractical. Claire Rayner was just too well known; on the occasions she had been on those wards nurses had been forced to spend more time keeping well-meaning well-wishers at bay than actually nursing. And anyway she wanted – hell, she deserved – privacy. Previously when she had been in hospital, the tabloids had been desperate to get hold of the story. We were determined it wouldn't play out like that. These last days were quiet, as infection began to close her down. The kindnesses we could show were increasingly small. One morning I was with her and she told me that more than anything else she craved fresh orange juice. The bright, crisp tang of freshly squeezed orange juice. That was all. The ward had told her there was no way they could squeeze oranges for her. As it happened, downstairs in the hospital shop they sold bottles of the stuff. I brought some up. She drank deep and for the morning at least, perhaps simply bolstered by the hit of fructose, rallied slightly.

But gently, after that, she began to slip away. One Sunday evening in October her consultant announced that there were decisions to be taken. The rest of my family moved off to another room for a case conference; I stayed with Claire to keep her company. She wanted to know if she was dying and I was as honest with her as I could be. At that point nothing was certain but it didn't look great. We fell to talking about last words, the way they were never as good as we might wish. Famously the last words of King George V when he died in 1936 had been recorded as 'bugger Bognor'. Something like that, we agreed, would not do. I suggested a reference to the NHS, under increasing threat of cuts by the relatively new Conservative–Lib Dem government. Together we formulated the words.

Her consultant returned. Her kidneys were failing. What? Both of them? she asked. Yes. She said, 'Double fuck.' We laughed. There were two possibilities. Either she could have a last stab at dialysis, which might give the kidneys a little space in which to recover, or they could simply keep her comfortable and let the inevitable happen. We thought she would go for the latter. She had been through so much, been so angry and distressed and miserable. As ever, Claire surprised us. She would not go gentle. She opted for the dialysis.

She died quietly the next evening at a little past seven. We managed to sit on the news until early the next morning, revealing then that she had wanted her last words to be recorded as, 'Tell David Cameron that if he screws up my beloved NHS I'll come back and bloody haunt him.' They became the headline on the story of her death and two days later were used as a question to the Prime Minister in the

House of Commons. What, the Tory MP Margot James asked, was Mr Cameron's response? On the opposition benches, while she spoke, the Labour MPs howled at the Prime Minister like ghouls. Cameron declared he had nothing but respect for my mother, which was not the same thing as promising to protect the health service.

Of course, Claire was a lifelong atheist. She was certain there was no hereafter and certainly nowhere for her to haunt the Prime Minister from. Except in the digital age, almost anything is possible. In the months and years that have followed, Claire's last words have become a rallying cry; they have turned up on placards during demonstrations, been referred to in speeches. And even now if you search Twitter under 'Claire Rayner' you are most likely to find some reference to them, usually with a simple question to David Cameron over how he's sleeping at night with my mother's ghost in hot pursuit. Even she would recognize that it really is a kind of haunting, social-media style.

To describe the humanist funeral as a quiet affair would be to misrepresent the torrent of hilarious, often filthy anecdote that filled the crematorium that afternoon. One image will stay with me: my brother, Adam, placing on the edge of the pulpit, as a prop, that wooden carving of a cock which Claire had received in the post so many decades before. It was, the humanist celebrant said during her address, the only funeral she had presided over where the word 'cunnilingus' had been used. There was a context, but let's just let it hang there so your imagination can run wild.

Afterwards we returned to my parents' house to mark her passing in the only way my family understood: with a luscious tea catered for us by her favourite local Italian restaurant. There was bubbly. There was chatter. There was laughter.

It was the sort of party Claire used to love; it was the only one she could not attend.

The funeral of my mother-in-law, Denise, had taken place just a few weeks before. It was an altogether quieter but equally sweet occasion, as we pushed back the memories of the pain and discomfort she had endured in her latter years to recall the woman we had all adored. Afterwards we went back to her home and the serious work began: hunks of Gruyère were grated into bowls, followed by even bigger blocks of Emmenthal. The two ceramic pots were rubbed with cut cloves of garlic and then filled with white wine, to be heated gently on the stove. At the dining table another team set to work sawing up French sticks into manageable-sized pieces of bread. The cheese was added, the stirring began and with it the familiar hubbub over whether it was thickening properly. Did it need more salt? Was now the time to introduce a teaspoon of cornflour to each, beaten into a glass of kirsch? We had been doing all this for decades. Each time we had asked ourselves the same questions. The questioning was a part of the ritual.

The burners were lit, the steaming pots brought to the table, and quickly the daffodil-yellow pools of melted cheese began a slow pop and boil. And so the tribe gathered, the evidence of a long life, fully lived: there were Denise's three children and their partners; the grandchildren, some of them now grown up so they in turn could be there with her great grand-children. We skewered hunks of bread and crowded around, some of us turning shoulder in to make a little more space. Denise may have begun her life in Switzerland but we were a very long way from there now. We were in a tidy bungalow on a tidy housing estate not far from the town of Stourbridge in that part of the West Midlands known as the Black Country, the deep, rolling accents of which could be heard around the table. But a single piece of food culture had managed to sustain and renew that link to Switzerland; it was a reminder of what united us, what bound us together.

We skewered pieces of bread on our long forks, and plunged them into the cheese with the usual teasing and jostling directed at making one of our number lose theirs and risk a forfeit. But somehow we all brought the bread up intact and raised our forks. Other families remember their loved ones with the clink of glass on glass and the alcoholic burst of whisky or wine. Not this family. We toasted Denise with the ends of our fondue forks and the thick, slow drip of fabulous, boozy cheese. It was the only thing that made any sense to us.

11.

A NEW GASTRONOMICS

I am still a greedy bastard.

And I still can't lie about it, even for the sake of appearances.

I can, however, take a little comfort from the fact that I am not alone. We are all greedy bastards now. From time to time policy makers talk intensely about the need for people in the West to alter their patterns of consumption. We need to eat less meat and dairy, less fat and sugar; we need more vegetables, more fibre. We need to be able to see our feet. All of this is true, even though I have really horrible feet. I would happily live without ever seeing them again. Up until a couple of years ago we were given these dietary instructions based solely on soaring levels of obesity and associated conditions like Type 2 diabetes and heart disease. Now we are given them, not just because we're worried about getting fat, but because in the near future there may not be enough food to go round.

Unfortunately, attacking the issue based solely on Western patterns of consumption is missing the point. Even if America and Western Europe introduced massive and unprecedented

257

changes to their diet – and some of that will happen out of economic necessity – that would still leave a vastly greater population in countries like China, India, Indonesia and Brazil scoffing all the meat-heavy, gravy-slicked, dairy-rich pies. Then again, this complication does rather come with the territory. For at the heart of too much that is said in the mass media about the problems in our global food system lies a big fat lie. That lie is simplicity. We are constantly told that it's all very simple: that if you want to do the right thing all you need do is follow a few simple rules.

Eat this, not that. Buy this, not that. Shun them, embrace those.

It is not simple. It is never simple. Anybody who tells you otherwise is fooling you. Worse still, they are probably fooling themselves. Reading books or newspaper articles or watching television programmes by chefs and food campaigners can be an exhausting, dispiriting business. They barrel from what appears to be one intensely ethical, perfectly made, morally unquestionable lifestyle choice to another. They source – nobody shops for food any more – their lunch from that lovely chap just down the road, who keeps only seven pigs and knows them all by name, and holds them dear, until the time comes to give them an aromatherapy massage, crank up the Vivaldi, and slaughter them under general anaesthetic. They eat only what the season is bountiful enough to supply. They till their own land by hand, share their gluts with their dear neighbours, and don't even know where the nearest supermarket is, let alone ever visit it.

Put aside the suspicion that it's a put-up job; that nobody really lives like this. Even if they do, it's not really surprising. They have built their entire careers out of doing so, constructed a persona that allows and requires it. Sourcing their food rather than just getting the shop in isn't simply what they do. It's who they *are*, and they are paid to do it. You, meanwhile, have a proper job, and kids to look after, and the bills to pay, and God knows money's too tight to mention. Who the hell are they to lecture you?

Oh, and one other thing: as we now know, a lot of what they've been telling you is simply wrong.

So, what have we learned?

1. Supermarkets are NOT evil.
2. Though, of course, they are also VERY EVIL INDEED.
3. Caring about how things taste, being obsessive about seasonality, perving over top-quality ingredients, rubbing yourself against the glossy pages of a Nigella Lawson cookbook: all of that is completely fine. But …
4. … it's not the same as supporting sustainable agriculture.
5. Local food is not all that. Except …
6. … when it happens to be.
7. And if localism is far less important and food miles too simplistic a measure, then eating imported ingredients out of season isn't necessarily a big moral issue any more. In fact …
8. … not all food imports are the devil's work. Some of them are the solution.
9. Farmers' markets are brilliant places. As are Ferrari showrooms, and glossy shops selling Chanel handbags. If you've got the cash, go right ahead. Knock yourself out. (I know I do.)
10. Organic food makes a pretty feeble argument for itself.

11. Big agriculture isn't all nasty, evil and dangerous and awful and unspeakable. Indeed …
12. … some big agriculture is necessary.
13. Turning our backs on biotechnology because it's, y'know, weird and involves science and people in white coats and nothing good can ever come from any of that is really, really dumb. Because a lot of people in the world do not have access to enough food.
14. We do need to eat less meat.
15. There's no such thing as natural and unnatural, so we need to find new words.
16. Biofuels are total bollocks.
17. All this stuff is ear-bleedingly, eyeball-gougingly complicated.

Yes, it is. It's why at various points in this book you may have spotted me contradicting myself. Bad Jay. Guilty as charged. On one page I argue that we need to increase the volume of apples – of everything, frankly – that is grown in Britain and Europe generally. On another page I say that the most sustainable option may well be stuff grown in New Zealand and shipped halfway around the world to us.

There is a reason for that: we live in a dirty and flawed world. In a clean and perfect world, with a truly perfect market, each country on the planet would exploit its environmental competitive advantage to grow the foodstuffs they are best suited to growing, with the lowest possible carbon footprint. All that food would then flow about the planet from places of surplus to places of deficit. Everybody would be fed. Sadly, because both that perfect world and perfect market do not exist, it doesn't work like that. Lamb, apples and dairy products produced in New Zealand may well have the smallest carbon footprint as a result of the country's ideal climate and landscape. Europe, however, is finding it harder and harder to buy them because the deformed business model of its supermarkets means consumers have become used to not paying enough for food. The rising economic might of China and India is cutting us out of the deals. We are moving further and further towards the back of the queue. We are becoming the poor relations.

Meanwhile the certainties are collapsing. Local food really may be great for local economies and therefore for the health of the communities that produce it. That has to be a good thing. Likewise, farmers' markets may well be lovely places full of top produce, which can provide small farmers with a living. As I've already said, I love a good farmers' market. But that is not the same as local food and farmers' markets being the most sustainable model. And just to make things even more complicated there will, of course, be some things grown locally to you or sold in farmers' markets that actually do happen to be the most sustainable. Finally there is the very idea of a fully sustainable food production system. As Professor Tim Benton put it to me, it is like happiness or intellectual fulfilment. It is, he said, 'an aim, not an actuality'; it is something we will constantly strive for and journey towards without ever completely reaching.

See. It's anything but simple. It's complicated. What, in God's name, is to be done?

As I said at the very outset, we need to embrace a new economic model around our food, one which is flexible and non-doctrinal. At its heart must be one idea: sustainability. I still think 'gastronomics' is a stupid word, but it's my word, and until someone else comes up with something better it will have to do. It does at least bring together an interest in aesthet-

261

ics – the greedy business of how it all tastes – with the issues around cost, production and environmental impact.

A lot of it comes down to hard cash, certainly from a British perspective – although the same principles apply in any country or culture governed by a strong supermarket sector. In the short term British supermarkets must simply start paying their suppliers more. That will enable farmers to invest in agriculture so, in turn, our food self-sufficiency can start to rise again. When I accused the supermarkets publicly of not doing this the British Retail Consortium, the trade body which acts as apologist-in-chief for the major food retailers, threw a report at me from May 2012 called 'Retail and Farming: Investing in Our Futures'. Boy, is that a fun read. It piously lists all the grants supermarkets have made to universities and trade bodies to help fund research into things like water and energy usage, the improvement of yield, carbon footprint reduction, and so on. For example, it included the thrilling fact that the Co-op makes an annual grant of £10,000 to one college to help study water management. Ten grand? Ten bloody grand? These are retail companies with turnovers of billions. Tesco alone makes an estimated £6,000 profit every minute. Even a few million pounds' worth of research grants is nothing compared with paying farmers enough so they can actually stay in business and expand. And, of course, all of these research initiatives put the onus on the food producers to improve their efficiency so they can better cope with the moment when the retailers roundly screw them on the deal.

Let's not pretend. Paying farmers more will mean a further, relatively small increase in the price of food in the supermarkets, on top of current food price inflation. Consumers had better get used to the idea because the era of cheap food is well and truly over. And if they don't do that Britain's self-sufficiency will continue to fall. If that happens those consumers will be left completely powerless when a global food supply shock happens, as has been increasingly predicted for 2013. Big businesses in Britain will try to keep supplying themselves from the global market only to discover that – oh my! – not only have prices shot up there too, but they can't even get their hands on the stuff because of all the other countries which have secured their own lines of supply. Suddenly food price rises won't just be modest. They will be dizzying. Meat will double or triple in price; bread, vegetables and fruit will do likewise. And all because we didn't pay enough for our food in the first place.

Hell, by the time you're reading this, it might already have happened. You might already be peering at your shopping bills with wide-eyed awe and fear, occasionally glancing across at the family pet and wondering just how much meat there might be on a 12-year-old tabby cat.

In October 2012, as the drought in America began to impact upon global grain prices, the United Nations issued a warning. 'Populations are growing but production is not keeping up with consumption. Prices for wheat have already risen 25 per cent in 2012, maize 13 per cent and dairy prices rose 7 per cent just last month. Food reserves are at a critical low level,' said Abdolreza Abbassian, a senior economist with the UN's Food and Agriculture Organization. 'It means that food supplies are tight across the board and there is very little room for unexpected events.' I am writing in the early winter of 2012. Did early 2013 bring deep floods or heavy snows? Was it an unseasonably hot spring or a late, late frost? Have we experienced 'unexpected events'?

I hope not.

Already in late 2012 British supermarkets were admitting they were finding it hard to keep the shelves stocked with fresh produce. Questions of supply had suddenly become real. So real that one supermarket chain, Sainsbury's, finally recognized what campaigners had been telling it for years. It stopped shunning fruit and vegetables purely on aesthetic grounds. In the past if a carrot or an apple or an onion wasn't the perfect shape, it didn't go on sale; between 20 per cent and 40 per cent of all fruit and veg grown in Britain is wasted in this way. Suddenly Sainsbury's realized it could no longer afford to do that. It was a light-bulb moment.

'We've taken the decision to radically change our approach to buying British fruit and vegetables as a result of this year's unseasonal weather,' said Judith Batchelar, director of food for Sainsbury's. 'This may mean a bit more mud on peas or strawberries that are a little smaller than usual, but our customers understand and love the idea.' If you want hard evidence of just how fragile global food supply is, you will find it in a misshapen carrot. Perhaps one of those that looks like the crossed legs of a man desperate for a pee. Laugh at it. Show it to your mates in the supermarket. Post pictures of it on Twitter. Then buy the bloody thing, cook it, and eat it.

What else can the consumer do?

Although it really is possible that the more sustainable products could come from abroad, for the moment it probably does make the most sense, on balance, to buy the food grown in your own country wherever possible. It's not about nationalism. It's not about patriotism. It's about cash: buying what farmers produce helps them to invest. The more they can invest, the more sustainable a model they can reach for. Because consumers really can drive this. However, to do so they need to be given the right tools.

Key to that, within the next few years, has to be a new kind of labelling. A genuinely robust gastronomics means that the food we buy needs to have a sustainability rating. The food industry will complain about bureaucracy and paperwork. I get their point: one study found there are currently around 400 certification systems in operation around food in Europe alone. They will moan about cost. They always do. But far too much depends upon this for vested commercial interests to be allowed to stand in its way. And in the long term it's in their interests. Already we would not dream of buying a fridge or a freezer or a car without first being made aware of its environmental rating. We want to know whether the choices we are making are good or bad, not just in terms of value for money, but also in terms of the environment. We all now have to make an active decision to buy an energy-inefficient washing machine. It isn't something that just happens.

The same should apply to our food. It will require international cooperation. It will require the creation of cross-industry bodies and a quite significant amount of patience, but it's nothing that hasn't been done many times before. Plus the professional skills to create sustainability ratings already exist. Significant numbers of food producers, both big and small, already audit their carbon footprints. It's clear to me from talking to people in the industry that they regard it as good business practice to do so. The closer to a carbon-neutral model you move, they tell me, the better your bottom line. So if businesses are already doing this, why would they not want to share that information with consumers, unless they have something to hide? Or, to put it another way, the food businesses you should be deeply suspicious of are the ones that do not wish to share their sustainability data with you. Sure, the best way to measure sustainability is still argued over. It is a work in progress. New measurements come in; others are dumped. But the fact that it's all in flux is absolutely not a good reason for not doing it.

Some will argue that this will baffle shoppers. That's to underestimate them. People are really quite smart. They become used to new ideas very quickly. All they need is something straightforward and readable. There could be a number of ways to do that. But imagine two ratings from light shades of green for highly sustainable to deep shades of blood red for less so. One of the ratings would show you where each foodstuff stood in relation to the rest of your basket. So meat and dairy would almost always be in the red zone compared with, say, apples or potatoes, which would almost always be in the green. The second rating would show you where products stood in relation to each other within their category, enabling you to choose the most sustainably produced dairy products or beef. Producers would have an incentive to reduce the carbon footprint of their food as much as possible so as to get the best sustainability rating possible and therefore win a place in the shopping basket.

This scale will need a name. And if you want to call it the Rayner Scale, well, I can just about live with that. Surely having my name slapped across the entirety of your food shop is only right and proper? No? Stupid idea? Please yourself. Call it what you like. Just get on with it and introduce the damn thing.

Elsewhere in the supermarket we need one other change. Nowhere in this book is there a section on food waste. Why? Because it's so blindingly obvious that it's a very bad thing. You really do not need to read pages of me traipsing across a rubbish dump and retching at the smell to understand it. In January 2013 a study by Britain's Institution of Mechanical

Engineers found that up to 50 per cent of all food produced globally is wasted or lost at various points along the food supply chain. It is a very special kind of obscenity. Get rid of both food waste and biofuels and the simple business of feeding the planet would probably stop being a hot-button topic (though questions of sustainability would remain). So how do we get consumers to stop buying more than they need and then throwing away perfectly good edible food?

Here's one small idea: ban the bagging of fruit and vegetables by supermarkets. The big supermarkets like bagging stuff up for a couple of reasons. First, it's much easier to promote single units, a bag of six apples, say, or three traffic-light-coloured peppers. You can do two-for-one deals on bagged fruit and veg in the way you can't on loose. Two-for-one deals encourage shoppers to buy more than they could ever need, only to throw it away later. Second, you can't put a 'use by' date on loose fruit and veg. You can put one on a bag. And all of a sudden consumers become infantilized. They are no longer making adult decisions about the edibility of potatoes or courgettes, based on experience. They simply read the side of the bag and if the date printed there – which always errs on the side of caution – has passed, out it goes. If we had to buy all this stuff loose we would be far more likely to buy only what we needed and far less likely to throw out food that was still perfectly good. Oh, and the law change would get rid of a whole pile of carbon-hungry packaging.

It's a no-brainer.

Big Agriculture, Big Food – call it what you like – is here to stay. A lot of people will still find the very concept distasteful. I understand that. Mega-corporations do seem to have a habit of trampling over the little people. They lack human scale. Still, we should take some comfort from the fact that a leviathan like Cargill now recognizes it has to be responsive to the demands of social media; that it can no longer act with impunity because the high-profile brands which use its products do not like being associated with scandals. Today, as myriad grassroots campaigns against big brands have proven, big business really does get called to account. Apple had to respond to social-media protests over working conditions in its Chinese manufacturing plants. The coffee chain Starbucks was forced onto the defensive by a campaign over the lack of corporation tax it paid in the UK. The tech company behind Blackberry, Research in Motion, had to apologize for the failure of its email service as a result of a chronic lack of investment in its infrastructure.

I could now call for an end to the involvement in the food chain of large corporations, but I've really never been one for futile grandstanding. They are a fact of life, and we depend upon their logistical power. Given the scale of the challenges we face in this century we need them to clean up their act and do the thing they do best: move food in volume from the place where it is grown to the place where it is needed. Small really ain't all that relevant here.

There will, of course, be other models; markets function best when there is diversity. Within Britain's food market there are a number of enterprises which have managed to plough a furrow between the fragile, self-serving economics of small scale and artisan on the one side, and gargantuan on the other. 'Big smallness' is also a pretty stupid term, but it does rather describe the family-owned supermarket chain Booths, based in the north-west of England. Booths doesn't have 1,000-plus branches like a Tesco or Sainsbury's. It has about thirty. This means it still has proper buying power, and can work to economies of scale, while at the same time staying very close to its suppliers and giving them a deal that enables them to prosper. Shopping there is a little more expensive than at its rivals, but as Edwin Booth, the current member of the family to run the company, said to me, 'You could argue it's a price the consumer should be paying. There are more and more people shopping with a conscience.' Hence the company runs an ongoing carbon-footprint audit and sustainability goals are built into its buying policies. When I suggested to Edwin that Booths sounds like the ultimate business for the middle classes he laughed. 'I like to talk about inclusive exclusivity. It's about loving the sense of community and that's not the exclusive domain of the middle classes.'

Edwin Booth is right. Too much about food has become a class issue. It's become about lifestyle. It's become about how we see ourselves. But global hunger isn't a lifestyle choice and nor is grinding poverty. We are still allowed to care a little bit too much about what we're going to have for dinner tonight. We're very much allowed to get excited over the best ingredients, or a killer recipe. And just because you slump on the sofa of an evening after a hard day at work to watch a bit of food television, that doesn't make you a bad person.

But as the twenty-first century gets into its stride it's time we had a very close look at all the assumptions we have been fed about the world of food. We need to stop reacting emotionally, and start thinking realistically. We need to read the numbers, understand the maths, focus on the science.

Because be in no doubt: all of this is far too important for us to risk getting it wrong.

EPILOGUE

Late one Saturday afternoon a couple of weeks after I bought it from Lidgate's, I took the £31 chicken from the freezer where I had stowed it. A chicken costing that much was not just to be dispatched quickly. I felt it needed its moment. It deserved a bit of an occasion. I let it defrost overnight. The next morning I took the bag of giblets from its cavity, put the bird in an oven tin, rubbed the skin with a little olive oil, and sprinkled it with flakes of expensive sea salt farmed from the waters off the Essex coast. I stuffed a few wedges of salted butter into the creases around the legs and wings and shoved it all into a hot oven, surrounded by those giblets. After about forty minutes I turned the bird over, seasoned its back, and let it cook in that position for another twenty minutes. For the remaining half hour after I had righted it, I basted it every ten minutes or so, and tried to resist the temptation to rip off bits of bronzed chicken skin from places where my larceny would not be spotted. I failed. I let it rest after cooking for a good half an hour.

We ate it for a late Sunday lunch, with lots of caramelized cauliflower, because my two boys love that, and a good, sticky gravy made by scraping up the bits left on the tin by roasting the liver and neck and heart from the giblet bag. It was a good Sunday lunch, the kind I really like. We chatted. We laughed. We told the boys not to eat so damn fast.

As to the bird, what can I tell you? It tasted of chicken.

ACKNOWLEDGEMENTS

It is customary, when writing acknowledgements, to save until the end the news that all views expressed in the text are the author's own. Given how controversial some of the opinions expressed in this book are, I'm getting that disclaimer in first. The fact that I thank people for their help does not necessarily mean that they agree with me (though, of course, they should).

While I undertook an awful lot of original research for this book, it also depends hugely on the stories I covered and the experiences I have had as a journalist elsewhere. I would therefore like to thank my colleagues at the *Observer* – editor John Mulholland, deputy editor Paul Webster, *Observer Magazine* editor Ruaridh Nicoll and *Observer Food Monthly* editor Allan Jenkins along with many others – all of whom have given me the opportunity and uncommon freedom to roam the waterfront as a journalist. Likewise, I am indebted to the exceptional team at the BBC's *One Show*, led first by Doug Carnegie and now by Sandy Smith, for allowing me to experience so much about food production through what must now be close to the 150 films I have made for them. I am immensely proud of my associations with both the *Observer* and *The One Show*.

For general and specific help I would like to thank (in alphabetical order): Adrian Barlow of English Apples and Pears, Edwin Booth of Booths, Tricia Braid of Illinois Corn, Rosie Childs and her colleagues in both Britain and Rwanda at Save the Children UK, Steve Dolinsky, Steven Fairbairn of Cargill, Firmdale Hotels, Jim Iuorio, Sir David King, the staff of F.W. Mansfield's Fruit Farms, Chris Marshall of QV Foods, Jennifer Middleton of Lemonzest PR, the press office of the National Farmers Union, the entire staff of J. Penny and Sons, Steve Sexton, Scott Shellady and Roger Thurlow. There are also a number of people who spoke to me on condition of anonymity, and at some professional risk to themselves. I am grateful that they did.

Tim Benton, Professor of Population Ecology at the University of Leeds and the UK Champion for Global Food Security, was hugely generous with both his time and his research database, providing me with enormous numbers of relevant academic research papers and studies. He always made himself available when I needed a little help understanding exactly what it was I was reading. I would also like to record a huge debt of gratitude to the marvellous Louisa Loveluck, the most talented researcher and journalist any chap could wish to have on his team. She was brilliant at digging up statistics, research papers and cuttings throughout the writing of this book; quite simply, she made it possible to complete this book in the time allowed. She comes highly recommended.

My agent Jonny Geller of Curtis Brown was, as ever, a source of encouragement and support and believed in this project from the very start. Iain Macgregor and his colleagues at my publishers HarperCollins have been equally enthusiastic and energetic in helping to turn the idea for this book into the work you now hold in your hands. They were everything an author could wish for.

But my biggest thank you must go to my wife, Pat Gordon Smith, who read every draft of this book as it was being written, put her trained editor's eye to work in keeping both me honest and the text clean, kept my spirits up when I found myself in the weeds, and my glass filled at the end of the day. I simply couldn't have done it without her.